YOUR
BEST
MEETING
EVER

YOUR BEST MEETING EVER

7 Principles for Designing Meetings That Get Things Done

Rebecca Hinds, PhD

SIMON ACUMEN

New York   Amsterdam/Antwerp   London
Toronto   Sydney/Melbourne   New Delhi

SIMON
ACUMEN

An Imprint of Simon & Schuster, LLC
1230 Avenue of the Americas
New York, NY 10020

For more than 100 years, Simon & Schuster has championed authors and the stories they create. By respecting the copyright of an author's intellectual property, you enable Simon & Schuster and the author to continue publishing exceptional books for years to come. We thank you for supporting the author's copyright by purchasing an authorized edition of this book.

First Simon Acumen hardcover edition February 2026

SIMON ACUMEN and colophon are registered trademarks of Simon & Schuster, LLC

Simon & Schuster strongly believes in freedom of expression and stands against censorship in all its forms. For more information, visit BooksBelong.com.

For information about special discounts for bulk purchases, please contact Simon & Schuster Special Sales at 1-866-506-1949 or business@simonandschuster.com.

The Simon & Schuster Speakers Bureau can bring authors to your live event. For more information or to book an event, contact the Simon & Schuster Speakers Bureau at 1-866-248-3049 or visit our website at www.simonspeakers.com.

Manufactured in the United States of America

10 9 8 7 6 5 4 3 2 1

Library of Congress Control Number: 2025037478

ISBN 978-1-6680-6748-2
ISBN 978-1-6680-6750-5 (ebook)

 Let's stay in touch! Scan here to get book recommendations, exclusive offers, and more delivered to your inbox.

To everyone who has ever sat through a pointless meeting, wondering, "Why am I here?"—this book is for you.

And respectfully, it's also about you.

CONTENTS

INTRODUCTION

How Meetings Turned into
Weapons of Mass Dysfunction

In 1943, during the height of World War II, agents from the Office of Strategic Services (OSS), the precursor to the Central Intelligence Agency, were hard at work developing a new form of warfare. But they weren't designing new battlefield tactics, cracking enemy codes, or planning espionage. They were writing the *Simple Sabotage Field Manual*.[1]

It wasn't meant for soldiers or spies. It was designed for ordinary citizens living in enemy territory. Open resistance was too risky, so the manual recommended subtle acts of sabotage.

It instructed civilians working in offices, factories, transportation hubs, and shops to inject inefficiencies into the systems that kept the enemy's operations running—by misfiling paperwork in an office, sending trains to the wrong destinations, dulling tools on a factory line, and misdirecting telephone calls. The goal? Clog the enemy's systems with so much dysfunction that they'd collapse under the sheer weight of their own inefficiency.

One of the most soul-sucking sabotage tactics? Meetings. The manual urged citizens to weaponize them. A civilian railway clerk, for instance, might lure enemy officers into a pointless, mind-numbing meeting, dragging out every excruciating detail under the noble-sounding banner of "coordinating train schedules."

The manual advised citizens to schedule meetings with groups "as large as possible—never less than five," derail discussions with pointless chatter and "problems which are largely imaginary," rehash old decisions, and avoid any shortcuts that might make things less painful.[2] In other words, turn meetings into productivity sinkholes, where time, energy, sanity, and brain cells go to die.

Sound familiar? What was once a wartime sabotage tactic now reads like a modern meeting. Today's meetings swell with people who contribute little beyond nods, sighs, and side-eyes. Discussions meander aimlessly around fake or trivial problems. Decisions get rehashed until no one remembers what problem they were trying to solve. And *poof*. Another hour gone, swallowed whole by a slow-motion time heist.

How did we get here?

After World War II, military leaders swapped their uniforms for suits, but they didn't leave their battlefield strategies behind.[3] The chain-of-command leadership, rigid hierarchies, and love of process didn't disappear. Instead, they were repackaged and redeployed in the office.

At the same time, the postwar boom gave rise to sprawling multidivisional, multinational corporations.[4] To manage the growing complexity, these organizations draped themselves in layers of red tape, built hierarchies so steep they could give you vertigo, and used meetings as a blunt instrument for control: a place to gather updates, delegate tasks, and reinforce the pecking order. Instead of coordinating work, meetings turned into mini battlegrounds where leaders asserted their power, commandeered the airwaves, and made sure everyone in the room knew exactly who was in charge.

Over time, meetings started to feel less like real work and more like theater. Executives took the stage like Broadway actors, delivering monologues designed more for applause than action. They strutted into conference rooms like generals inspecting their troops, puffed up with pride over their ever-expanding calendars. Meeting invites turned into status symbols—proof you were important enough to be pulled into the spectacle. The ultimate flex? "Sorry, I'm double-booked," which became corporate speak for "I'm just too important."

And while the performance unfolded, the real work piled up. The more time meetings chewed up and spat out, the less time anyone had to actually get things done. And because most meetings didn't solve real problems, they set off a chain reaction of follow-ups, clarifications, and cleanup meetings to fix what the original meeting failed to accomplish. Soon enough, the dysfunction that the OSS once weaponized to sabotage the enemy had turned into just another day at the office.

Today, even executives, with all their power and perks, are drowning in calendar carnage. Back in the 1960s, they spent fewer than ten hours per week on average in meetings.[5] By 2007, that number had ballooned to twenty-three hours a week according to some estimates.[6] That's like spending your workweek trapped in meetings from Monday morning to Wednesday afternoon, leaving two measly days for heads-down work.

The financial toll is staggering. Elise Keith, the founder of the meeting management platform Lucid Meetings, estimates that up to eighty million meetings happen every day in the US,[7] costing well over $1.4 trillion annually,* more than 5 percent of the country's gross domestic product.[8]

It's gotten so bad that complaining about meetings has become a workplace sport. A sponsored Harris Poll found that 18 percent of US

---

* Keith originally ran this calculation in 2022 and estimated the cost to be around $1.4 trillion. In 2025 she shared an updated estimate with me, now well over that amount.

adults would rather sit at the DMV, 17 percent would rather watch paint dry, 12 percent would rather endure a four-hour commute, and 8 percent would prefer to suffer through a root canal than attend a status meeting.[9] When surveys start comparing meetings to dental procedures and bureaucratic hellscapes, you know something has gone spectacularly wrong.

Then the pandemic hit and things got even worse. Stripped of their ability to "manage by walking around," many leaders panicked. Their knee-jerk solution? More meetings. Couldn't swing by someone's desk? Schedule a meeting. Worried your team wasn't working hard enough? Schedule a check-in to micromanage them. Miss the sound of your own voice? Fire up Zoom.

Within two months of the pandemic lockdowns, meeting volumes had surged. A study of 3.1 million people across sixteen global cities found that workers attended 13 percent more meetings than before, and these meetings were packed with 14 percent more attendees.[10] Meetings replaced hallway chats, quick check-ins, coffee breaks, and even those painfully awkward happy hours. They became corporate duct tape: the lazy fix slapped onto every problem, whether it fixed anything or not.

In the post-pandemic era, as uncertainty has sunk its teeth into our workplaces—fueled by remote and hybrid work shifts, AI hype, economic whiplash, and a general sense of what-the-hell-is-happening—unproductive meetings have reached soul-crushing new lows. When we're unsure what to do, our slap-happy meeting reflex kicks into overdrive. Meetings give us the comforting illusion of progress, but behind the smoke and mirrors, they're often just unproductive time sucks.

In 2024 individual contributors, managers, and executives spent an average of 3.7, 5.8, and 5.3 hours per week, respectively, in *unproductive* meetings, an increase of 118 percent, 87 percent, and 51 percent since 2019.[11] Managers now spend more time languishing in unproductive meetings than anyone else. They're stuck in the middle, ping-ponging between high-level strategy meetings that are too abstract to do anything with and low-level status updates that regurgitate what happened instead of what matters. Hours get burned passing information up and down the org chart—work that a well-built communication system could handle without dragging everyone into another dead-end meeting.

For over fifteen years, I've studied the good, the bad, and the utterly broken realities of workplace meetings. Few things frustrate me more than watching bad meetings gobble up time, energy, and sanity from good people. And I've seen some truly epic time guzzlers. Like the designated notetaker who, when asked for meeting notes, handed over a pile of Post-its. Or the executive who nodded off mid-meeting, not long after urging everyone to "stay focused." Or the manager who called an urgent hour-long meeting to discuss reducing pointless meetings—and then ended it without assigning a single action item.

When I joined Dropbox in 2014 fresh out of college, I had a front-row seat to the aftermath of its radical Armeetingeddon, a company-wide crusade to eliminate unnecessary meetings.[12] That was my first glimpse of how a bold meeting reset could jolt people out of their broken meeting habits, at least temporarily.

Over the years, as I've studied, advised, and consulted for organizations across industries, including some of the largest in the world, I kept seeing the same slow-motion train wreck. Meetings multiplied, while productivity and engagement nosedived. Instead of doing real work, people sat in circles discussing work, slowly suffocating under the dead weight of broken meetings.

Eventually, I wanted to do more than help organizations manage the symptoms of bad meetings. I wanted to help them find a real cure. So in 2019 I enrolled in a PhD program at Stanford's Center for Work, Technology, and Organization to study how organizations adapt their work practices for the future of work—just months before COVID-19 turned the workplace upside down.

Over the next few years, I saw how organizations tried to repair their crumbling communication systems, including their meetings. For many, the pandemic was the wake-up call they desperately needed. But for others, it just meant doubling down on dysfunction. Instead of solving the root problems, they flooded calendars with even more meetings, turning an already bad situation into a full-blown dumpster fire.

When I finished my PhD in 2022 I launched the Work Innovation Lab at Asana,* an external-facing research and innovation center focused on fixing broken ways of working with evidence-based strategies (and pressure-testing them inside Asana, too). It didn't take long for one problem to shoot straight to the top of our dysfunction leaderboard: bad meetings.

Our first mission was to declare Meeting Doomsday at Asana, a full-scale calendar cleanse designed to eliminate the bloated, pandemic-era meeting overload.[13] People reclaimed their time. Their sanity returned. They rediscovered the joy of getting real work done. And for the first time, I had real hope. Maybe it was possible to escape the nightmare of bad meetings for good.

Since then, I've worked with dozens of companies around the world to help them improve how their teams collaborate. Each organization has its own special brand of dysfunction, but the root cause is almost always the same: Their meetings weren't intentionally designed. They just happened. And then they kept happening.

The true scale of the problem hit me when one of the world's largest videoconferencing companies reached out for help. It turned out that

---

*   Asana is a leading work management platform.

the folks engineering the tools we rely on for meetings couldn't figure out how to fix their own. If they were willing to shell out big bucks for help, what does that say about the state of our meetings? It's a sobering reminder that even the fanciest video tools, or the most buzzed-about AI, won't magically rescue us from bad meetings.

What we need isn't just better meeting technology. We need a full-scale reset in how we think about and design meetings.

YOUR MOST BROKEN, OVERLOOKED, AND EXPENSIVE PRODUCT

Quick meeting fixes are everywhere. Some folks think slapping an agenda on a meeting invite is a magic bullet. Others pin their hopes on meeting cost calculators, convinced that flashing a daunting dollar sign will guilt their people into canceling. Then there are No-Meeting Day evangelists who are under the illusion that cramming five days of dreadful meetings into four will miraculously make them less miserable. And now AI has joined the list of false prophets, with people sending digital twins to sit through meetings on their behalf.

If these quick fixes were all it took, we'd have fixed this mess years ago. Meetings aren't broken just because someone forgot to add an agenda. They're broken by design. And no amount of duct tape can fix a fundamentally flawed system.

This book isn't about halfhearted hacks. It's about rolling up your sleeves and rebuilding your meetings from the ground up. The secret? Treat your meetings like products. And not just any products. They're the most important, most expensive, and most overlooked products in your entire organization.

Meetings are where decisions are made—or die slow, painful deaths in circular debates. They're where teams align—or spiral wildly off course. They're where relationships deepen—or fracture. And they devour time, energy, money, and sanity at spectacular rates.

Unfortunately, most meetings aren't treated like products. They're treated like junk drawers: overstuffed, disorganized, rarely cleaned out, and crammed with things no one needs or wants. And that tangled mess doesn't just waste time. It drags down morale and chips away at job satisfaction. Research shows that how employees feel about their meetings is a significant predictor of overall job satisfaction, even after controlling for factors like the nature of their work, pay, their boss, and their colleagues.[14] In other words, bad meetings don't just eat up your workday. They can rot your culture and leave your employees feeling miserable.

And yet, instead of treating meetings as the high-stakes, high-cost product they are, companies view them as an unavoidable workplace tax. Something to endure rather than design.

Imagine if companies launched products the way they run meetings: without a clear purpose, riddled with bugs, bloated with useless features, zero user feedback, and no one held accountable when they flop. Customers would riot. Stock prices would tank. Competitors would pounce like vultures. The products would crash and burn. And yet that's how most meetings operate.

Meetings need to justify their cost. If we sink this much time, energy, and money into them, they should deliver real value. Otherwise, they're just painfully expensive illusions of productivity.

In this book, you'll learn how to design meetings worth your time. We'll rebuild them from the ground up using the same principles behind great products. Each chapter tackles a common meeting dysfunction and fixes it with a proven product design principle, giving you a blueprint for designing meetings that don't just fill the calendar. They actually work.

THE 7 MEETING DESIGN PRINCIPLES

Each of the seven meeting design principles is essential, but you don't need to tackle them in order. Start with the ones that address your team's biggest dysfunctions. Your first priority isn't to fine-tune what's already working. It's to eliminate what makes your meetings pointless and painful. Research shows that "bad is stronger than good": negative experiences have a far greater impact than positive ones.[15] So, stop the bleeding first.

Once you've addressed your biggest dysfunctions, you can refine, improve, and double down on what's working well enough but still can be improved.[16] That's how you design your best meeting ever.

Because great meetings aren't happy accidents. They're the result of intentional design.

Principle 1
Volume: Cut Your Meeting Debt

Are you drowning in too many meetings? Start here. It's time for a calendar reset. We'll confront your "meeting debt" (yes, you've got some) and reclaim your team's time for actual work.

Principle 2
Measurement: Choose the Right Metrics

Not sure if your meetings are working? Don't get seduced by metrics that are easy to track but useless for improving your meetings. I'll show you how to measure what actually matters.

Principle 3
Structure: Become a Meeting Minimalist

Are your meetings bloated? Do they have too many minutes, too many people, too many agenda items, or pop up too often, like calendar spam? It's time to cut the clutter. I'll show you how to strip meetings down to their essentials, so they stop bleeding time and start delivering results.

Principle 4
Flow: Apply Systems Thinking

Are your communication channels a disorganized mess: lost messages, buried files, scattered updates, and constant pings? Meetings won't fix that. In fact, they're often a symptom of a bigger problem, not the cure. I'll help you design a communication system where meetings have a clear purpose, and the right information reaches the right people at the right time.

Principle 5
Engagement: Prioritize User-Centric Design

Do your meetings leave people bored stiff, zoned out, or silently plotting their escape? I'll show you how to design meetings people don't dread and, yes, even look forward to.

Principle 6
Timing: Get Your Meetings in Rhythm

Do your meetings feel more like interruptions than progress? Scheduling a meeting at the wrong time kills momentum, shatters focus, and grinds work to a halt. I'll show you how to sync your meetings with the natural rhythm of work, so they propel work forward instead of slamming on the brakes.

Principle 7
Technology: Innovate and Iterate

Zoom fatigue? Death by PowerPoint? Drowning in AI tools that promised to fix your meetings but somehow made them even more painful? I'll help you decide which tools will enhance your meetings, and which are overpriced, overhyped distractions.

By the time we're done, your meetings will be well-built products—built with purpose, stripped of waste, and worth the time they consume. This book is your blueprint to reclaim your meetings, your time, and your sanity. Once and for all.

PRINCIPLE 1

Meeting Volume: Cut Your Meeting Debt

As the sun crept over the San Francisco skyline on an otherwise ordinary August morning in 2013, employees at Dropbox—the up-and-coming file-sharing service—woke up to an unexpected company-wide email. The subject line was as dramatic as it was intriguing: "Armeetingeddon has landed."[1]

The name was a tongue-in-cheek nod to Armageddon, the term for world-ending catastrophes, and the 1998 apocalyptic blockbuster film where Bruce Willis saves Earth from a giant asteroid.

But at Dropbox, the looming threat wasn't an asteroid hurtling toward Earth. It was meetings. Bloated, sprawling, soul-crushing meetings that had piled up like space junk during the company's meteoric rise. Armeetingeddon was more than a calendar purge. It was an all-out declaration of war on the dysfunctional meetings devouring employees' workdays.

In one sweeping move, Dropbox's IT department wiped recurring meetings from employees' calendars overnight. The email gleefully explained the carnage: "If you check your calendar, you'll notice that it's feeling a bit light—[at] midnight we flipped the switch." And it practically grinned through the screen: "Ahhh, doesn't it feel fantastic?"

Before Armeetingeddon, meetings were relentless at Dropbox. Employees pinballed from one meeting to another, some zipping through the hallways on RipStik scooters to keep up with their overstuffed calendars. Meetings didn't just clutter the workday. They *were* the workday.

And then, in an instant, they were gone.

For two weeks, Dropbox imposed a strict "meeting moratorium." Each night, the IT department swept through calendars like merciless janitors, scrubbing away any recurring meetings employees tried to sneak back in. Only a select few meetings were spared—the ones considered essential to the company's operations: recruiting meetings, heads of staff meetings, and meetings with external stakeholders like customers. Everything else was wiped clean. No exceptions. No mercy.

What followed was an eerie, unnatural calm. The relentless drumbeat of meetings vanished overnight, leaving behind something unfamiliar: uninterrupted time for employees to do their work.

By the time I joined Dropbox a year later, Armeetingeddon had become company lore. New hires heard the story during onboarding, passed down like a war story. Our own Bruce Willis moment. But instead of saving Earth, Dropbox had saved its people from the crushing doom of endless meetings.

Dropbox isn't the only company that has waged war on meetings. In 2023 Canadian e-commerce giant Shopify launched its own calendar purge, cheekily named Chaos Monkey.[2] The name paid homage to *chaos engineering*, the practice of deliberately disrupting or crashing IT systems to test their resilience.[3]

But Shopify's version didn't crash servers. It crashed calendars. A bot descended on employees' calendars, ruthlessly deleting any recurring meetings with two or more people. In an instant, thousands of hours were freed from the cold, dead grip of standing meetings that had long outlived their usefulness.

Meanwhile, at Slack, employees had been drowning in a swamp of recurring meetings so overgrown that no one remembered why they existed. These so-called "legacy meetings" had become corporate heirlooms, passed down from employee to employee, and growing more irrelevant each time a new meeting host took over. Eventually, Slack's leaders had enough. They hit the nuclear button and declared "calendar bankruptcy."[4]

"There are lots of legacy meetings that have changed owner, purpose, scope—let's start with a blank slate to determine what's *really* important," they told employees.[5] And just like that, recurring meetings vanished overnight.

Are meetings so fundamentally broken that the only viable solution is to tear them down and start over?

The short answer is yes, especially if your organization is drowning in what I call *meeting debt*: the ever-growing pileup of outdated, bloated meetings that choke productivity and smother real work.

In product development, there's a concept called *technical debt*. It builds up when teams cut corners and slap on quick fixes instead of addressing problems the right way. At first, it's manageable. But over time, those patches pile up and the system becomes a bloated, inefficient mess that's costly to maintain and nearly impossible to fix. Eventually, there's only one option left: Scrap it and start over with a full rewrite.

Meeting debt forms in much the same way. It's the quiet, creeping accumulation of outdated, unnecessary, and utterly pointless meetings that clog calendars. Like technical debt, it builds up quietly. It's the weekly check-in that lingers long after it has outlived its purpose, kept alive by the excuse "That's how we've always done it." It's the monthly steering committee meeting that outlasts the project it was meant to oversee. It's the calendar invite fired off with all the thoughtfulness of a sneeze—and accepted just as reflexively. No questions asked.

Before you know it, your calendar has become a junkyard of useless meetings, smothering real work under heaps of dysfunctional debris.

FIVE STEPS FOR CUTTING MEETING DEBT

In this chapter, you'll learn five practical steps to help you identify and eliminate your organization's meeting debt, and prevent it from building back up.

Step 1: Launch a Calendar Cleanse

When meeting debt spirals out of control, sometimes the only solution is to hit the reset button and make bold, sweeping cuts. Think Dropbox's Armeetingeddon, Shopify's Chaos Monkey, or Slack's Calendar Bankruptcy.

Step 2: Equip Employees to Defend Their Time

A calendar cleanse is just the beginning. The real challenge is preventing meeting debt from accumulating again. Employees need tools, scripts, and a culture that makes pushing back on bad meetings the norm, not an act of defiance.

Step 3: Build a Meeting Debt Repository

You also need a system to catch calendar crimes early. Set up a meeting debt repository (*repo*): a simple system for reporting dysfunctional meetings so they can be reviewed, redesigned, or shut down before they waste even more time.

Step 4: Add Guardrails to Prevent Meeting Debt

The best way to stop accumulating meeting debt is to cut it off at the source. Add a little friction—or, if necessary, a lot. Raise the bar for who is allowed to hit "Schedule" on yet another calendar invite.

Step 5: Commit to Regular Maintenance

Meeting debt will continue to accumulate unless you develop a habit of clearing it. Schedule regular meeting cleanses and build in ongoing maintenance to prevent meeting debt from piling up.

Clearing meeting debt may seem daunting and time-consuming, but I've seen teams slash their meeting debt and reset their meeting cultures in just a couple of weeks. In the rest of this chapter, we'll break it down—step by step—so your organization can finally reclaim its time, focus, and sanity.

Let's get pruning.

STEP 1: LAUNCH A CALENDAR CLEANSE

In 2024 a fast-growing cybersecurity company reached out to me in full-blown meeting panic mode. "We're in too many meetings. It's chaos," their head of communications confessed. She'd experienced the sweet relief of an Armeetingeddon-style reset I'd led at her previous company and was desperate for a similar overhaul. But then she hesitated. "Our leaders are not ready for anything that bold," she said. "There'd be too much pushback."

When companies hesitate to make bold cuts, it's often because their outdated routines have become so ingrained that breaking free feels risky, uncomfortable, and simply exhausting.

Sure, you can trim a meeting here and there. But if your calendar's already a raging dumpster fire, a few nips and tucks won't cut it. You need a complete reset. Too often, though, executives reach for safe half measures—like the classic "meeting audit."

Audits might tidy things up around the edges, but they won't fix the deeper rot. In 2022 I teamed up with Stanford organizational psychologist Bob Sutton to evaluate which approach had a greater impact: a standard meeting audit or a full calendar cleanse.[6] We called it the Meeting Reset. We randomly split fifty-eight Asana employees into two groups:

- **THE AUDIT GROUP.** These participants performed a standard meeting audit. They reviewed their calendars one meeting at a time, trimming and tweaking meetings to make them more useful.

- **THE MEETING DOOMSDAY GROUP.** This group started with the same audit but then wiped their calendars completely clean of recurring meetings for forty-eight hours. After the reset, only meetings that proved their worth were resurrected. Some were brought back in their original form, but most returned leaner and more useful.

Both groups cut meeting debt, but the Meeting Doomsday group reclaimed far more time: five hours per week per participant compared to three.

To understand why, we consulted Gabrielle Adams, a professor and behavioral scientist at the University of Virginia.[7] She explained that wiping the slate clean forces people to pause and seriously question whether each meeting deserves a place on their calendar. Adams pointed to research from Nobel Prize winner Daniel Kahneman's *Thinking, Fast and Slow*, which shows that people are far more likely to break old habits and spark fresh ideas when they step back and reflect deeply.[8] By starting from scratch, the Doomsday participants weren't just pruning their meetings. They were putting each one on trial before it earned a spot back on their schedules.

That's the power of a full calendar cleanse. Sure, it frees up time. But the bigger payoff is forcing participants to confront their long-standing habits and assumptions about meetings. And once they break free of the inertia of "it's always been there," cutting deadweight meetings becomes much easier. In the Meeting Doomsdays I've led, participants have reclaimed up to eleven hours per week each on average, and those gains can last for months.[9]

Pulling off a successful Meeting Doomsday[10] takes guts, but the payoff is worth it. Here's how to pull it off.*

Four Weeks Before Doomsday: Nail the Logistics

Meeting Doomsday doesn't begin on the day you cancel the meetings. It starts with the prep work. Without the right preparation, it'll just be a temporary detox from the dysfunction, not a cure.

---

* These steps are adapted from the Asana "Fixing Meetings Playbook" that I co-authored with Bob Sutton and Joshua Zerkel, but I've updated them based on what I've learned since.

INVOLVE EMPLOYEES OR RISK REVOLT. Heavy-handed moves like Dropbox's Armeetingeddon, Shopify's Chaos Monkey, and Slack's Calendar Bankruptcy can wipe out meeting debt overnight. But they also risk ambushing employees. And when employees feel ambushed, they don't buy in—they comply begrudgingly. That's when the old habits come back with a vengeance.

One of the keys to a successful Meeting Doomsday is codesigning it with your employees. When people help build the solution, they're more likely to buy in, a phenomenon that Harvard Business School professor Michael Norton calls the IKEA Effect.[11] We value things more when we've had a hand in creating them, whether it's a bookshelf or a rebuilt calendar.

If you want people to commit to your organization's changes, give them a real say in which meetings stay, which get cut, and which undergo a total overhaul. Unlike Armeetingeddon, Meeting Doomsday isn't an IT-led mass calendar wipe. It's a human-powered reset. Meeting owners decide which meetings to cut. Attendees get a voice too, opting out of meetings they find useless and pushing to redesign the ones worth saving.

GET THE TIMING RIGHT. Whether you're planning a Meeting Doomsday for a single team, a department, or your entire organization, timing matters. Schedule it for early in the week (Monday or Tuesday) and during a lighter workload period, like right after a major project wraps or at the start of a new quarter. If you launch it during a high-stakes deadline or crunch period, you're less likely to fix your meetings and more likely to spark a revolt.

KICK IT OFF WITH A BANG. Meeting Doomsday should feel like a movement. Kick it off on the same day for all participants. Then, to keep the momentum going, set up a shared virtual space, like a Slack channel, where employees can swap calendar horror stories, ask questions about Doomsday, and celebrate their newfound calendar freedom. Let them vent. Let them cheer. Let them bask in the sweet joy of reclaiming their time.

ENGAGE YOUR ADVOCATES. You'll need to recruit a few "energizers" to help lead the effort. Babson College professor Rob Cross describes energizers as the people who light up the room, spread enthusiasm, and make bold initiatives like Meeting Doomsday feel exciting instead of daunting. Their energy is contagious. Cross's research shows that energizers are more likely to get their ideas heard and implemented than non-energizers.[12] When they're in, others follow.

But enthusiasm isn't enough. You also need an executive sponsor with real clout. Employees have seen too many "change initiatives" come and go to take another one at face value. If higher-ups just nod along from the sidelines, employees won't take it seriously. But when leaders roll up their sleeves and slash their own bloated calendars, it sends a clear message: fixing broken meetings is everyone's job, starting at the top.

Three Weeks Before Meeting Doomsday: Declare Doomsday

It's time to make it official: Meeting Doomsday is coming.

MAKE THE ANNOUNCEMENT. Draft an announcement that's clear, bold, and jargon-free. No corporate BS. Explain exactly what's happening, what employees need to do, and when they need to do it.

But don't just lay out the logistics. Your job is to start a move-ment. Make bad meetings the enemy. This isn't just some ho-hum change effort. Turn it into a rallying cry. Give employees a reason to care. This is their chance to take back their calendars, reclaim their time, and finally put an end to the soul-crushing meetings that have worn them down for years.

GET LEADERS AND ENERGIZERS ON BOARD. Before you hit "Send," line up your executive sponsors and energizers. Get them to follow the announcement with a strong, public endorsement: a quick Loom video, a Slack post, or a shout-out during a team or all-staff* meeting. Their visible support gives Doomsday credi-bility and turns it into a battle worth fighting.

GET THE TIMING RIGHT. Announcing Meeting Doomsday three weeks before the calendar gutting begins strikes a good balance. It gives participants enough time to prepare, but not so much that momentum fizzles and people start finding excuses to weasel out. And believe me, they'll try. Someone once told me they were "too busy with meetings" to participate in Meeting Doomsday.

One Week Before Doomsday: Meeting Doomsday Audit

One week before Doomsday, it's time to assess what to cut and what to keep. Kick things off with a rallying cry: "Today, we take back our calen-dars, once and for all!"

---

*   I use the term *all-staff meeting* instead of *all-hands meeting*. The term *all-hands* is ableist. It assumes everyone has physical hands. It's a small shift, but language matters if we want our workplaces to be truly inclusive.

The first step is for participants to conduct a meeting audit. Before wiping their calendars clean, they need to decide which meetings are worth bringing back. Have them evaluate every recurring meeting on their calendar, either by exporting from Google Calendar or Outlook, or by going old-school and writing them down manually. Then, ask them to rate each one on a simple scale of 1 to 3 across two dimensions:

- **IMPACT:** To what extent does this meeting help you reach your work goals?

- **EFFORT:** How much work does this meeting require, including prep time, the meeting itself, and follow-up work?

In the first Meeting Doomsday I led, we asked participants to rate meetings based on how "valuable" they were. But *valuable* is a slippery word—vague enough to let any bad meeting weasel its way back onto the calendar. One person described a meeting as "valuable" simply because it filled the full hour. (That's a terrible measure of success. You'll learn why in chapter 3.)

The impact-versus-effort framework, a staple in product design, is more effective. Instead of reflexively justifying meetings based on habit, tradition, or a vague sense of "value," it forces employees to put them under the microscope and ask: Is this really worth the effort?

Give participants one week to complete the audit. By the end, they'll have an inventory of their meetings—what's worth keeping and what's just calendar junk.

Meeting Doomsday: Purge Your Calendar

This is the boldest—and most liberating—step: the actual Meeting Doomsday. For the next forty-eight hours, participants must delete every recurring meeting they listed on their audits, including the ones that scored a 3 for impact.

Hitting "Delete" on every meeting forces a hard reset. Even a forty-eight-hour pause gives people enough breathing room to rethink what's worth keeping. Once the slate is clean, participants often realize that even their "best" meetings weren't fully optimized. With a fresh perspective, they start spotting improvements, even if it's just shaving off five unnecessary minutes. And sometimes, they come to a bigger realization: The best version of a meeting is the one that doesn't exist at all.

If a full purge feels too extreme, or if your entire organization isn't participating in Meeting Doomsday, start small. Target recurring meetings with five or fewer attendees. They're easier to kill off without sparking backlash.

But don't let the larger meetings off the hook. They're often the worst offenders of meeting debt, and the hardest to kill off. Once a big meeting latches on to the calendar, it clings on for dear life. Canceling or redesigning it turns into a bureaucratic horror show: fielding complaints from loyal attendees and fending off that one person who insists the meeting is "critical for alignment." So the meeting lumbers on, week after week, slowly bleeding your team dry.

This is where your audit results come in. If a meeting with more than five attendees didn't score a 3 for impact, take it directly to the organizer. If they won't commit to redesigning it, tell them to put attendees out of their misery.

One Week After Meeting Doomsday: Bring Back the Essentials

After the forty-eight-hour meeting detox, it's time to rebuild. Instruct participants to reinstate only the meetings that earned their place back on the calendar.

- MEETINGS THAT SCORED A 3 FOR IMPACT BUT A 1 FOR EFFORT? These are obvious keepers. But don't just bring them back on autopilot. There's almost always room for improvement.

- MEETINGS THAT SCORED A 3 FOR EFFORT BUT ONLY A 1 FOR IMPACT? Good riddance. Do not resuscitate them.

For the intermediate ratings (like meetings that scored a 2 for impact), encourage participants to rethink their design. Can they be shorter? Do they need to happen as often? Is everyone on the invite list necessary? (We'll dive deeper into more strategies in chapter 3.)

Four Weeks After Doomsday: Crunch the Data

Four weeks after the hard reset, take stock of the impact. How much time did participants claw back? Which meetings survived the purge, and which ones were rightly tossed into the calendar graveyard? What patterns emerged that can help your team spot (and squash) meeting debt before it starts creeping back in?

During one Meeting Doomsday I led, I teamed up with Stanford computer science student Steven Li to develop a model to predict low-value meetings based on participants' audit results. We analyzed over a dozen factors, but one insight stood out: Meetings with vague titles (like "catch up" or "coffee chat") consistently ranked among the most useless.

Meanwhile, meetings with clear, purpose-driven titles (like "Project Bluebird Milestone Planning" or "Q3 Sales Strategy Review") consistently ranked higher on impact. The takeaway was clear: If the meeting title doesn't tell you exactly why you're there, it probably isn't worth showing up. We shared this and other red flags with participants to help them sniff out low-value meetings moving forward.

Don't just crunch the numbers. Gather qualitative feedback from participants as well:

- Did they feel relief after the purge?
- Were they more focused or energized?
- Was it easier to get meaningful work done?

Then, spotlight the best success stories. Celebrate the people who made bold, high-impact cuts. Call out the most brilliant meeting redesigns. Because when people see the real, tangible benefits—and taste the sweet freedom of reclaiming their time—they'll wonder why they didn't do it sooner.

As for the folks who didn't participate? They'll still be stranded in calendar purgatory, shuffling from one pointless meeting to the next, watching the Doomsday participants finally move their work forward.

STEP 2: EQUIP EMPLOYEES TO DEFEND THEIR TIME

Bad meetings are relentless. Without guardrails, they start creeping back shortly after your reset ends. That's why employees need the tools and permission to push back when the calendar landfill starts piling up again.

Companies like Dropbox[13] and GitLab[14] know this. They arm employees with pre-written scripts to politely decline low-impact meetings. Here are a few adapted scripts you can use:

- "Thanks for including me! I'm wondering if we could try to solve this over email instead?"

- "I've been in so many meetings lately, but I'm trying to be more disciplined about my schedule. Could we try to solve this without a meeting, first?"

- "I'd be happy to give you feedback on that! Before we schedule a meeting, could I review it in a shared doc?"

At GitLab, these scripts are baked right into their employee handbook. Employees know exactly what to say. No awkward fumbling for the right words. No second-guessing. The handbook spells it out: "If you're invited to a meeting that may not need to exist, it's OK to respectfully decline and point GitLab team members back to this handbook section."

Why are scripts like these so liberating? Because the moment a meeting hits your calendar, it sets off a chain reaction of social pressures, strong-arming you into hitting that "Accept" button, whether the meeting is worth your time or not.

In his book *Influence*, Arizona State University psychology professor Robert Cialdini outlines several psychological principles that help explain why declining a meeting can feel awkward, guilt-inducing, and sometimes downright risky, even when you know it's the right move:[15]

- **RECIPROCITY.** When someone takes the time to invite you, you feel like you "owe" them your attendance.

- **COMMITMENT.** When a meeting invite comes from a boss or
  senior leader, declining it can feel like an act of defiance. Or
  like stepping on a career land mine.

- **LIKING.** If the inviter is someone you admire or want to impress,
  declining feels personal. Like you're rejecting them, not just
  the meeting.

These psychological forces help explain why over half of employees
(53 percent) feel obligated to attend meetings they're invited to, even
when they aren't critical to the agenda, according to a 2022 survey by
transcription company Otter.ai.[16] Lower-level employees were 16 percent more likely to report feeling this pressure than more senior-level
employees. They're trapped in a catch-22: skip the meeting and risk appearing uncommitted or disrespectful, or show up and sit through yet
another pointless slog.

This is where those go-to scripts can cut through the calendar crap.
They ease the pressure by giving employees ready-made, socially accept-
able, company-sanctioned language to decline unnecessary meetings,
without the guilt trip.

But words alone aren't enough. Employees need enough psychological safety to use them. That means building a culture where people can
push back on inefficiencies and decline invites without worrying that
they'll be sidelined or scolded. Creating that kind of culture takes time.
(And it deserves its own book.*)

Yet even in workplaces where psychological safety is in short sup-
ply, employees can still push back on dysfunctional meetings. Harvard
Business School researcher Tijs Besieux and Harvard professor Amy Ed-

---

* Amy Edmondson's book, *The Fearless Organization*, tackles this brilliantly.

mondson suggest three strategic ways to challenge bad meetings based on your organization's level of psychological safety.[17]

The Helpful Workaround

In workplaces with low psychological safety, calling out bad meetings can feel like playing with fire. Say the wrong thing, and suddenly you're not fixing the problem. You *are* the problem. But that doesn't mean you have to sit there helplessly suffering under the weight of broken meetings. Besieux and Edmondson recommend an approach they call the *helpful workaround.*

Here's how it works: Instead of bluntly calling out what's wrong with a meeting, ask a seemingly innocent question that subtly calls attention to the dysfunction. For example, if the discussion spirals off-topic, you might say, "This is an interesting conversation. But do you think we'll still be able to get through today's agenda if we keep discussing this?" Translation: "This meeting has gone off the rails. Can we stop this soapbox session before it swallows up another twenty minutes?"

The brilliance of the helpful workaround is its subtlety. It doesn't come off as an attack. You're not criticizing. You're just being "curious" (even if, deep down, you're gritting your teeth at the inefficiency). It's a subtle nudge toward a better meeting. So subtle, in fact, that the organizer might even walk away believing *they* were the one who first spotted the problem.

The Solution-Centric Proposal

In workplaces with moderate psychological safety, calling out bad meetings doesn't feel like stepping into a minefield, but you still need to tread carefully. One wrong move and you could find yourself knee-deep in someone's bruised ego. Here, Besieux and Edmondson recommend the *solution-centric proposal*: Point out the issue, but pair it with a question that proposes a solution. For example, you might say, "I've noticed our status updates sometimes take up most of the meeting, which leaves little time for discussion. What if we tried sending status updates asynchronously and used the meeting time for real discussion instead?"

Like the helpful workaround, this approach lets you package your feedback as curiosity rather than criticism, which helps disarm people's defensiveness. And because psychological safety is higher, you can go a step further: not just naming the problem but suggesting how to fix it.

The Constructive Confrontation

In workplaces with high psychological safety, employees don't need to rely on clever phrasing or disguised "curiosity." Besieux and Edmondson recommend the *constructive confrontation*: Name the problem head on and pair it with a clear solution. For example, you might say, "I've noticed our meetings regularly go past the scheduled time. Can we tighten up the agenda and end on time?" It's direct and solution-oriented. Name it. Fix it. Move on.

No matter how much or how little psychological safety exists in your organization, leaders set the tone. If executives treat bloated, pointless meetings as an unavoidable cost of doing business, so will everyone else. But if they openly call out inefficiencies and demand improvement, it gives everyone else permission to do the same.

Yet, according to Otter.ai's survey, a whopping 80 percent of employees report that their managers have never talked to them about declining meetings.[18] That silence is toxic. It forces employees into a high-stakes guessing game. Should they skip the pointless meeting and reclaim their time? Or play it safe and show up, driven by the fear that declining might sideline them when the next promotion season rolls around?

Most people don't take the risk. They stay silent, open the meeting link, and brace for impact. Employees accept 83 percent of meeting invites that are sent to them, even though they report wanting to decline 31 percent.[19]

But when leaders break that silence and challenge meetings publicly, they send a powerful message:

- It's OK to say no to pointless meetings.
- It's OK to ask if a meeting needs to happen.
- It's OK to walk out if a meeting isn't serving a purpose.

Meetings aren't obligations. They're investments. And if they're not paying off, it's time to pull the plug.

STEP 3: BUILD A MEETING DEBT REPOSITORY

Even in workplaces with high psychological safety, some people still hesitate to call out bad meetings, script or no script. Some are introverts who would rather suffer through a useless hour than voice their concerns. Others hate confrontation. And some have spoken up so many times without seeing change that they've given up trying.

That's where a meeting debt repository (or *repo*) comes in. It's a centralized, easy-to-use system, which can be anonymous, where employees can flag broken, bloated, or time-sucking meetings without needing to confront the meeting organizer directly.

Think of it as a bug-tracking system, but for meetings. Software developers don't just ship code unchecked. They perform code reviews, set up automated tests, and deploy debugging tools to catch problems before they snowball into full-blown technical debt. Your meetings deserve that same level of scrutiny.

In 2024 Amazon CEO Andy Jassy rolled out his version of a debt repo, called a "Bureaucracy Mailbox." It was an email inbox that gave employees a direct line to report broken processes like time-wasting meetings.[20] His commitment? "I will read these emails and action them accordingly," with the goal of "rooting out" and "extinguishing" bureaucratic bloat.

To launch your own meeting debt repo, set up a portal where employees can easily flag meeting debt. It can be a dedicated email inbox (like Jassy's), a Slack channel, or an anonymous form. One company I worked with named theirs the "Fighting Friction" form: a digital whistleblower tool that enabled employees to flag broken processes like meetings that bogged them down with needless friction.

If you want your meeting debt repo to drive real change, don't leave it in the hands of middle managers. Some will take action. Some will ignore it. And the worst will treat it like a witch hunt, trying to hunt down whoever dared to complain. If you're serious about fixing meeting debt, the repo needs executive oversight. Ideally, the CEO or COO should review submissions, call out the worst offenders, and prove—through actions, not empty platitudes—that this isn't just another "we value your feedback" charade.

STEP 4: ADD GUARDRAILS
TO PREVENT MEETING DEBT

Clearing meeting debt feels great. But the real victory isn't wiping the slate clean. It's keeping it that way. That's where guardrails come into play: systems and tactics that prevent meeting debt from accumulating in the first place by cutting it off at the source.

There are three types of guardrails:

- **SPEED BUMPS.*** Gentle nudges that encourage people to pause before adding another meeting to the calendar.

- **GATEKEEPERS.** Approval checkpoints that require a designated person (like a manager, department head, or senior executive) to sign off before a meeting can be scheduled.

- **BLOCKS.** Hard stops that prevent certain meetings from ever making it onto the calendar.

Let's start with the gentlest guardrail: speed bumps.

Speed Bumps: Think Before You Click

When Shopify introduced No-Meeting Wednesdays, its leaders knew a policy wasn't enough. So they paired it with a speed bump: a Slack bot that automatically nudged anyone who attempted to book a meeting on the forbidden day to reconsider. The bot didn't block Wednesday meetings outright. It just reminded the scheduler they were about to violate the norm, prompting them to think twice.[21]

The little speed bump worked. According to COO Kaz Nejatian, 85 percent of employees comply with No-Meeting Wednesday, far better than the typical no-meeting-day compliance rate I see (which is usually 50 percent or worse).[22]

If you want speed bumps that actually reduce meeting debt, go

---

*   I first learned the concept of speed bumps from Bob Sutton; he writes about them in his wonderful book with Huggy Rao, *The Friction Project*.

straight to your biggest problem areas. Are your meetings bloated with too many attendees? Add a calendar pop-up that says, "Whoa! This meeting has more than eight people. Are all these folks necessary?" (Why eight? You'll find out in chapter 3.) Are employees' calendars packed with legacy meetings? Trigger an automated warning before they can create a new recurring meeting series: "This meeting is set to recur indefinitely. Try setting it to expire after ninety days and then reevaluate if it's still useful."

Tools like Slack, Google Calendar, and modern project management platforms allow you to create these automated nudges through built-in features or APIs.

Speed bumps don't block meetings outright. They just make people pause. And sometimes that brief moment is all it takes to stop someone from reflexively adding a meeting and plunging straight into a time-wasting pileup.

Gatekeepers: If You Want the Meeting, Prove It

Gatekeepers don't just nudge people to think twice. They require explicit approval from a manager, a team lead, or even the CEO before a meeting can be scheduled. This extra step forces people to justify why a meeting is necessary, rather than scheduling it by default. Because if a meeting isn't worth the effort to get sign-off, it's not worth stealing an hour of everyone's time.

For years, Google clung to the idea that holding more interviews meant better hiring decisions.[23] Candidates were dragged through marathon interview loops, sometimes interviewing with a dozen different employees for a single role. But then Google crunched the numbers to see if those extra interviews made a difference. They discovered that just four interviews were enough to predict whether a candidate should be hired with 86 percent confidence.[24] Beyond that, every additional interview improved the prediction accuracy by less than 1 percent.

So Google introduced a gatekeeper rule: the Rule of Four. No more than four interviewers could be scheduled with a candidate. If someone wanted a fifth, they had to submit a written justification directly to the then director of people operations, Laszlo Bock.[25] Unsurprisingly, needing Bock's sign-off made that fifth interview seem a whole lot less appealing.

Suddenly, the interview bloat evaporated. According to Shannon Shaper, Google's hiring innovation manager, the Rule of Four saved Googlers hundreds of thousands of hours, reduced the average time-to-hire by approximately two weeks, and spared candidates from slogging through endless interview loops.[26]

Blocks: No Means No Meeting

Blocks are the strictest meeting guardrails of all. They don't just discourage meetings. They stop them dead in their tracks.

Some blocks are self-imposed, like Josh Braun's "three strikes" rule.[27] When he was head of sales at the software company Basecamp, Braun had a simple policy: If a sales prospect racked up three strikes, he refused to meet with them. Strikes were earned for:

- canceling a meeting because of a "competing priority";
- canceling a meeting because they were "running late"; or
- canceling a meeting without giving any explanation.

Three strikes and you were out. If someone didn't respect Braun's time, they didn't get it.

Technology can enforce blocks, too. Take Clockwise's Focus Time feature. It can automatically decline meeting requests during protected hours, regardless of how "urgent" someone claims their quick sync is.

One of my favorite blocking strategies is a simple Google Calendar hack. Mark yourself as OOO (out of office) on no-meeting days, and Google will auto-decline any invites that try to sneak in. It won't explain or negotiate. And it certainly won't apologize for defending your time and sanity.

Want to send an even louder message? A former colleague of mine, Ashley Waxman, now VP of brand marketing at the influencer marketing platform CreatorIQ, took it a step further by labeling her block: "No-Meeting Wednesday. I will decline to protect my sanity."

I never dared to schedule over that. And even if I had, Google would have blocked me.

STEP 5: COMMIT TO REGULAR MAINTENANCE

Two years after Dropbox's Armeetingeddon, Sutton and I followed up with CEO Drew Houston to see if the meeting purge was still keeping meetings under control.

His verdict? "It's worse than ever."[28]

The post-purge bliss lasted about a year, but then meeting debt came roaring back. Familiar complaints about chopped-up workdays and bloated calendars resurfaced. The writing was on the wall: Dropbox needed another Armeetingeddon.

Schedule a Regular Cleanse

Meeting debt is relentless. A one-time cleanup won't cut it. As Houston told us, cutting meetings is like mowing the lawn. Do it only once, and the weeds will grow back before you know it.

That's why you need a recurring calendar cleanse. Pick a set date at least once per year—ideally twice—for a Meeting Doomsday. Don't wait until your calendar looks like a neglected jungle and you need a weed whacker just to find thirty minutes of focus time. Treat it like preventive maintenance. You wouldn't let outdated code pile up until your entire system crashes. You wouldn't ignore customer complaints until you need a product recall. So why let meeting debt pile up until your team is stuck in calendar quicksand?

Wait too long and you'll find yourself right back where you started: trudging through a jungle of pointless meetings, wondering how your calendar turned into an unruly mess all over again.

Reward Good Meeting Design

One of the best ways to keep meeting debt from creeping back is to hold people accountable for their share of it.

We obsessively track budgets, revenue, and profits, often down to the decimal. We penalize overruns and missed key performance indicators (KPIs). But somehow, wasting hours in pointless meetings rarely shows up on anyone's performance review.

Meetings aren't free. They just feel that way because the costs are hidden. But every meeting is a payroll line item in disguise. When you stuff ten employees into a meeting for an hour, you burn ten hours' worth of salaries. So why don't we hold meetings to the same standards as any other major business expense? Why don't we incentivize and reward the kind of collaboration that drives results, instead of just draining resources?

High-performing organizations do. According to research from the Institute for Corporate Productivity (i4cp), they're up to five and a half times more likely to reward effective collaboration.[29] Effective meeting management should be treated as a core competency, factored into performance reviews, 360-degree feedback, and even compensation.

You don't need to overhaul your entire performance review process to start rewarding good meeting design. Ask your team for honest feedback on how you run meetings. Use AI tools to measure your meeting effectiveness. (We'll cover the best tools in chapter 7.) And make it fun. Give out awards for Most Valuable Meeting of the Month. Celebrate the hero who turned a sixty-minute slog into a fifteen-minute power meeting. Give out a prize for Least Likely to Schedule a Meeting That Could've Been an Email.

When designing great meetings becomes a badge of honor, your meeting culture shifts. Meetings stop being mindless calendar fillers and, instead, become proof that your organization values people's time.

And that's a skill worth mastering—and celebrating.

MEETING DEBT WILL BANKRUPT YOUR WEEK— UNLESS YOU FIGHT BACK

Calendar cleanses can free up massive amounts of time. When Shopify launched its Chaos Monkey initiative, it wiped out 12,000 recurring meetings,[30] equivalent to approximately 322,000 hours of meeting time saved over a year across its roughly 10,000 employees.[31]

But as Dropbox's Armeetingeddon made clear, purges alone aren't permanent fixes. Without long-term strategies in place, meeting debt creeps back in. Soon enough, your once-pristine calendar turns into an overgrown jungle of calendar crabgrass.

The five debt-clearing steps we've covered—calendar cleanses, giving employees tools to push back, setting up meeting debt repos, adding guardrails, and committing to regular maintenance—aren't silver bullets. They work only if you treat them like habits, not one-off heroic efforts.

If you're not actively paying down your meeting debt, it's quietly racking up interest. And before long, those pointless meetings won't just nibble away at your time. They'll bankrupt your workweek.

PRINCIPLE 2

Measurement: Choose the Right Metrics

You're about to hit "Schedule" on a thirty-minute meeting when a number flashes across your screen.

Five hundred dollars. A thousand dollars. Maybe more.

That's the price tag for pulling everyone into the room. Would you still click "Schedule"?

That cold slap of reality is exactly what COO Kaz Nejatian wanted Shopify employees to feel when the company rolled out its meeting "cost calculator." As part of the company's Chaos Monkey initiative, the tool was integrated directly into employees' calendaring systems. Every time someone tried to schedule a meeting, it automatically crunched the numbers, added up the hourly salary rates of every attendee, and slapped a price tag on the invite. The goal was to make the hidden cost of meetings painfully visible and force employees to confront the uncomfortable question: Is this meeting worth *that* much?

But it didn't take long for Shopify's calculator to stir up controversy. *Bloomberg* accused the company of "shaming" employees into canceling meetings.[1] Meanwhile, *Business Insider* labeled the tool "gimmicky," pointing out that it used generic salary estimates, meaning two engineers with vastly different paychecks could still trigger the same cost.[2] Others worried that fixating on meeting costs would discourage collaboration and stifle creativity by turning every invite into a guilt trip.

Love it or hate it, the calculator proved just how tricky—and polarizing—meeting metrics can be. That's why you need Meeting Design Principle 2: Choose the right metrics.

THE METRICS TRAP

Metrics like meeting costs can be as tempting as they are treacherous. As in product development, they can reveal what's working and what's broken. But if you measure the wrong thing—or the right thing in the wrong way—metrics won't fix your meetings. They'll just help you run terrible ones more efficiently.

The product world is littered with cautionary tales of metrics gone wrong. In 1985, after years of Pepsi chipping away at its market share, Coca-Cola decided to reformulate its iconic soda and launch New Coke. On paper, it looked like a slam dunk. Taste tests showed people preferred New Coke over both Pepsi and the original formula.[3]

But when New Coke hit the shelves, customers revolted. The backlash was swift and brutal. Protest groups popped up across the US with names like Society for the Preservation of the Real Thing and Old Cola Drinkers of America.[4] This fierce response forced Coca-Cola to backpedal and bring back the original formula as Coca-Cola Classic.

What went wrong? Coke measured the wrong thing. The taste tests were conducted in sterile lab environments, disconnected from the real-life moments that made Coke iconic. They didn't measure the nostalgia: the ice-cold bottle cracked open at a backyard barbecue or that sneaky sip from a parent's glass at a ball game.

As Coke learned the hard way, if you don't choose your metrics wisely, they'll lead you down the wrong path. And with meetings, it's even trickier because they're volatile, improvisational, and human to the core. You can't just measure user satisfaction and expect to know if the meeting worked.

THE FOUR MANTRAS OF MEANINGFUL MEETING MEASUREMENT

Most organizations don't measure their meetings at all, let alone in ways that reveal whether they actually drive results. To avoid costly flops like Coke's blunder, stick to four core mantras of meaningful meeting measurement:

MANTRA 1: AVOID MISLEADING METRICS. Don't confuse what's easy to track with what's useful. Just because a meeting metric feels credible, doesn't mean it will help you improve your meetings.

MANTRA 2: USE RETURN ON TIME INVESTED (ROTI). The simpler your feedback loop, the better your insights. If you want honest, actionable feedback, focus on the metric that matters most: return on time invested (or ROTI).

MANTRA 3: MEASURE WHAT MATTERS. A metric is worthless if it doesn't influence decisions or change behavior. If your meeting metrics don't drive people to design better meetings, they're just vanity metrics.

MANTRA 4: BEWARE OF METRICS AS TARGETS. As economist Charles Goodhart once warned, "When a measure becomes a target, it ceases to be a good measure." If people start gaming the system to hit a number instead of solving a real problem, your metrics will cause more harm than good.

There are only three good reasons to measure your meetings:

- To prevent meeting debt from piling up by using metrics as speed bumps, like Shopify's cost calculator.

- To assess whether a meeting is effective by measuring return on time invested (ROTI).

- To improve the meetings that stay on the calendar by using meeting analytics.

Follow the four mantras, and you'll be able to achieve all three.

MANTRA 1: AVOID MISLEADING METRICS

Numbers are seductive. Research shows that people trust information more when it includes them.[5] It's why simply slapping a number onto something can instantly make it feel more credible. But that false sense of precision can lure you into a data-driven illusion.

When measuring meetings, four metrics can be especially misleading: meeting sentiment, self-ratings, meeting cost, and meeting time savings. They look useful, but they usually just give you a false sense of precision, while quietly steering you off course.

Meeting Sentiment: The "Meetings Suck" Reflex

You've seen the clickbait headlines:

- "Half of All Meetings Are a Waste of Time"[6] (*Forbes*)
- "Meetings Are a Productivity Killer—and 3 in Every 4 are Totally Ineffective"[7] (*Fortune*)

These stats go viral because they tap into a universal workplace ritual: our collective love of bashing meetings. It's right up there with griping about the weather or roasting your company's latest reorg.

Even when a meeting isn't a complete train wreck, people still grumble. Why? Because complaining about meetings is social glue. Few things bond two coworkers faster than trading war stories about an hour-long meeting that could've been a three-line email.

But a lot of that trash talk isn't about the meeting itself. People bash meetings because they think that's what they're supposed to do. They've been socially conditioned.

In one study, Steven Rogelberg, chancellor's professor of organizational science at the University of North Carolina, asked employees to rate their meetings both publicly and privately. Publicly, over half complained about them. But privately, when they weren't performing for their peers, only 15 percent rated their meetings as poor. In fact, 42 percent called them "good," and 17 percent even described them as "excellent."[8]

People aren't always reacting to the meeting itself. They're reacting to how they think they're supposed to feel.

Another reason bad meetings stick in our brains is *negativity bias*. Research shows that we remember negative experiences more vividly and for longer than positive ones.[9] Blame it on our brains' survival instincts. Our ancestors didn't stay alive by admiring sunsets. They survived by panicking at rustling in the bushes, because it may have meant a predator was lurking nearby. That sunset? Beautiful, but not a matter of life or death.

Fast-forward to today, and that same bias means one bad meeting gets seared into our memory, drowning out several good ones. It also explains why broad, sentiment-based questions about meetings in general—like "How effective are your meetings?" or "What percentage of your meetings are effective?"—are mostly useless. They trigger knee-jerk negativity. It's like asking people how they feel about Mondays. Cue the groans.

Instead of triggering automatic complaints, anchor your questions to specific meetings. Ask about a concrete experience (like their last meeting or this morning's 9 a.m. stand-up), rather than a vague "How do you feel about meetings?" That helps you bypass the default "meetings suck" reflex. When you get concrete, people stop griping in generalities and start giving feedback you can actually use.

Self-Ratings: "It's Not Me, It's You"

Asking people to rate their own meetings might seem like a smart way to measure meeting effectiveness. But there's one big problem: Humans are world-class blame deflectors. When a meeting flops, it's never our fault. It's usually someone else's.

Before I joined Adam Grant on his podcast *WorkLife* to discuss why meetings often suck, he posted a simple question on LinkedIn: "I hate meetings . . . What was the worst meeting you've ever attended?"[10]

The floodgates opened. Hundreds of horror stories poured in, and the blame flew in every direction:

- the "incompetent senior managers" who berated everyone;
- the "HIPPOs" ("Highest Paid Person's Opinion") who hijacked the conversation;
- the attendees who showed up late.

Meeting expert Elise Keith combed through the responses and spotted a clear pattern: People always saw themselves as the victim. The innocent bystander. The poor soul trapped in another dysfunctional meeting, but certainly not the one causing it.[11]

Psychologists call this *self-serving bias.*[12] When things go well, we pat ourselves on the back and take credit. When they crash and burn, we point fingers. Magically, we're surrounded by clueless, incompetent colleagues who couldn't run a meeting to save their lives.

Asking a meeting host to rate their own meeting is like asking a chef to review their own cooking. You'll get five-star reviews a lot of the time, even if the soup's so salty it could kill a slug.

If you want genuine feedback, skip the self-ratings and go straight to your attendees. They have the clearest perspective on what's working, what's broken, and whether what you're serving is undercooked, over-done, or downright inedible.

By the end of this chapter, you'll know how to get honest feedback, and use it to serve up better meetings.

Meeting Cost: A "Shock Metric" for Slashing Meeting Debt

When meetings feel "free"—just another block on the calendar—they become dangerously easy to misuse. As consultant Tom Goodwin put it: "These days, it's harder to expense a Twix from a hotel mini bar than it is to call a meeting that costs $20,000 of other people's time."[13]

Submitting a fifteen-dollar lunch receipt requires four approvals.

But schedule a meeting that burns through a week's worth of salaries? No receipt required.

Few things grab people's attention like slapping a price tag on something they assumed was free. Shopify understood this when it rolled out its meeting cost calculator. It was designed to jolt people out of their mindless meeting habits. I call this a *shock metric*: a number meant to make you squirm. Suddenly, instead of casually clicking "Schedule," you're staring at a $500, $1,000, or even $5,000 price tag. Is that status update really worth that much?

When used wisely, meeting cost metrics act like speed bumps to prevent meeting debt. They make people think twice before adding another meeting to the pile. But dollar signs alone don't tell the whole story.

In 2014, a *Harvard Business Review* article described a weekly ninety-minute mid-level-management meeting at a large manufacturing company that cost over $15 million a year in salaries. Shockingly, when managers were asked who approved the meeting, no one had an answer.[14] "Tom's assistant just schedules it and the team attends," they said.

That $15 million price tag is jaw-dropping (and the lack of oversight is even more damning). But a high-cost meeting isn't automatically a wasteful one. That $15 million meeting might have prevented a $75 million lawsuit or sparked a $150 million revenue idea. As Warren Buffett put it, "Price is what you pay; value is what you get."[15]

Organizational expert Michael Arena witnessed this firsthand at a global retail company. He once attended a meeting with between seventy and eighty highly paid senior leaders. On paper the meeting looked like a colossal waste of time. However, in just sixty minutes, the group made a dozen high-impact decisions, sliced through weeks of bureaucratic sludge, and dodged countless rounds of email Ping-Pong. That meeting didn't just break even. It delivered serious returns.

Shock metrics like meeting costs can jolt people into rethinking their knee-jerk scheduling reflex. But guilt-tripping people gets you only so far. If you want to fix your meetings for real, you need to go beyond sticker shock and ask a far more important question: Was the time well invested? (More on that shortly.)

Meeting Time: The Easiest Metric to Love and Abuse

One of the easiest metrics to track is meeting time (by meeting, person, or company-wide). Just add up the minutes. Once people see how many hours are disappearing into the calendar vortex, they become much stingier about tossing another one in.

But don't just look at totals across a series of meetings. Clocking time within a single meeting is a simple way to prevent marathon meetings from becoming another entry on your meeting debt ledger. That's what New York City Mayor Michael Bloomberg aimed for in 2011 when he installed "count-up" clocks in City Hall meeting rooms.[16] At the start of each meeting, staffers would hit the timer and watch the seconds climb up and up. Bloomberg's press secretary bluntly said, "We're not here to sit around and chat—we're here to get things done."[17]

Folks at Google Ventures had a similar "aha" moment in 2013 when they started measuring meeting time with an unlikely tool: the Time Timer.[18] Originally designed to help kids with autism and ADHD stay focused, the oversized red countdown clock found its way into Silicon Valley meeting rooms. Inspired by how effectively it worked in his son's first-grade classroom, Jake Knapp, a design partner at Google Ventures, decided to try it on executives. (Because, let's be honest, we all know a few executives who could use a little first-grade discipline. More on that in chapter 5.)

And it worked. Meetings became shorter and sharper. "Setting that bad boy on the table instantly makes meetings more urgent and efficient," said Knapp.[19]

Why do countdown clocks work? Because they make time loss feel real. They tap into what psychologists Amos Tversky and Daniel Kahneman call *loss aversion*. Their research shows that the pain of losing something feels about twice as intense as the joy of gaining it.[20] Time doesn't feel abstract anymore. It's bleeding out on a giant screen, second by second, right before your eyes. When you see your minutes dying in real time, you start treating them like they matter.

Like measuring the financial cost of meetings, tracking meeting time makes the toll impossible to ignore—and it lights a fire under your team to avoid meeting debt. But time alone doesn't tell you if that hour was well spent, or how to make the next one more productive. And if you're not careful, time-tracking can backfire, turning meetings into a frantic race against the clock. Meaningful discussions get rushed. Complex problems get flattened into sound bites. Ideas don't get the oxygen they need. Not because they aren't valuable, but because they don't fit inside a thirty-minute calendar cage. In chapter 3, I'll show you how to prevent that by giving each agenda item a clear finish line—so you'll know exactly when to move on and when to slow down.

MANTRA 2: USE RETURN ON TIME INVESTED (ROTI)

The truth about meetings usually gets swallowed rather than spoken. Honest feedback is tough to pry out of people.

Ask the wrong way, and you can trigger the "meetings suck" reflex or wear people out with survey fatigue. Neither will get you the insights you need to fix what's broken.

That's where return on time invested (ROTI) comes in.[*] To assess the real value of your meetings, ask participants one simple question: Was the meeting worth their time? That's ROTI. At the end of a meeting, participants rate it on a 0–5 scale:

0: COMPLETE WASTE OF TIME. This meeting was a total interruption. It didn't help move my work forward and made it more challenging to get back on track.

1: SIGNIFICANT WASTE OF TIME. This meeting had a few useful moments that helped me move my work forward, but overall, it wasn't worth the time I invested.

2: BREAK-EVEN. The time I invested matched the progress the meeting helped me make in moving my work forward.

3: MODERATE RETURN ON TIME. The meeting helped me move my work forward, but hardly enough to justify the time I invested.

4: GOOD RETURN ON TIME. The meeting was a worthwhile investment of my time. It helped me make clear progress on my work.

5: EXCELLENT USE OF TIME. The meeting was well worth the time I invested. It helped me move work forward more than almost anything else I could have done with that time.

You can use an online form or a digital poll to collect responses.

---

[*] I first learned about ROTI from Elise Keith.

ROTI started as a low-tech system used by agile and lean develop-ment teams. After a meeting, participants would hold up their fingers to rate it: zero (a closed fist) if the meeting was a complete waste of their time and five if it was well worth it. But let's be honest: Most employees don't want to flash a big, closed fist while making awkward eye contact with the person who just led the terrible meeting.

Unless psychological safety is high, anonymous digital tools are often more effective for collecting feedback. They strip away social pres-sure and make it more likely that people will tell you what they really think, not just what you want to hear.

ROTI borrows its logic from a familiar product metric: ROI (re-turn on investment). In product development, success isn't measured by how long something takes to build. It's measured by the value it delivers. ROTI applies the same lens to meetings. It dislodges the meeting suck reflex by pushing people to judge value against the most finite resource they have: their time. Everyone has an instinctive sense of when their precious time has been wasted.

To make ROTI more actionable, Elise Keith suggests asking attend-ees a simple follow-up question: "What would it take for you to improve your rating by one point?" That will give you specific, actionable feed-back on how to improve.

That's it. No bloated post-meeting surveys. Just two sharp questions that cut straight to the truth and tell you whether the meeting delivered a return worthy of the time people put in.

ROTI isn't meant for every meeting.* Use it strategically—about

---

* ROTI isn't the right tool for meetings where the main goal is to build rela-tionships. These meetings won't always deliver a quick payoff or score high on ROTI. But over time, these slow-burn investments build the kind of trust that opens doors, moves work forward, and saves your ass when things go sideways.

10 percent of the time—to spot patterns and make smart design changes. If you ask too often, you'll get junk data. Some people will auto-tap "5" just to make the survey overload stop. Others will dole out "0" ratings purely out of spite.

Between your ROTI assessments, let meeting analytics do the heavy lifting (we'll get to those soon). Software tools are better at crunching numbers, are more objective, and don't require any effort from participants, making them the perfect sidekick to ROTI.

Want to go even further? Tie ROTI to employee performance reviews. As we covered in chapter 1, running effective meetings should be treated as a measurable skill. Imagine a workplace where employees proudly share their high ROTI scores instead of flaunting their overstuffed calendars like twisted badges of honor. That's the kind of meeting culture worth building—and rewarding.

MANTRA 3: MEASURE WHAT MATTERS

Shock metrics can jolt people into canceling bad meetings. And ROTI helps you evaluate whether the time was worth it, without the guilt trip that shock metrics sometimes deliver. The follow-up question ("What would it take for you to improve your rating by one point?") gives ROTI even more backbone. It surfaces what's not working and helps make sense of split ratings. Maybe the agenda mattered to half the participants and bored the rest to tears. In that case, you can refine the agenda or stop inviting people who don't need to be there.

But ROTI takes you only so far. If you're serious about improving your meetings, you need to dig deeper. The biggest dysfunctions aren't always obvious. They lurk within patterns, bottlenecks, and bad habits that people can't see or don't think to question.

Debugging Your Meetings with Analytics

When we analyzed the impact of the Meeting Reset at Asana, one unexpected culprit behind bad meetings emerged: Wednesdays.

At Asana, Wednesdays are sacred, officially designated No-Meeting Wednesdays. And so, when someone broke protocol and booked a meeting anyway, frustration spread quickly. Employees weren't just annoyed—they resented the organizer for hijacking their protected focus time.

We discovered this through meeting analytics. We started by analyzing participants' detailed meeting audits, which tracked everything from when the meetings were scheduled (day of the week and time of day) to the number of attendees, how often they happened, what they were titled, and more. Then we built a model to predict each meeting's average perceived impact and effort based on the participants' audits. The results were clear: Employees consistently rated Wednesday meetings as less impactful.

That's the difference between meeting metrics and meeting analytics. Metrics are just the raw numbers: how many meetings, how long they last, how often they recur. Analytics, on the other hand, is the detective work. It goes beyond the numbers to spot patterns, expose what's broken, and serve up insights on how to make things better.

You can surface meeting analytics manually, as we did by analyzing meeting audits and building a model. But there's a more efficient way: digital exhaust.[21] Every video meeting leaves behind a trail of digital DNA: data from calendar invites, meeting logs, chat activity, and more. When you piece it all together, you can finally see what's dragging your meetings down:

- Are some leaders treating the calendar like their personal fiefdom, scheduling endless, mind-numbing status updates?

- Are people multitasking during meetings, firing off Slack messages to their coworkers instead of paying attention?
- Do your most important meetings consistently run late or get hijacked by ramblers?

Most companies don't realize they have access to such a wealth of insights. But once you dig in and the patterns start to surface, it becomes a lot harder to pretend everything is fine. You start spotting meeting dysfunction in places you never even thought to look.

That's what happened when a global tech company with tens of thousands of employees took a closer look at its meetings. At first, executives assumed the company had a meeting volume problem: too many meetings and not enough focus time. But when they brought in the meeting analytics firm Worklytics, a different culprit emerged.

The meetings that employees loathed the most weren't just frequent. They were one-sided status updates led by VPs while everyone else mentally checked out. How could Worklytics tell? Slack and email activity spiked during those meetings—a clear sign that employees were multitasking their way through the dead air.

Once these insights surfaced, the CEO issued a blunt directive. He asked the monologuing VPs who were scheduling the meetings to rein in their brain-draining status dumps.

If the company's leaders had tracked only total meeting hours as a standalone metric, they would've missed the real problem. The issue wasn't just *how many* meetings they had. It was who was running them (the VPs) and how they were structured (as one-way status snooze-fests).

Tools like Zoom, Microsoft Teams, and Read AI can surface these kinds of analytics: who's dominating the airwaves, which meetings engage people, how often meetings start late, and even how frequently people multitask.

You can use analytics to improve your in-person meetings, too. Just create a virtual meeting link and have everyone join from a shared conference room or their own devices. That way, you'll capture key metrics like talk time and engagement—the raw data your analytics engine needs to spot what's working, what's not, and where your meetings need a tune-up.

Just like a buggy product, bad meetings need a full diagnostic. They're filled with hidden design flaws. But fortunately, like any malfunctioning product, they can be inspected, debugged, and redesigned into something people actually want to use.

Five Analytics That Unmask Meeting Dysfunction

Meeting dysfunction comes in many flavors. Some teams are buried under back-to-back calendar clutter. Others are stuck on a hamster wheel of status updates. Some are held captive by overtalkers who can't resist the sound of their own voice.

But no matter where your meeting dysfunction is hiding, there are five universal metrics that can help you sniff it out and shut it down. They're the perfect complement to ROTI. On their own, they're just raw metrics. But when you track them over time, compare them across teams, and tie them to real outcomes, they become powerful analytics that expose the calendar gunk.

1. Time in Meetings: Hours Spent in Meetings per Week

In May 2024, Nvidia CEO Jensen Huang sat down with Stripe cofounder and CEO Patrick Collison for a fireside chat. Huang gave a brutally honest glimpse into his daily routine: "I wake up at 6 a.m. . . . . I get my work done before I get to work . . . And then when I get to work [I have meetings] pretty much all day long."[22]

Let that sink in: "I get my work done before I get to work."

The CEO of one of the most innovative companies doesn't count the meetings that dominate his day as "real" work. And he's not alone. Employees at all levels find themselves squeezing their most important work into the margins of their day—before dawn, after dinner, or claustrophobically wedged between back-to-back meetings. Productivity isn't the only casualty. Employee morale takes a beating, too.

How much meeting time is too much? According to Worklytics, the tipping point is ten hours per week.[23] Once employees exceed that threshold, the negative effects start piling up: longer work hours, not enough time for deep, focused work, and lower engagement.

Of course, meeting loads vary by role. A product manager generally needs more meetings than an engineer. But if your team is regularly blowing past the ten-hour mark, or if one poor soul is racking up double or triple their peers' meeting hours, it's time to hit the brakes and figure out what's broken.

Carnegie Mellon University professor Vivek Wadhwa envisions a future where calendars have built-in warning systems.[24] Imagine you hit the ten-hour threshold and a bright red pop-up flashes across your screen: "WARNING: Your week is now 25 percent meetings. Proceed with caution."

That's the kind of speed bump that can help you avoid scheduling your workweek straight into a productivity sinkhole.

2. Airtime: Share of Voice in Meetings

Communication in most group settings is wildly unequal. According to Leigh Thompson, a management professor at Northwestern University, in a typical six- or eight-person group setting, just three people are responsible for about 70 percent of the talking.[25] That's why so many meetings feel less like conversations and more like hostage situations dominated by a few voices.

Hogging airtime isn't just bad etiquette. It skews our perceptions of others' competence and leadership. It fuels what researchers call the Babble Hypothesis: The more someone talks, the more we perceive them as a leader—even if they're just spewing verbal diarrhea.

In one study, Neil MacLaren, a researcher at the US Army Research Institute for the Behavioral and Social Sciences, observed thirty-three groups working on a task together. At the end, participants voted on who they believed was the leader.[26] For every additional roughly thirty-nine seconds someone spoke, they scored another "leadership" vote. And men received an extra leadership boost equivalent to the number of votes participants received for forty-five seconds of speaking time.[*]

Equal speaking time is one of the strongest predictors of team performance (we'll unpack that more in chapter 7).[27] When a few voices take over, you end up with shallow debates, flimsy decisions, and outcomes built on shaky ground.

If a vocal minority is monopolizing the mic while everyone else sits there like potted plants, your meeting needs a redesign. If people aren't speaking up because they have nothing to contribute, leave them off the invite list and send a recap. But if they're staying silent because a few overtalkers are steamrolling the room, it's time to intervene. In chapters 5 and 7, I'll give you strategies to rebalance airtime, rein in chronic overtalkers, and make sure your meetings serve everyone—not just the blabbermouths.

---

[*] A more recent study (Loignon et al., 2025) found a similar relationship between speaking time and leadership emergence, but notably did not find a gender difference.

3. Multitasking: Frequency of Task-Switching During Meetings

In 2023, Stanford economics professor Nick Bloom and colleagues surveyed approximately four thousand workers in the US and uncovered some eyebrow-raising meeting habits:[28]

- 40 percent admitted to texting or talking with family or friends during video calls;
- 26 percent confessed to doing this weekly; and
- 38 percent admitted to "double Zooming" (yes, being on two video calls at once).

This so-called "multitasking" isn't multitasking at all. It's task-switching, and humans are terrible at it. Our brains can't skillfully juggle two tasks at once, so we rapidly switch between them, tricking ourselves into feeling productive while doing both tasks worse.[29]

Microsoft Teams can track how often participants toggle away from the meeting window to check other Microsoft apps like Outlook or Word—a sign that their bodies are present in the meeting, but their brains are somewhere far away. Read AI takes it further, analyzing participants' micro-behaviors to gauge engagement and sentiment. If the software detects someone's eyes darting toward a second monitor, it flags them as possibly less engaged (but it also knows that glance might mean they're working on something relevant to the meeting and it can tell the difference). And if their speech patterns shift abruptly—starting fast and then trailing off mid-sentence—it's another sign that something has hijacked their focus.

Even without these tools, you can look for telltale signs of multitasking: delayed responses, background typing, and that distracted nod of someone pretending to listen while secretly adding items to their Instacart.

The goal isn't to bust people for multitasking. It's to use analytics to figure out what's broken about the meeting that's leading people to check out. Because if attendees are mentally somewhere else, the problem probably isn't their distraction. It's your meeting.

And if people don't feel the need to be fully present in your meeting, maybe they don't need to be there at all.

4. Punctuality Rate: Percentage of Meetings That Start Late

In a 2013 study, Steven Rogelberg and his colleagues asked 195 participants to reflect on one or two meetings they'd recently attended. When meetings started late, even by just a few minutes, other participants responded negatively:

- When meetings started one to five minutes late, 50 percent reported negative emotions like frustration, disrespect, and disappointment.[30]

- When meetings started six to ten minutes late, 61 percent reported negative emotions.

Tracking punctuality isn't about playing time cop. It's about hunting down the real issues. Why are meetings running late in the first place? Are people starting late because they're sprinting between back-to-backs? Or because everyone knows the meeting will be a monumental time suck, so they figure, "Why bother putting in the effort to show up on time?"

Either way, lateness is rarely the real problem. It's usually a symptom of deeper dysfunction. (We'll explore how to tackle lateness in meetings in chapter 5.)

5. Attendance Rate: Percentage of Invitees Who Show Up

People show up for what matters. If attendees are dodging your meetings, you need to understand why.

Analytics can expose what's really driving the no-shows, like if meetings are scheduled during time slots that are chronically double-booked or that clash with other recurring meetings. In a study of a pharmaceutical organization, my coauthors Rob Cross, Michael Arena, and Greg Pryor found that half of all meetings on employees' calendars were double-booked with other meetings.[31] Given the choice, employees vote with their feet.

Instead of chasing RSVPs or mindlessly rescheduling, treat poor attendance like a warning light. Diagnose the problem and decide whether to redesign the meeting or shut it down.

Big Brother Won't Fix Broken Meetings

Meeting analytics can be powerful. But mishandle them and you'll erode employee trust.

Rachel saw this play out at her company. HR quietly rolled out a meeting analytics system to track employee activity across Zoom, Slack, and other platforms. But instead of being transparent, they spent months debating whether they were legally required to inform employees. When they decided they weren't, they kept it a secret. Eventually, some employees found out and felt spied on. What could have been a tool for better collaboration became a symbol of surveillance and shattered trust.

If you're tracking meeting metrics, start with transparency. Tell employees what you're tracking, why it matters, and how it will benefit them. Because no matter how valuable the insights are, if people feel surveilled, they won't care about the insights. They'll care only about the betrayal.

Whatever you do, don't weaponize the data. Make it clear that employees won't be penalized for having too many meetings or speaking too much in them. If people think the data will be used against them, they'll either shut down or start gaming the system.

Build trust instead. Give employees the option to opt out. More importantly, give them a reason to opt in. If the analytics genuinely help them improve their work, they'll want the insights.

The best way to earn that buy-in? Put the data in their hands. Let employees see and act on their own meeting data. Give them access to key metrics and analytics, like how often they show up on time, how frequently they multitask, and how effective their meetings are. But don't just fling a dashboard at them. Make it actionable. Give them clear guidance for interpreting the data, spotting bad habits, and deciding whether a meeting is necessary or deserves to be deleted.

When employees take ownership of their meeting data, they stop being passive victims of broken meetings and start becoming active codesigners of better ones. They take back control of their time. And they become better stewards of everyone else's.

Metrics That Don't Sting, Don't Stick

Meeting metrics and analytics can surface all kinds of dysfunction. Still, if leaders don't believe there's a problem, good luck getting them to fix it. You can hit them with charts, heat maps, and dashboards, but if the data doesn't strike a nerve, all you'll get is a shrug: "That's just how it is. My meetings aren't any worse than anyone else's."

Worse, you might trigger a full-blown allergic reaction. I once witnessed someone try to convince a sales leader to cut back on meetings. It backfired spectacularly. "Meetings are where deals are made and quotas are crushed," the leader snapped. "Cut meetings, and you cut sales." End of discussion.

If you want meeting metrics to drive real change, don't lecture leaders about "bad meetings." Instead, show them how their meetings are actively sabotaging what they care about most: missed deadlines, unhappy clients, stalled projects, or declining revenue.

At one company I worked with, work velocity had become painfully slow—so much so that employees turned it into a running joke, peppering Slack messages with snail emojis whenever a decision or project dragged on. HR had piles of meeting analytics showing that employees were spending way too much time in meetings (well above the ten-hour-a-week tipping point), but leaders shrugged. They didn't think it was *that* bad.

So I suggested flipping the script. Instead of focusing on generic metrics like time in meetings, zero in on what leaders cared about: speed. The HR team whipped up a dead-simple graph: weekly meeting hours on the *x*-axis and velocity scores (from employee surveys) on the *y*-axis.

Boom. It hit like a sucker punch.

Correlation doesn't equal causation, but the pattern was now too loud to ignore: The more time teams spent in meetings, the slower their work crawled. Now, meetings weren't just nibbling away at their time—they were actively slowing the company down. That's when leadership finally snapped to attention. And that's when things started to change.

Benchmarking: Turn Meetings into a Winnable Game

Humans are wired for competition. We can't help but compare ourselves to others. And meetings are no exception. Show people how their meeting metrics stack up against those of their peers and you'll trigger some serious soul-searching, calendar gutting, and a healthy dose of workplace rivalry. Few things jolt people into action as quickly as realizing they're dead last in a race they didn't even know they were running.

In 2022, my colleagues Rob Cross, Michael Arena, Greg Pryor,

Tim Bowman, and I built a "collaborative intelligence" dashboard for a group of Asana employees.[32] The dashboard displayed how often employees collaborated on the Asana platform and how they stacked up against their peers' averages (aggregated by role and function to avoid any name-and-shame). For two weeks, participants checked their dashboards daily, adjusted their work habits based on the data they saw, and recorded their reflections in diary entries.

By the end of the experiment, a whopping 93 percent of participants had made concrete changes to how they worked. The over-collaborators (the ones flooding their teammates with tasks and triggering a flurry of distracting notifications) realized they needed to pump the brakes and carve out some more focus time. Meanwhile, the under-collaborators saw they were lagging behind and likely dragging their teams down so they stepped up and collaborated more.

More than half (55 percent) of participants said the most valuable part of the dashboard was the benchmarking: seeing how their collaboration habits measured up. Raw individual metrics didn't have the same impact. They needed something concrete to measure against.

You can use that same kind of benchmarking to jolt people into fixing their meetings. When employees see their meeting metrics stacked against those of their peers and get a clear picture of what "healthy" looks like, it's a cold slap of reality. Suddenly, those low-value meetings aren't just annoying. They're embarrassing.

That wake-up call hit hard at one multinational tech company. Engineers were drowning in meetings, self-reported productivity was sinking, and critical projects were stalling because meetings chopped calendars into tiny, unusable bits of time. To tackle the problem, the company rolled out dashboards that ranked teams on key metrics, including how much focus time employees had left each day after meetings were done pillaging their day.

The rankings kicked off a wave of friendly competition. Teams raced to climb the leaderboard, gutting low-value meetings left and right. Meeting time across the engineering department plummeted, focus time increased, and two years later, those dashboards are still doing their job and keeping bad meeting habits in check.

But benchmarking only works if you're tracking the right metrics. Focus on what matters: meeting quality (using ROTI), the five key meeting analytics we've covered in this chapter, and real business outcomes. Don't rely on any one metric in isolation. A low meeting load might look like a win—until you realize decisions are stalling and no one's aligned. To fix what's broken, you need a more complete picture.

You don't need a data scientist or a six-figure dashboard to pull this off. Tools like Tableau, Looker, or even a well-built Google Sheet are enough to help teams visualize their meeting trends, track improvements, and spot problem areas in real time. When you add benchmarking to the mix, you're not just nudging your team toward better meetings—you're handing them a scoreboard. Suddenly, fixing meetings stops feeling like a lost cause and starts feeling like a winnable game. After all, the proof is right in front of them. Other teams are already cutting bloat and seeing results. So what's their excuse?

MANTRA 4: BEWARE METRICS AS TARGETS

On his first day as a technical adviser at the Canadian Digital Service in Ottawa (part of the Canadian government), Sean Boots showed up ready to make an impact. Coming from the tech industry, he was struck by the sheer scale of meeting bloat in the government. Hour after precious hour vanished into bureaucratic black holes.[33]

Boots rolled up his sleeves and built a meeting cost calculator to expose how much time (and taxpayer money) was swirling down the drain.[34] Unlike Shopify's version, Boots's calculator didn't rely on salary averages. He used real salary data for each civil servant on the meeting invite, slapping a more accurate price tag on every meeting.

Boots even joked about adding a "high scores" leaderboard to rank the most expensive meetings. Then he took to Twitter with a cheeky challenge: "Ever wonder how much your public sector meetings cost? Shame your enemies. Impress your friends!"[35] It was clever. It was bold. And it was begging to be misused.

When a metric becomes a target, people stop fixing the real problem and start gaming the system instead. That's Goodhart's Law in action: "When a measure becomes a target, it ceases to be a good measure." We've seen this before with misleading metrics. Start dangling incentives for shorter meetings and you risk getting rushed discussions and half-baked decisions. The meeting's original purpose gets pummeled in the push to hit some superficial metric.

That's why ROTI works when other metrics fail. It's tough to manipulate because it comes straight from participants. And since scores are anonymous, there's no incentive to sugarcoat or suck up.

Bad Metrics Breed Productivity Theater

Goodhart's Law helps explain why *productivity theater* (the performative art of prioritizing looking busy over getting things done) runs rampant in so many organizations. About two-thirds (65 percent) of workers admit they sometimes prioritize looking busy over doing meaningful work, according to the 2024 State of Work Innovation report my team led at Asana, which surveyed more than 13,000 knowledge workers across six countries.[36]

Workers get credit for staying late, typing furiously, keeping their Slack status lights glowing bright green, firing off instant replies, and stuffing their days with meetings, no matter how pointless.

I once worked with a colleague who was a black belt in meeting productivity theater. His calendar was a masterpiece of fiction: stuffed with a dozen recurring one-on-ones that he'd often cancel the day before. When I asked him why, he sheepishly admitted, "It shows my manager I've got a lot going on." He wasn't managing his time. He was performing it.

Meaningful metrics like ROTI are the antidote to this charade. Instead of rewarding jam-packed calendars, organizations should incentivize, celebrate, and reward meetings that deliver real value. Don't applaud a full calendar. Applaud a high ROTI.

WHAT GETS MEASURED, GETS MANAGED

You've probably heard the saying "What gets measured, gets managed." But measure the wrong things, and you'll end up with bad meetings or more productivity theater. Busier calendars, not better meetings. As sociologist William B. Cameron once said, "Not everything that can be counted counts, and not everything that counts can be counted."[37]

When you start measuring what truly matters, you stop just spending time in meetings and you start investing it. And when you treat time as an investment, meetings stop being mindless obligations and start becoming strategic products for getting work done.

The real goal isn't to make meetings shorter or cheaper. It's to cut the unnecessary ones so you can reinvest that time in what matters most: deep work, meaningful collaboration, building relationships, and inspiring your team.

The meetings worth keeping are the ones that drive real business impact. Those meetings deserve to be protected—and perfected—using ROTI, meeting analytics, and the seven principles in this book. That's how you turn meetings from a soul-sucking tax into something worth showing up for.

Before implementing the strategies in this chapter, start with this brilliantly simple assessment that I picked up from Zapier CEO Wade Foster.[38] I call it the Calendar Reality Check. It's a lightweight form of analytics that uses your own calendar to reveal whether your time is aligned with what matters most. Here's how it works:

1. **LIST YOUR TOP WORK PRIORITIES.** Write down your top priorities at work (for example, meeting with customers, coaching your team, driving strategy, professional development). Next to each, estimate the percentage of time you *should* be spending on them.

2. **COMPARE IT TO YOUR CALENDAR.** Now, pull up your actual calendar. Does it line up with those top priorities? Or are your days clogged with meetings that don't support those priorities—or worse, actively distract you from them?

Your real priorities aren't what you say they are. They're what appears on your calendar. As Foster puts it, "Doing a compare and contrast between what you think your priorities are versus where you actually spend your time will give you a lot of insight into whether you're on the right track."

So, what's the verdict? Are you making smart investments with your time, or are you letting pointless meetings pickpocket your productivity? Time is your most valuable asset. Start investing it like it is.

PRINCIPLE 3

Structure: Become a Meeting Minimalist

In 2023 a major US university found itself in a bind. Google was rolling out new cloud storage fees for faculty and students, but the university's budget was already locked. Instead of making the uncomfortable ask for more funding from university leadership, IT leaders proposed a complex decentralized funding system: any student or faculty exceeding fifteen gigabytes would be required to cover their overage out of pocket.

Seasoned IT staff warned that this would be a logistical nightmare, but no one wanted to go back to leadership with the budget request to fund it centrally. So the decentralized plan chugged forward, dragging an avalanche of meetings behind it as teams scrambled to sort out the logistics.

IT leaders formed a sprawling sixty-person advisory group made up of campus IT staff, plus a smaller, tighter-knit advisory group of IT leaders. These groups met monthly for over fourteen months. Each meeting surfaced new complications and questions, which triggered even more meetings. Who would foot the bill for storage drives shared across departments? How do you bill students who don't even have budgets? One IT leader recalled weeks when he sat through five meetings about the funding plan. In total, the initiative spawned *hundreds* of meetings.

After all that, they scrapped the whole thing. It was too complex to implement. Instead, they did what would've been more efficient to do from the start: They asked university leadership to fund the storage centrally. Leadership agreed, eager to avoid the bureaucratic chokehold aimed squarely at students and faculty.

The university experienced a full-blown case of meeting clutter, which occurs when meetings bloat unnecessarily. They become too frequent, too long, too packed with agenda items, or too overloaded with attendees.

Meeting clutter tends to form when people dodge tough decisions. It feels safer to pile on more agenda items, more people, more minutes, or more meetings than to make the tough call. In the university's case, no one wanted to ask leadership for more funding so they scheduled their way into oblivion. Hundreds of spin-off meetings could have been avoided if the people holding the purse strings had been in the room from the start.

To avoid that kind of downward spiral, you need Meeting Design Principle 3: Meeting Minimalism. In chapter 1, we confronted the sheer overload of meetings choking your calendar. Now it's time to deal with what's left and turn those meetings into high-impact collaboration products. Meeting minimalism means stripping meetings down to their essentials so what's left is lean, purposeful, and built to deliver results.

Minimalism is infused into the world's most iconic products. Take the iPhone. When it was launched in 2007, it eliminated the clunky keyboards, endless buttons, and confusing menus of its competitors in favor of a single sleek touchscreen. Or Google, whose home page is the digital poster child for minimalism: one search bar, a couple of buttons, and nothing else to get in your way. That ruthless simplicity didn't just make

Google easy to use. It made using it so intuitive and purposeful that it became a verb.

The best minimalist products don't try to do everything. They just do the important things better.

The same brutal simplicity applies to meetings. With every shorter meeting, every pruned agenda, every nonessential attendee left off the invite list, and every spin-off meeting you axe, you're reclaiming precious brain space. It's like Marie Kondo-ing your meetings: If those extra minutes, topics, people, or follow-up meetings don't spark value, thank them for their service and show them the door.

THE FOUR MEETING DIMENSIONS
TO MINIMALIZE

Meetings are clutter magnets. They will spread in every direction if you let them. To curb the bloat, apply minimalism to four key dimensions of your meetings.

DIMENSION 1: AGENDA. A long agenda isn't a sign of thorough planning. It's a sign of clutter. More agenda items mean more detours, distractions, and dead ends.

DIMENSION 2: DURATION. The longer a meeting drags on, the more room for tangents, rabbit holes, and Bob's unsolicited updates on his marathon training. (Yes, Bob, we get it. You're fast. We're exhausted just from listening).

DIMENSION 3: ATTENDEES. Cram too many people into a meeting, and it's like Thanksgiving dinner gone wrong. Everyone's talking over each other, nobody agrees on anything, and Aunt Susan keeps insisting that the turkey needs another thirty minutes.

DIMENSION 4: FREQUENCY. When meetings happen too often, whether because the cadence is too frequent or there are too many "meetings about the meeting," they lose their purpose and grind your team into dust.

Meeting clutter might not look like piles of old magazines, tangled cords, and stale coffee cups, but it overloads your brain all the same. Walk into a meeting with sixteen agenda items or twenty-four attendees and your mental alarm bells wail: "Mayday! Get out while you still can!" Before you know it, the meeting feels less like a workspace and more like stumbling into a hoarder's living room: overwhelming, claustrophobic, and full of mental tripping hazards.

When faced with meeting clutter, your survival instincts kick in. You start punting tough topics, nodding along to bad ideas, and perfecting the art of looking busy while mentally checking out. Anything to make the misery end sooner.

THE RULE OF HALVES: ONE RULE TO SLASH MEETING BLOAT ACROSS EVERY DIMENSION

How do you declutter your meetings? Start with ruthless subtraction.

In a world addicted to "more," we've become victims of what Bob Sutton calls "addition sickness": our knee-jerk reflex to solve problems through addition.[1] Add a few extra agenda items? Sure, why not? Invite a couple more people? The more, the merrier. Schedule a follow-up meeting? Of course—just to double-check (and then triple-check) what was already decided.

But all that addition doesn't make your meetings better. It makes them bloated, exhausting, and utterly ineffective.

University of Virginia engineering professor Leidy Klotz dissects this "more is more" trap in his book, *Subtract: The Untapped Science of Less*.[2] Our brains are wired to pile on more, even when subtraction would be faster, simpler, and smarter.

But here's the good news: Klotz's research also shows that you can short-circuit this reflex by explicitly encouraging subtraction. That's why radical moves like Meeting Doomsday and Armeetingeddon from chapter 1, where teams wipe their calendars clean and start from scratch, are so effective. It's like spring cleaning for your calendar. Intimidating and painful at first, but oh, so satisfying once the clutter is gone.

Subtraction isn't just about wiping meetings off the calendar. It's about trimming the dead weight from the ones that stick around. In the Meeting Doomsdays I've led, the biggest time savings haven't come from mass cancellations, but from trimming the fat off the survivors. Thirty-minute meetings drop to twenty-five. Monthly meetings move to quarterly. Invite lists shrink to only the people who need to attend.

And all those small cuts add up. During the 2022 Meeting Reset that I ran with Sutton at Asana, sixty participants audited 1,160 meetings and then went to work redesigning their calendars. Most (70 percent) of the time savings came from small adjustments, like shortening meetings and holding them less frequently, rather than outright cancellations.[3]

One of the most efficient—and gutsiest—ways to declutter your meetings is what Sutton and Klotz call the Rule of Halves.[4] Take a cold, hard look at the length, attendees, agenda, and frequency of your meetings and slice each by 50 percent. It'll feel extreme. It might even feel reckless. That's the point. The discomfort forces you to confront what's truly essential—and mercilessly cut the rest.

In the rest of this chapter, I'll show you how to apply the Rule of Halves to the four key dimensions of your meetings (agenda, duration, attendees, and frequency), along with specific sniper-like strategies for cutting clutter and reclaiming precious time for more productive work and collaboration.

DIMENSION 1: AGENDA

The first key dimension of your meetings to declutter is the agenda. Too often, agendas—like the meetings themselves—are treated as theater props. Scribble down "Discuss strategy" or "Team updates," and *ta-da!* Your meeting will be productive, right?

Not even close. It creates the illusion that you've prepared. But behind the curtain, it's often just smoke, mirrors, and recycled nonsense. As Steven Rogelberg has found, half of all agendas are recycled versions of past ones. Just mindless regurgitations of the same tired topics.[5] And when they're not recycled, agendas become bloated grab bags of random musings, pet projects, and half-baked ideas. In both cases, it's a sign that the meeting wasn't designed. It was just dumped together.

It's time to rethink the role of agendas entirely:

- **OLD WAY OF THINKING:** Agendas are just a list of topics to cover and check off. If we have one, the meeting will be productive.

- **NEW MINIMALIST MINDSET:** Agendas must be intentionally designed. Each item has a clear job to do and a clear finish line. If it doesn't, it doesn't belong in your meeting.

Think of your agenda like a product blueprint. You wouldn't cram a product full of random features just to make the roadmap look full. That's how you end up with gimmicky bloatware and piles of support tickets. Meetings work the same way. Every agenda item should be built to move work forward. If it doesn't, it's just clutter.

Apply the Rule of Halves

Once you've built your agenda, try cutting it in half. Have ten items? Reduce them to five. Five items? Shrink them to two or three. Prioritize what truly needs a real-time discussion. If it's just a routine update, a minor decision, or a status check, punt it to Slack, email, or a dashboard—safely away from your precious meeting minutes.

Every Agenda Item Should Pull Its Weight

A minimalist agenda isn't just about having fewer items. It's about having the right ones. To avoid agenda items that do nothing but clutter your meetings, turn them into verb-noun combinations that spell out exactly what needs to happen (the verb) to achieve a specific outcome (the noun). Every item should have a job to do. No freeloaders.

For example:

- Instead of "Budget Discussion," try "Approve Q3 Budget."
- Instead of "Project Update," try "Finalize Q2 Feature Priorities."

If you can't turn an agenda item into a verb-noun combination, that's a red flag. It's probably not a real action. It's likely an information dump or pointless agenda filler in disguise. Think "Team Update" or

"Budget Overview"—the kind of vague, time-sucking fluff that eats up minutes without moving the work forward.

Switching to action-oriented agendas won't always shrink your agenda list, but it'll make your meetings more efficient. Every item gets a clear finish line, so you'll know exactly when to move on. It also kills the lazy habit of recycling the same tired topics week after week. When every item has a real job to do, it gets checked off and retired. Not mindlessly recycled in next week's meeting.

Beware the Law of Triviality

Even with an action-oriented agenda, your meeting can still derail thanks to the Law of Triviality. British historian Cyril Northcote Parkinson coined this law, which states that "the time spent on any item of the agenda will be in inverse proportion to the sum [of money] involved."[6] In other words, the more insignificant the issue, the more time people will waste discussing it.

This phenomenon is better known as *bikeshedding*, a term that comes from the example Parkinson used to illustrate it back in 1958.[7] Imagine a financial committee reviewing three proposals:

- a £10 million nuclear plant;
- a £350 bike shed;
- a £21 annual coffee budget.

Where does the committee spend its time? Not on the nuclear plant. That gets rubber-stamped in minutes (if there's a decent proposal on the table) or punted to a future meeting. It's complex, intimidating, and risky. Nobody wants to admit they don't fully understand it or be held responsible if things go sideways.

But the bike shed? Suddenly, everyone's an expert. Should it be blue or green? Does it need a skylight? Finally, something safe and low-stakes to weigh in on.

And the coffee budget? That's when the real debate begins: oat milk versus almond, French vanilla versus hazelnut, and a passionate debate over whether pumpkin spice deserves a spot in the fall lineup.

Bikeshedding poisons modern meetings, too. Dan Pilat and Sekoul Krastev, cofounders of the behavioral science think tank The Decision Lab, describe a meeting agenda with two items:[8]

- reducing carbon emissions
- deciding on standing desks for the office

The carbon emissions discussion should take up most of the meeting time. It's complex, high-stakes, and loaded with big consequences. But what really happens? Attendees either rubber-stamp whatever the most powerful or charismatic person proposes, or they kick the can down the road to avoid taking the heat.

Then the standing desk takes over. Suddenly, the room is full of self-declared ergonomic experts, debating desk heights, footrests, and whether standing boosts productivity. It's low-stakes. It's safe. And it's a spectacular waste of time.

To avoid bikeshedding, don't just move the most important items to the top of your agenda. Cut the trivial ones entirely and handle them asynchronously. Then, set your attendees up to tackle the real issues. Send a pre-read with enough context to make sure people show up ready to contribute with informed opinions that move the work forward.

And be ruthless with your invite list. If someone doesn't add real value, leave them off. When people don't feel qualified to weigh in on the important topics, they overcompensate by clinging to the safest, shallowest topics on the agenda. That's how serious conversations get hijacked by trivial nonsense like pumpkin spice. Be clear about the input you expect from each person. Then hold them accountable for showing up with more than safe takes on throwaway topics.

Use a Parking Lot to Keep Your Meetings Out of the Ditch

You can build the perfect agenda, stacked with high-stakes, verb-noun items, and your meeting can still veer off road thanks to rogue tangents. One minute you're aligning on a key decision. The next, you've swerved off into a debate over whether Bring Your Kids to Work Day should include pets.

To prevent your agenda from skidding off course, borrow a maneuver from the marketing analytics platform AppsFlyer: the "parking lot."[9] When someone steers the conversation off road, "park" their idea in a shared virtual document or whiteboard (if you're all in-person). After the meeting, revisit the list asynchronously. Or, if needed, schedule another meeting to review what's been parked.

Jeff Roth, CEO of an executive coaching firm, suggests two clever upgrades to get even more mileage from the parking lot.[10] First, assign a "valet": someone responsible for capturing detours and parking them. Second, encourage "self-parking." When someone realizes they're about to take the meeting off road, they park their tangent before anyone needs to grab the wheel.

DIMENSION 2: LENGTH

Now let's tackle the second dimension of meeting clutter: length.

Most meetings drag on far longer than they should. One of the biggest culprits is Parkinson's Law, which states that work expands to fill the time allotted.

Cyril Northcote Parkinson (the same guy who gave us the Law of Triviality; he had a real knack for exposing time-wasting nonsense) coined the term in 1955 after noticing something bizarre. Even as the British Empire shrank, losing two-thirds of its navy and a third of its personnel, the number of bureaucrats overseeing it kept growing.[11] To justify their jobs, they buried themselves in mountains of busywork.

Meetings fall into the same trap. Any leftover time at the end gets stuffed with tangents, rabbit holes, and rambling. Michael Ridgway, Chief Engineer at Culture Amp, calls it "padding out."[12] "There is nothing worse than a thirty-minute meeting that 'pads out' to sixty because everyone knows an hour has been scheduled," Ridgway says. Once the time is on the calendar, people feel obligated to fill it.

To prevent meetings from turning into time-sucking marathons, adopt a new minimalist mindset:

- **OLD WAY OF THINKING:** Meetings should fill the time allotted.

- **NEW MINIMALIST MINDSET:** Meetings should last only as long as it takes to accomplish their goals.

The first step is to put the Rule of Halves to work.

Apply the Rule of Halves

Take a merciless look at your calendar. That hour-long meeting? Slice it to thirty minutes. Your thirty-minute meeting? Shrink it to fifteen. At first, it might feel uncomfortable—like squeezing into pants two sizes too small. But that discomfort is exactly the point. Shorter meetings create more urgency. People arrive prepared, skip the fluff, and get straight to the point. There's no time for rambling monologues, meandering updates, or that pesky "one last thing" that magically mutates into three more.

Worried about cutting too much? Don't be. If every agenda item is framed as a verb-noun combination, you'll know exactly when each item's job is done. If you run out of time before finishing the verb, that's a signal you may have trimmed too deep. This also helps protect against the artificial time pressure created by shock metrics, where the ticking clock drives the meeting's pace instead of the actual progress being made.

And if you overshoot and cut too deep, no problem. You can always add time back if needed. But chances are, you'll realize you didn't need nearly as much time as you thought.

Tame the Clock with the 50/25 Rule

If the Rule of Halves feels too extreme (or your attendees start sharpening their pitchforks), ease into minimalism with the 50/25 Rule.

Google cofounder Larry Page hated meetings so much that he once fired his assistant to avoid being scheduled for them.[13] But even Page couldn't completely escape the relentless march of executive calendar bloat. So he fought back with a rule: no hour-long meetings. He told his assistant to cap them at fifty minutes. "An hour-long meeting must include time for a bathroom break," he explained.

Inspired by Page's minimalist approach, Rajiv Pant, then CTO of *The New York Times*, rolled out the 50/25 Rule at the newspaper giant.[14] Sixty-minute meetings were capped at fifty minutes, and thirty-minute meetings were slimmed to twenty-five.

Pant experimented with two ways to apply the 50/25 Rule, either ending meetings at the twenty-five- or fifty-minute mark or starting them at five or ten minutes past the hour or half hour. The first approach (ending early) backfired more often than he'd like. Parkinson's Law reared its ugly head, and the meeting expanded to fill the time anyway. Those extra five or ten minutes didn't turn into a precious break. Instead, they were gobbled up by tangents, chit-chat, and "just one last thing" detours.

So Pant flipped the script and began meetings late (five or ten minutes past the hour or half hour), a tactic he borrowed from William Lewis, the former CEO of Dow Jones. That protected against Parkinson's Law. You can't pad out time that hasn't even started.

Once Pant made the switch, he noticed an unexpected upside: The 50/25 Rule didn't just save time. It curbed multitasking. Knowing they'd have a built-in window to check emails and messages afterward, attendees stopped pecking at their phones and flicking through distractions—and tuned into the meeting.

If you're ready to try the 50/25 Rule, let your calendar do the heavy lifting. Google Calendar's Speedy Meetings feature sets the default meeting length to fifty or twenty-five minutes. Microsoft Outlook offers a similar feature.

But beware: Buffer thieves are everywhere. They lurk like seagulls, ready to snatch your hard-earned free minutes. They'll schedule meetings at 11:55 a.m. or 4:50 p.m., chewing into your break. Or worse, they'll spot your carefully carved-out ten-minute buffer and pounce, wedging in a ten-minute meeting.

To prevent this, block off the full thirty or sixty minutes on your calendar but add a note for attendees: "Meeting starts at 10:05" (or whenever your buffer ends). This way, you protect your buffer and avoid spending your day ping-ponging between meetings.

Stop Defaulting to 30- or 60-Minute Meetings

If your meetings consistently spill over past their scheduled end times, you might need to ditch the predictable thirty- or sixty-minute defaults. Instead, experiment with something unconventional, like a fifty-two-minute meeting. Or forty-one minutes. Or twenty-seven.

Juan Perez, a Special Forces commander, discovered the power of odd meeting durations during a six-month overseas deployment.[15] He noticed that thirty-minute meetings had become meaningless. They had grown so familiar that attendees treated the end time more like a loose suggestion than a firm stop. "A half hour just seems to be something we are so comfortable violating that we breach its constraints without a second thought," Perez explained.

So Perez made a radical but simple shift: He capped the meeting length at twenty-seven minutes. The oddly specific timing snapped his team out of autopilot. They couldn't help but wonder, "Why twenty-seven?" Perez recalls attendees fixating over the number twenty-seven, thinking, "There had to be a reason for the boss to want it to be exactly twenty-seven minutes." Instead of coasting until the clock ran out, they became hyperaware of the time.

The result? They stuck to the twenty-seven-minute rule for the entire six-month deployment.

Yank the Chairs, Shrink the Clock

Another way to jolt your meeting lengths out of autopilot? Take away the chairs.

In 1999 Allen Bluedorn, a management professor at the University of Missouri, studied 111 groups and found that sit-down meetings ran about 34 percent longer than their stand-up counterparts. But the faster pace of stand-up meetings didn't come at the cost of decision quality. Teams made equally strong decisions.[16]

Modern leaders are still cashing in on the benefits of standing meetings. When Neal Taparia, cofounder of Imagine Easy (creator of EasyBib), implemented them, he slashed his average meeting time by 25 percent, from forty-eight minutes to thirty-six.[17]

Some organizations take it even further. At Just Fearless, a business development consulting firm, they yank the chairs if a meeting goes over time.[18] Want to keep talking? You'll have to do it standing up. It creates a sense of urgency—because nobody wants to monologue when gravity is telling their legs to wrap it up.

Standing meetings come with other perks. Andrew Knight, a professor of organizational behavior at Washington University, discovered that when participants stand, they have higher levels of "physiological arousal," which makes them more alert, engaged, and ready to contribute.[19]

Knight also discovered something oddly primal about standing versus sitting in meetings: People were more territorial and less collaborative when seated. Sitting carves the room into little plots of land that feel like "mine": my chair, my slice of the table, my turf. But when people stand, those bubbles burst. The room turns into shared ground and so do the ideas. As Knight puts it, "A workspace that encourages people to stand up is going to lead to more collaborative and more creative outputs."[20]

End the Meeting Early. Throw Some Confetti

Whether you're following the 50/25 Rule or experimenting with oddly precise meeting lengths, one golden rule always applies: End the meeting as soon as it's done. Don't drag it out just because the clock hasn't run out. If the decision's made, the debate's over, or the problem's solved, cut people loose.

Ending meetings early isn't just about sparing people a few extra minutes. It's about giving them something they rarely get: a little more control over their day.

Laurie Santos, who teaches Yale's wildly popular course The Science of Well-Being, calls these surprise minutes *time confetti*.[21] * It's like finding a crumpled five-dollar bill in your jacket pocket—small, unexpected, and oddly delightful. And when you spend that time doing something you genuinely enjoy, Santos says, you feel more "time affluent."[22] And it pays off: Research has shown that time affluence lowers stress, boosts happiness, and improves mental health.[23]

So don't hoard the minutes. Throw some confetti instead.

DIMENSION 3: ATTENDEES

It's time to put the third dimension of meeting clutter on the chopping block: your attendee list.

According to former Google Product Manager Alex Diaz, Larry Page had clear guidelines for making meetings "meaningful" at Google. One was "No more than eight participants, but widely circulated notes after."[24]

Unfortunately, most meetings aren't that disciplined. They're more like kids' birthday parties: Everyone gets an invite to avoid hurt feelings. But silent spectators aren't harmless. Like bored party guests, they suck energy from the room. One well-timed sigh, an eyeroll, or a loud keyboard clack can sour the vibe. Before long, people are wondering why

---

* As Santos pointed out to me, the term *time confetti* originated in Brigid Schulte's book *Over Work: Transforming the Daily Grind in the Quest for a Better Life* (New York: Henry Holt and Co., 2024).

these extra bodies are even there. Then comes the sugar crash. Attention tanks, patience wears thin, and everyone's eyeing the exit.

To apply meeting minimalism to your attendee list, start by flipping your mindset:

- **OLD WAY OF THINKING:** More attendees mean more perspectives, more inclusion, and more learning. The more, the merrier.

- **NEW MINIMALIST MINDSET:** Only invite people with clear, indispensable roles. No spectators, just stakeholders.

Once you make that shift, it's time to start trimming.

Apply the Rule of Halves

Take a ruthless look at your invite list and cut it in half. Yes, half. If someone's input isn't essential, they don't need to be there.

Don't worry. You're not exiling anyone for life. If you realize later that someone essential is missing, you can always loop them in. But starting lean forces you to break the habit of inviting people "just in case" and helps you kick your addiction to bloated, overstuffed meetings.

If Two Pizzas Can't Feed Your Meeting, It's Too Big

If your meeting has more than eighteen people, the Rule of Halves (which cuts it only to nine) won't be bold enough. You need something stricter: the Rule of Eight.

Larry Page didn't pull the number eight out of thin air when he called it the ideal meeting size. At Google, eight was the sweet spot: enough brains in the room to get diverse input, but small enough to keep things focused and productive. Jeff Bezos had a similar revelation at Amazon with his Two-Pizza Rule: no meeting should have more people than two pizzas can feed (which translates to about six to eight people, depending on their appetites).[25]

Steve Jobs was just as ruthless about bloated attendee lists. In 2011, when he advised President Obama to meet with a group of CEOs to discuss innovation, Jobs insisted that the guest list be capped at six or seven. When White House aides tried to invite more attendees, Jobs flat-out refused to attend. The guest list was too bloated for a productive discussion.[26]

He was right. The bigger the meeting, the less relevant it becomes to each person. The bystander effect also kicks in. The more people in the room, the less responsibility anyone feels. Everyone assumes that someone else will speak up, ask the tough question, or make the call. So no one does.

And when people don't feel accountable, they check out. Microsoft's research found that multitasking climbs steadily as the number of attendees in remote meetings increases.[27] The more people in the meeting, the easier it is to fade into the background and the faster you start treating the meeting as background noise. Research by Otter.ai shows that when employees don't feel their presence in a meeting is necessary, they spend 70 percent of the meeting multitasking.[28]

According to Bain & Company, the optimal group size in decision-making meetings is even smaller. Their research has found that once a meeting exceeds seven participants, decision quality drops by 10 percent per extra person.[29] Bain partners Michael Mankins and Jenny Davis-Peccoud explain, "If you take this rule to its logical conclusion, a group of seventeen or more rarely makes any decisions."

Resist the temptation to overstuff your invite list. Just because someone's affected by a decision doesn't mean they need to be in the room making it. If they need to know only what was decided or act on it afterward, skip the invite. Send the notes or recording and let them get back to work.

Invite Stakeholders, Not Spectators

Cutting your attendee list isn't just about shrinking the number of Zoom tiles or the number of chairs in the room. It's about making sure every person present has a good reason to be there.

After Armeetingeddon, Dropbox implemented a new rule: Only invite stakeholders, not spectators.[30] Bain & Company has an even less flattering term for these spectators: "meeting tourists."[31] They show up out of curiosity, snap a few mental souvenirs, and mostly stay on the outskirts of the discussion. Every now and then, they toss in a generic comment (like "Let me double-click on that" or "This is a helpful discussion") and then they continue to nod along as if they're admiring the scenery from a tour bus.

To weed out the spectators and tourists, use the Three-Word Test. Summarize each attendee's role in three words. For example:

- "Provides technical insight"
- "Approves budget decision"
- "Represents user needs"

If you can't sum up someone's contribution in three clear, meaningful words, cut them. A lean, engaged group will always outthink, outdecide, and out-execute a bloated room.

Implement a "One In, One Out" Policy

Before adding another name to a meeting invite list, pause. As Ken Segall, Apple's former ad agency creative director, said, "Every time the body count goes higher, you're simply inviting Complexity to take a seat at the table."[32]

Use the One In, One Out rule to keep complexity in check. Inspired by "feature budgeting" in software, it's a strict but straightforward method to keep your meeting-invite lists lean. For every new attendee you add, one existing name needs to go. If you can't justify the trade, the new addition probably doesn't need to be there.

Of course, being left out can sting, so it's important to be careful about how you frame the exclusion. In a leaked memo to Tesla employees, Elon Musk wrote, "It is not rude to leave; it is rude to make someone stay and waste their time."[33]

That's the right mindset. Being left off a meeting invite isn't a snub. It's a sign of respect. It means your time is so valuable that it's best spent elsewhere.

Great meetings don't hoard people. They protect their time.

Stop Using Meetings for "Learning by Osmosis"

Some managers romanticize "learning by osmosis." It sounds noble: Invite junior employees to meetings so they can soak up wisdom from the sidelines and walk out enlightened. But in practice, it usually just adds clutter. Senior attendees begin to self-censor, tiptoeing around sensitive topics they would otherwise discuss openly. Meanwhile, junior employees sit there like deer in headlights, unsure when to speak—or whether they're even supposed to.

If someone doesn't have a clear role in the meeting, they should sit it out. Record the session and let junior employees watch it on their own time. That way, they can skip the irrelevant parts, rewatch key moments, and absorb the key takeaways without disrupting the flow of the actual meeting. Then turn it into a genuine learning opportunity with follow-up questions like:

- What did you notice about how decisions were made?
- How would you improve the way the meeting was run?
- How would you handle a situation like this in the future?

But if a junior employee *does* have a clear role, don't leave them off the invite list just because they lack a fancy title or a plush corner office. The people closest to the work often have the most useful insights, so give them a real seat at the table. Don't mindlessly plop them in the room and hope for the best. Set clear, bounded expectations, like "Your role is to share insights on what you've seen and heard from customers, not to weigh in on final decisions."

Because a seat at the table means nothing if you don't know why you're sitting there.

Uphold the Law of Two Feet

The strategies in this chapter aren't just for trimming a bloated invite list. They apply to you, too. Make sure you're not the source of the clutter.

At the Fedora Project, the open-source community behind the Fedora Linux operating system, members follow the Law of Two Feet: If you're not gaining or contributing value in a meeting, use your two feet and walk out of the room (or, in virtual meetings, drop off the call).[34]

Meeting leaders should champion this rule. Say it out loud. Put it on the agenda. Give attendees explicit permission to walk out.

Carrie Goucher, who has a PhD from Cambridge University in meeting culture, takes it a step further by awarding prizes to the first person who uses the Law of Two Feet in her meetings. As Goucher explained to me, "When someone walks out, it shouldn't be a sign of rudeness but instead that you are making good choices for the organization overall."

Sometimes, the most valuable action you can take in a meeting after sharing your input or gathering the necessary information is to simply walk away, log off, or leave however you can.

DIMENSION 4: FREQUENCY

You've decluttered your agendas, trimmed your meeting durations, and slashed attendee bloat. Now it's time to take on the sneakiest dimension of them all: meeting frequency. Meeting frequency isn't just about having too many meetings in general or spending too much time in them. It's about the cadence: certain meetings are happening too often. When that's the case, meetings stop being useful and become repetitive, performative, and disconnected from real progress.

Frequency-related meeting clutter builds up for all kinds of reasons. Sometimes it's because recurring meetings happen too frequently, like a "daily" meeting that only needs to happen weekly. Other times, it accumulates because the cadence keeps chugging along long after the meeting has outlived its purpose. That's how zombie meetings—lifeless meetings that refuse to die—survive. (We'll tackle those pesky monsters soon.) And then there are the "meetings about the meetings," where a single meeting spawns its own micro-cadence. You end up with a mess of spin-off meetings (like the university fiasco) or endless pre-meetings that bury real work under layers of meeting mulch.

A well-executed Meeting Doomsday can clear out some of that clutter. But if you want to keep your calendar lean for the long haul, you'll need ongoing strategies to rein in your meeting frequency.

It starts with a mindset shift:

- **OLD WAY OF THINKING:** Frequent meetings mean better communication, coordination, and alignment.

- **NEW MINIMALIST MINDSET:** If your meetings are happening too frequently, that's a red flag. It usually signals poor communication, unclear roles, or a broken decision-making process—and a lazy reflex to default to meetings.

Begin by applying the Rule of Halves to detoxify your calendar. After that, it'll be time to move on to more surgical strategies to eliminate unnecessary pre-meetings and spin-off meetings.

Apply the Rule of Halves

If a recurring meeting happens every day (like a stand-up), slash it to twice a week. If it's weekly, try every other week. Monthly? Experiment with every other month.

You can always adjust later. But chances are, no one will grieve the death of that weekly sync where everyone recites status updates without truly getting anything "synced." If that daily meeting turns out to be essential, great. You'll finally know why.

When we conducted the Meeting Reset at Asana, the changes that participants made to the frequency of their meetings (like shifting a weekly meeting to a monthly one) accounted for 17 percent of the total time saved.[35] And once meetings stopped lurking around every corner, people arrived more prepared, focused, and ready to contribute. Because when tomorrow's meeting isn't an option, today's meeting gets taken more seriously.

And something else glorious happens when tomorrow's meeting isn't on the calendar. People stop waiting for permission to move work forward. They hash things out over Slack, send a decisive email, or—best of all—solve the problem all on their own.

Meetings stop being the default dumping ground for every minor issue and finally become what they should be: a last resort.

Give Every Meeting an Expiry Date

Decluttering your calendar of frequent meetings also involves confronting the zombie meetings: those recurring meetings that have outlived their usefulness yet refuse to die. They often start with good intentions: aligning teams, breaking down silos, and kicking off big projects. However, as teams align and start to develop other communication channels, the meeting parrots updates people already read in email or logged in the project tracker. Yet it lurches on, week after week, kept alive by inertia and a recurring calendar invite.

Meeting Doomsdays can help kill off zombie meetings. But unless you're vigilant, they'll keep rising again. To stop them from becoming immortal time thieves, give every recurring meeting an expiration date of three months, max. When it's up for renewal, ask: Is this meeting still delivering value, or has it decayed into another time-sucking corpse? If it's the latter, the expiration date gives you an excuse to pull the plug and let it die.

**How Warren Buffett
Keeps Zombie Meetings Off His Calendar**

Warren Buffett preempts zombie meetings with a radical strategy:
He allows meetings to be scheduled only one day in advance.[36]
Want a meeting with Buffett? You have to schedule it the day
before. Try scheduling something for next Wednesday? Tough
luck. His assistant will tell you to call back on Tuesday. This rule
keeps Buffett's calendar clear of stale, irrelevant meetings made
weeks or months earlier.

While most of us don't have Buffett-level clout to pull
this off, his rule is a blunt reminder: Just because a meeting is
squatting on your calendar doesn't mean it deserves to stay there.
Give yourself permission to pull the plug.

Kill Pre-Meetings Before They Kill Collaboration

When meetings start multiplying, it's often because the cadence is too
frequent—daily, weekly, monthly. But there's another, more insidious
culprit: pre-meetings. These behind-the-scenes alignment calls, prep
sessions, and dry runs multiply like a Hollywood blockbuster franchise.
One meeting spawns a prequel, a sequel, and a spin-off trilogy—none of
them worth producing or sitting through.

At VMware, one executive described a culture bogged down by frequent meetings. Every major meeting came with an entourage of prep
calls to align key players. By the time the actual meeting rolled around,
it wasn't a meeting. It was a performance. Slides were rehearsed, and

talking points were polished. If you weren't part of the pre-meeting club, too bad. The conversation had been scripted, and going off-script felt like interrupting a Broadway show mid-act.

CEO Zeb Evans saw this same dysfunction at the project management company ClickUp. Pre-meetings had become behind-the-scenes lobbying campaigns.[37] Decisions weren't made in the real meeting. They were quietly brokered beforehand, turning the actual meeting into a pre-scripted formality.

Pre-meetings are often a symptom of a lack of clarity. When roles, responsibilities, and decision-making authority are murky, people panic. Calendars bloat with pre-meetings as attendees scramble to pitch ideas, rehearse arguments, and smooth over conflicts before the main event begins.

Pre-meetings don't just waste time. They waste the potential of the actual meeting. Decisions aren't made based on merit or data. They're stacked in favor of whoever has the most insider access. And when employees realize that the real decisions were made three days ago during a hush-hush prep call, they check out. They stop contributing. Why bother? The meeting isn't real collaboration. It's corporate theater, and the curtain went up without them.

Before scheduling a meeting about a meeting, hit pause. Ask yourself: Is this meeting solving a real problem, or just compensating for a lack of clarity? If people don't know their roles, aren't sure who's responsible for what, or can't clearly state the problem, another meeting won't fix anything. Start with written communication instead. Define each person's role. Spell out exactly who owns what. Clearly state the problem you're trying to solve. If you can't do that in an email or shared doc, you're not ready for a meeting.

If a pre-meeting is truly necessary, don't let it happen in secrecy. Share the pre-meeting agenda with everyone attending the main meeting, even those who didn't participate in the pre-meeting. Record it. Document key takeaways and share them with everyone. Transparency eliminates backroom deals, secret handshakes, and shadow decisions. And it keeps collaboration where it belongs: in the real meeting.

Stop Spin-Off Meetings from Colonizing Your Calendar

Pre-meetings can be annoying, but at least they die off when the main event starts. Spin-off meetings are more relentless. These follow-ups get scheduled because the original meeting either didn't deliver or spawned more questions than answers.

If your calendar keeps getting colonized by spin-off meeting clutter, set some hard guardrails. As with Google's Rule of Four from chapter 1, impose a strict limit: no more than two follow-up meetings per topic. Beyond that, the meeting isn't solving problems. It's creating more of them.

Disagree and Commit. No Boomerangs Allowed

One of the nastiest kinds of spin-off meetings is the *boomerang meeting*. Just when you think you've made a decision or resolved an issue, someone utters the cursed words: "Let's schedule a follow-up to make sure we're aligned."

And just like that, you're back in another meeting, rehashing the same debate, sometimes with a newly invited cast of characters bringing their own fresh batch of opinions. The follow-up meeting hurls the conversation back to square one, like a boomerang.

Jim Kilts, the former CEO of Gillette, didn't tolerate this kind of calendar mutiny. He realized executives would nod along in meetings, pretending to agree, only to quietly undo the decisions later through back-channel politicking and side deals.[38] So Kilts laid down a blunt rule: Debate openly during the meeting, but once a decision is made, it's final. Every executive was expected to leave the room fully committed to the decision—even if they had fought tooth and nail against it moments earlier.

But he didn't stop there. Kilts added more teeth. He rolled out a quarterly review where execs were evaluated by peers, direct reports, and Kilts himself on how well they upheld meeting agreements, including sticking to decisions. This wasn't just a toothless 360-degree feedback loop. The ratings impacted a "sizable" chunk of employees' bonus pay.[39]

Jeff Bezos enforced a similar rule at Amazon called Disagree and Commit.[40] You didn't have to agree with every decision, but you were expected to back it once it was made. No "let's circle back" sneak attacks. No foot-dragging. No back-channel lobbying or shadowy puppetry in the hallway or Slack chat afterward.

No Decision-Maker? No Meeting

Spin-off meetings often occur because the right decision-makers weren't in the room. If no one has the authority to make the tough calls, teams become trapped in a cycle of endless debates, follow-ups, and calendar carnage.

Even if everyone in the meeting is perfectly aligned, it doesn't matter if no one has the authority to act. Sometimes people fake it. They pretend to make decisions above their pay grade, only to watch it all unravel when the issue gets kicked up the chain to the real decision-makers. Or, just as likely to boomerang, they build workarounds to stay within their limited remit. But these makeshift fixes usually create more problems (and more spin-off meetings) than they solve.

That's what happened at the university from the beginning of this chapter. What could have been a single, decisive top-down decision exploded into hundreds of meetings, all because the people with real authority (the university higher-ups) weren't in the meeting from the start.

Bullpens: One Room, Zero Spin-Offs

Another way to wipe out spin-off meetings is with bullpens. In baseball, the bullpen is where relief pitchers wait, ready to jump in when needed. Similarly, bullpen meetings are shared spaces where key stakeholders can jump in, solve problems on the spot, and move on.

The concept first gained traction at YouTube, where leaders would gather in their largest conference room, the Double Rainbow (named after the viral video of a man marveling at a double rainbow).[41] There was no set agenda. People showed up, and if they didn't have pressing issues to discuss, they worked independently. But if someone overheard something relevant, they could jump in, share input, and kill a spin-off meeting before it sank its teeth into the calendar.

Shishir Mehrotra, a veteran of YouTube's bullpens who later introduced the practice at Coda, recalls, "Regularly, we would see discussions spontaneously construct between a product lead from one area, an engineering lead from another, a lawyer who was left out of an original conversation, and a marketer who was unaware a launch was taking place." They could hash things out in real time. No damage-control meetings required.[42]

At first glance, bullpens seem to violate the rules of minimalist meetings. They usually involve more people than necessary and don't follow a strict agenda. But in the right context, that rule-breaking isn't a bug. It's a feature. Bullpens are designed for messy, fast-moving work—where problems don't show up on schedule and answers can't wait a week.

They make meetings "multi-threaded": instead of splintering every issue into its own stand-alone meeting, multiple conversations can happen in parallel.[43] That way, problems get solved in real time, without dragging through weeks of follow-ups and calendar clutter.

Bullpens work best in high-stakes environments where teams are tightly interdependent but don't have frequent meetings. When a problem surfaces, the right people are already in the room. There's no need to fire off a meeting invite or spiral into a Slack black hole. The issue gets handled on the spot, and the work keeps moving.

It's like taking your car in for an oil change, only to discover that your tires need rotating and your wipers need replacing. Instead of scheduling three separate appointments, the bullpen knocks it all out in one go, sparing you from a calendar chokehold of meeting sprawl.

Stop Spin-Off Meetings with DRIs

One of the fastest ways to eliminate spin-off meetings is to assign a Directly Responsible Individual (DRI). Steve Jobs made this a non-negotiable principle at Apple.[44] Every task, whether it was launching the iPhone or following up on a meeting action item, had a single, accountable owner. The DRI was responsible for getting the job done, either by doing it themselves or coordinating with the right people to make it happen.

Every meeting action item needs a DRI. It removes the guesswork about who's doing what, saves you from playing accountability whack-a-mole, and keeps next steps from falling through the cracks.

Don't stop at action items. Assign a DRI for the meeting itself. Someone needs to own the meeting, ensuring it stays focused and produces tangible outcomes—not just another slow swirl down the calendar drain.

And if the meeting DRI isn't responsible for every agenda item, then each item needs its own DRI. Someone has to make sure the verb gets done, like *approve* in "approve budget" or *decide* in "decide on proposal." Otherwise, agenda items won't do their job. They'll drag on without resolution and spawn a fresh batch of calendar clutter.

ALWAYS BE MINIMALIZING

Meetings shouldn't feel like a hoarder's den: crammed with pointless minutes, redundant attendees, aimless chatter, and endless follow-ups. Like the best products, the best meetings are ruthlessly stripped down to their essentials. No fluff. No filler. No freeloaders. If it doesn't spark value, it doesn't belong. Period.

Clear the meeting clutter so you can focus on what really matters. As Apple's Ken Segall put it, "Simplicity . . . needs a champion—someone who's willing to stand up for its principles and strong enough to resist the overtures of Simplicity's evil twin, Complexity."[45]

Be that champion. Fight for minimalism as if your team's time, focus, and sanity depend on it. Because they do.

PRINCIPLE 4

Flow: Apply Systems Thinking

More than a decade ago, MIT professor Sandy Pentland made a breakthrough that would change our understanding of what makes teams successful. By 2012, Pentland and his team had spent seven years outfitting about 2,500 people across twenty-one organizations with wearable sensors that captured over one hundred data points per minute, measuring everything from tone of voice and body language to who spoke and who stayed silent.[1]

After analyzing thousands of hours of interactions, Pentland's team discovered that what mattered most for team success wasn't intelligence, skills, or personality. It was the teams' communication patterns. Did everyone have a chance to speak, or did a few voices dominate? Did people communicate directly with each other, or did everything bottleneck through a single person? Were conversations buzzing with energy—or flatlining.

Remarkably, Pentland didn't need to know what people said. He could predict a team's success just by studying their communication patterns. In fact, those patterns were stronger predictors of success than intelligence, skills, and personality—combined!

Communication patterns determine how information flows across teams. When communication flows well, the right people get the right information at the right time, whether it's delivered directly to them or easy to find on their own. No one's left chasing down updates, rummaging through Slack threads, or stitching together scraps of information from different tools to figure out what's happening.

But good communication flow isn't a happy accident. It's something you have to design.

Think of your organization's communication system as a network of pipes. When everything's clear and connected, information flows smoothly, just like in Pentland's high-performing teams. But when those pipes are clogged or cracked, you get leaks, bottlenecks, and frustration spraying everywhere.

Meetings are just one pipe in that system. Trying to fix communication by tweaking meetings alone is like patching a single leaky pipe in a busted plumbing system. You might stop a drip here and there, but you're still ankle-deep in communication sewage. Most communication breakdowns don't start or stop in meetings. They build up before, after, and in between.

This is where systems thinking comes in: Meeting Design Principle 4. Great product designers think in systems. Take Apple. Your iPhone doesn't work in isolation. It syncs with your Mac, pairs with your Air-Pods, and shares data with your iPad. Apple doesn't just sell gadgets. It designs systems where everything works together.

Meetings need the same approach. They're not isolated events. If your other communication pipes—email, Slack, project management tools—are clogged, misused, or leaky, no amount of meeting optimization will fix the problem. And if your go-to fix for communication issues is scheduling more meetings, you're not solving anything. You're just cranking open another faucet and flooding the system.

THREE UPGRADES TO OVERHAUL
YOUR COMMUNICATION SYSTEM

To fix your broken communication system, you don't need more duct tape. You need a full-blown plumbing overhaul. Here are the three upgrades to stop the leaks, clear the gunk, and get things flowing:

UPGRADE 1: STANDARDIZE YOUR COMMUNICATION TOOLS. Every tool in your system needs a clear job. When meetings, email, and Slack all try to do the same job, communication becomes a traffic jam: messages pile up, signals get crossed, and essential information gets stuck in gridlock.

UPGRADE 2: DEFAULT TO ASYNCHRONOUS COMMUNICATION. Not every problem warrants a meeting. Make asynchronous (async) communication your default, so meetings become the last resort, not the knee-jerk calendar-clogging reaction.

UPGRADE 3: DESIGN FOR DISTANCE. If your system works only for people who sit next to each other, it's not a system. It's a bottleneck. Whether your team is spread across cities, countries, time zones, or even different floors, your system needs to work for everyone.

If you're drowning in meetings that could be emails or playing Slack archaeologist just to track down a decision, your communication system needs a serious tune-up. It's time to grab the plunger and wrench to unclog the mess.

UPGRADE 1: STANDARDIZE YOUR COMMUNICATION TOOLS

Imagine if every pipe in your house were a different size, made of mismatched materials, and held together with duct tape. You wouldn't get clean, flowing water. You'd get a flood in the kitchen, a trickle in the bathroom, and a geyser in the hallway. That's what happens when teams patch together communication tools without standardizing them across their organization.

This mess is made worse by what UC Santa Barbara professor Paul Leonardi calls the *credit card problem*.[2] Desperate for quick fixes, teams swipe their corporate credit cards and grab whatever new tool catches their eye. Software companies make it easy, often pricing their tools just low enough to dodge IT approval and scrutiny.

When the pandemic hit, things got even messier for many organizations. They scrambled to keep communication flowing without face-to-face contact and began stockpiling apps like survivalists hoarding toilet paper—except there was no shortage. Marketing grabbed Slack. IT clung to Microsoft Teams. HR doubled down on email. Engineering scattered files across Trello, Google Drive, and Notion, leaving behind digital breadcrumb trails only they could follow.

Everyone picked tools that worked for them, but nobody asked the most important question: Do these tools work together? Stanford professor Chip Heath and the late Duke University professor Nancy Staudenmeyer call this *coordination neglect*.[3] Teams patched their own leaks without realizing they were flooding the entire system.

The result? A Frankenstein's monster of mismatched tools that created mass confusion and frustration. Should you hop on Zoom? Drop a message in Slack? Fire up Microsoft Teams? Ping someone in four different places and hope one sticks? Communication became a scavenger hunt with critical information scattered, siloed, and scrambled across platforms.

All that tool-switching chews up your focus and dumps it straight into a productivity sinkhole. In the 2024 State of Work Innovation report that my team led at Asana, we found that the average knowledge worker wastes about six hours a week hopping between collaboration tools like Slack, Zoom, and Google Drive as they figure out which ones to use.[4] That's more than half a workday lost every week to digital hopscotch— time that should be spent doing real work.

Define Your Tools or Drown in a Digital Swamp

If you want your communication system to stop leaking, start by simplifying it. Standardize a core set of communication tools that everyone in your organization is expected to use. Let teams keep their specialized, purpose-built apps (like Jira for engineering, or Canva for marketing), but create a shared foundation for communicating across teams and functions. Ban build-your-own-adventure tech stacks.

And for everyone's sanity, pick *one* meeting platform. During the pandemic, I worked with a government organization where some employees pinballed between WebEx, Microsoft Teams, and Zoom in a single day. No one should have to run that kind of digital triathlon. But alas, according to the CEO of Read AI, David Shim, this hop-a-thon isn't unusual: Over 50 percent of Read's users juggle at least two video conferencing platforms a month.

Every tool in your system needs a clear purpose. No two tools should compete for the same role. And none should try to take on every role. It's like plumbing. You wouldn't run hot water, cold water, and sewage through the same pipe. It'd be a disaster (and a biohazard).

Take Slack, for example. It was originally designed as a "Searchable Log of All Conversation and Knowledge" (yes, that's what *Slack* stands for), a tool meant for retrieving documents and other information.[5] But today, people use it for *everything*: brainstorms, project updates, file storage, and cat memes. Before long, it stops being a searchable log and turns into a digital swamp. Instead of a steady flow of communication, employees end up slogging through the muck, plugging their noses, and wondering why everything feels so broken—and smells so bad.

To avoid this, cloud infrastructure company HashiCorp defines company-wide "standard communication tools" and assigns them clear roles.[6] For example, Slack is strictly for real-time conversations that don't need to be referenced later. Employees are reminded, "Slack is like talking in a room, you don't expect people who are not there to hear you."[7] Despite what its acronym claims, Slack isn't treated as a searchable library of all knowledge. It's just treated as a virtual hallway.

Similarly, at Sourcegraph, a code intelligence platform, employees are told, "Slack is not a source of truth."[8] To drive the point home, the organization auto-deletes all Slack messages in employees' public and private channels after eighteen months. This policy forces teams to store important information in the right places so Slack doesn't become a digital junk drawer overflowing with lost files and forgotten conversations.

Make sure your communication tools have clear rules. Start with naming conventions. Standardize how documents, folders, and channels are named. The average knowledge worker spends nine hours a week just searching for information.[9] And when their digital archaeological digs come up short, they call a meeting. Not because it's necessarily needed, but because it feels easier than continuing the dig.

Set rules for response times, too. What's the expected reply window for Slack? Email? Without clear expectations, meetings become a substitute for patience. People panic and schedule a meeting because they can't trust other tools to do their jobs.

Here's an example of how to define your communication system, clarifying each tool's purpose and the ground rules for keeping everything running smoothly:

PURPOSE	TOOL	RULES
Urgent communication (needs an immediate response)	Slack with @mention	Outline the rules for each tool, including naming conventions, response times, archiving protocols, and etiquette rules.
Communication that passes the 4D-CEO Test	Zoom or in-person meetings	
Non-urgent communication (FYIs, general updates, low-priority questions)	Slack without @mention	
Document creation/ editing (proposals, reports, notes)	Google Docs	
Work coordination (tasks with actions, deadlines, dependencies)	Asana	
Permanent document storage (best practices, final decisions)	Google Drive	

Don't expect employees to magically absorb the rules. Document them, add them to reference documents, pin them to Slack channels, and include them in new-hire onboarding. Systems work only when everyone plays by the same rules. And that won't happen through osmosis or wishful thinking.

Cutting Tool Bloat Starts at the Top

Setting rules and clear swim lanes for your communication tools is straightforward if you're starting from scratch. But most organizations aren't. They're already neck-deep in legacy tool bloat, juggling too many overlapping communication tools. In these cases, fixing the plumbing takes more than just guidelines. It takes decisive, top-down leadership and the stomach to make hard calls and rip out old plumbing.

In 2023, Paul Leonardi, Bob Sutton, Federico Torreti (former head of product at Amazon Web Services), and I launched an intervention we called the *collaboration cleanse* to help employees at Amazon and Asana escape tool bloat.[10] We asked fifty-eight employees from the companies to audit their workplace communication tools (like Slack, Zoom, and Figma) and then go cold turkey on some of them for two weeks. Half of our participants applied the Rule of Halves, cutting their communication tool set by 50 percent. The rest had free rein to slash as many tools as they wanted. Everyone logged their progress daily, including every time they caved and used a "banned" tool.

We learned a lot. But not all of it was good news.

The good news? Over half (53 percent) of our participants realized they could permanently ditch at least one communication tool. Several people discovered they didn't need two competing meeting platforms (like Zoom and Microsoft Teams) duking it out in their tech stack.

The bad news? We measured what Paul Leonardi calls *digital exhaustion*: the fatigue employees feel from using their digital tools. And it worsened during the cleanse.

Why? Because even though participants experienced the sweet taste of a leaner, saner tool stack, they also saw just how entrenched the clutter was. They wanted their teams, bosses, and clients to streamline their tools, too. But instead, everyone clung to their favorite tools, refusing to let go.

Rather than feeling relief, many felt trapped. That sinking realization that "this system is broken, and I'm stuck in it" wasn't just enlightening— it was exhausting.

And for the group forced to cut their tools in half, it was even worse. They became tool minimalists trapped in a maximalist world, butting heads with colleagues who refused to give up the sacred cows in their tool stacks.

This is where leaders need to intervene. At one organization Paul Leonardi studied, the CTO became so fed up with tool bloat that he staged a SaaS (Software as a Service) apocalypse. He mandated that every software subscription not authorized by IT be canceled.[11] If employees wanted a tool reinstated, their manager had to submit a written request directly to him. Six months after the mass cancellation, the company had thirty fewer tools in circulation.

Without top-down direction, fixing fragmented tools becomes an uphill battle. Teams can beg, barter, and nudge their colleagues to use the right tools, but they can't fix a system-wide problem alone. And as our participants discovered, it is utterly exhausting to try.

Some leaders flinch at the mention of tool standardization, worrying that it will limit employees' autonomy. But, according to a survey that my team led at the Work Innovation Lab, 67 percent of knowledge workers in the US and UK say they want their organization to adopt a single set of core collaboration tools.[12] They're tired of information scavenger hunts, app toggling, and negotiating where work is supposed to happen.

Standardization doesn't strip away autonomy. It clears the way for it. When employees stop burning brainpower figuring out *how* to work, they can focus on actually *doing* the work. That's the kind of autonomy worth designing for.

Standardize Meeting Scheduling with the 4D-CEO Test

Standardizing your communication tools also involves setting clear rules for when to use meetings as communication tools and when to skip them. Meetings are just one pipe in your communication system, and not everything deserves to flow through them.

That's where the 4D-CEO Test comes in. It's a ruthless, two-round filter designed to eliminate unnecessary meetings before they ever hit your calendar. Before you hit "Send" on that calendar invite, your meeting must pass both rounds of the 4D-CEO Test:

ROUND 1: THE 4D TEST. If the purpose of your meeting isn't to do one of these four things, cancel it:

- Decide
- Discuss
- Debate
- Develop (yourself, someone else, or your team)

Even if a meeting passes the 4D Test, it still needs to survive Round 2.

ROUND 2: THE CEO TEST. Your meeting must also meet at least one of these three criteria:

C: IS IT COMPLEX? Some decisions, debates, and discussions are too complex for asynchronous back-and-forths. If you're dealing with a strategic pivot, a cross-functional product launch, or a crisis full of "unknown unknowns," a real-time meeting is often more efficient. Here's a gut check: If it takes more than three async exchanges (emails, Slack messages, comments) to reach a resolution, and you've already provided the necessary context, it's probably complex enough to warrant a meeting.

E: IS IT EMOTIONALLY INTENSE? If you need to read emotions (like picking up on hesitation in a negotiation), express emotions (like showing empathy when delivering tough feedback), or manage emotions (like de-escalating conflict or motivating a disengaged team), then a meeting is probably the better choice.

O: IS IT A ONE-WAY-DOOR DECISION? Jeff Bezos made a crucial distinction at Amazon: Some decisions (like signing a multimillion-dollar deal or major strategic pivots) are "one-way doors." Once you walk through, it's very difficult to go back.[13] These often deserve a meeting. But most decisions are "two-way doors," possible to reverse if needed. Those can be handled asynchronously, unless they're complex or emotionally intense.

A word of caution: Don't be too quick to put development meetings (the fourth D in the 4D-CEO Test) on the chopping block. These are meetings that develop people, teams, and relationships. Think mentorship, learning, skill-building, and real human bonding. Unlike other meetings, these shouldn't be ruthlessly efficient. They're an investment in people, and that takes time.

Cutting development meetings isn't trimming fat. It's starving your team. Conflicts fester. Trust dries up. And skill gaps widen. As Henry

Ford is credited with saying, "The only thing worse than training your employees and having them leave is not training them and having them stay."[14]

UPGRADE 2: DEFAULT TO ASYNCHRONOUS COMMUNICATION

The most powerful antidote to meeting overload is an asynchronous (async) culture, where people communicate and collaborate without needing real-time conversations.

But most workplace technology isn't designed for async communication. And even when it can be used asynchronously, we've been conditioned to treat it like a real-time digital walkie-talkie. Take email. A 2015 study by Yahoo Labs of over 2 million people and 16 billion emails found that the most common reply time to email was just two minutes.[15] That's not async. It's a trained reflex.

We've become addicted to the thrill of constant pings. Every notification dangles the promise of something exciting: a big client win, a glowing shout-out, or maybe just a meme worth a chuckle. But most of the time, it's not exciting at all. And it shatters our focus. UC Irvine professor Gloria Mark found that it can take twenty-three minutes and fifteen seconds to recover from a single interruption.[16] In other words, one Slack ping or "quick question" can hijack your focus for nearly half an hour. Multiply that by dozens of interruptions a day, and it's no wonder deep work feels like wishful thinking.

Fixing this takes more than superficial hacks, like hiding behind giant headphones as a human Do Not Disturb sign or setting a smug email autoresponder that says, "I check email once a day." What you need is a total reset to a culture that defaults to async, not always-on.

If It's Not Documented, It Didn't Happen

Here's the golden rule for async success: If it's not documented, it didn't happen.

Every decision, task, update, and meeting (including agendas, notes, and follow-ups) needs to live in a single source of truth. When information is scattered across Slack threads, buried in email chains, or (worst of all) lodged in someone's leaky memory, you're just setting the stage for more meetings to fill in the blanks.

Documentation should go beyond just recording the final decision. In her research, University College of London professor Jen Rhymer has found that to make async work, you need to capture the messy guts of the process: the debated ideas, the vetoed options, the ugly trade-offs.[17] Without this "rich decision trail," as Rhymer calls it, teams fall into collective amnesia and end up rehashing the same debates in déjà vu meetings.

Documentation used to be a slog. It was manual and time-consuming. But AI makes it a lot less painful. Now meetings can be automatically transcribed, summaries generated in seconds, and key insights made instantly searchable. No more combing through pages of transcripts or digging through digital rubble to figure out what really happened.

Tools like Glean can turn scattered conversations across meeting transcripts, emails, project docs, and Slack messages into a single searchable system. Need context for a decision? Just ask: "We're deciding on a new pricing model. What past discussions should we consider?" and get an answer. No more chasing hazy recollections, second-guessing what was said, or scheduling a meeting just to remember what happened in the last one. We'll dig deeper into AI in chapter 7.

Memos Before Meetings

In 2004 Jeff Bezos sent a dagger of an email to Amazon's senior leadership team (the "STeam") with the subject line "No PowerPoint presentations from now on at Steam."[18] Instead, he replaced slide decks with memos. But not just any memos. Bezos demanded rigor. He wanted two-to-six-page documents that were "narratively structured," with full sentences, clear logic, and well-formed arguments. Some took a week or longer to write. "Clear writing leads to clear thinking, and vice-versa," Bezos insisted.[19] "There is no way to write a six-page, narratively structured memo and not have clear thinking."[20] In other words: If you can't explain it on paper, you're not ready to talk about it in a meeting.

Bezos' memo-first approach split meetings into two phases:

- **PHASE 1: THE "STUDY HALL."** Employees spent around ten to thirty minutes reading and annotating the memo in silence, without distractions. If the memo was unclear, the meeting was canceled. And if attendees had nothing left to add after reading and annotating, they invoked the Law of Two Feet and walked out.

- **PHASE 2: THE LIVE DISCUSSION.** After everyone read and absorbed the memo, the meeting shifted to a live, real-time discussion. If you were in the room and hadn't invoked the Law of Two Feet, it meant you had something meaningful to contribute that warranted a live discussion or debate.

By baking pre-reading time into the meeting itself, Bezos avoided the common scenario where attendees either skim or skip the memo and then bluff or bobblehead their way through the discussion. Instead, you get a room full of people who've done their homework, ready to contribute, challenge ideas, and move work forward.

If You Can't Explain It in Writing, You're Not Ready for a Meeting

In an async communication system, writing is the core operating language. It needs to be clear, direct, and self-explanatory. People should be able to self-serve the information they need without burning through meeting time or lighting up someone's Slack with a "quick question."

That's why GitLab urges employees to use "low-context communications by being explicit when communicating."[21] In other words, don't make your colleagues play detective. Don't force them to rummage through Slack threads or dig through email chains to figure out what you need. Lay it all out: links, documents, deadlines, and clear instructions.

ICF, a consulting and technology services company, enforces a "no lazy asks" policy.[22] Here's the difference:

- **A LAZY ASK:** "Can you take a look at this?"
- **A CLEAR ASK:** "Please review this draft for accuracy by Thursday at noon PST, and upload the final version to Confluence."

Lazy asks don't just slow things down. They breed unnecessary meetings. When your communication is vague, you force people to flood your inbox with clarifying questions—or worse, schedule a meeting just to decipher what you really meant. If you can't clearly explain what you need in writing, you're not ready to ask. And you're definitely not ready for a meeting.

Strong written communication weeds out lazy thinking, cuts down on misunderstandings, eliminates pointless back-and-forths, and preserves synchronous meeting time for the communication that deserves it. It builds a culture where thinking happens before talking. That's why Bezos called Amazon's memo culture one of the company's smartest decisions ever. It's a bold claim from a man whose company redefined online shopping, built a cloud empire, and launched rockets into space.[23]

Bullshit Doesn't Survive in Strong Async Cultures

A strong async communication culture—built on clear, disciplined writing—comes with an underrated perk: It doesn't reward bullies or bullshitters. Live meetings often reward smooth talkers, overconfident hand-wavers, and self-appointed visionaries, while quieter folks get steamrolled. But writing doesn't care how charismatic you are. It strips away theatrics and hot air, forcing every idea to stand on its own merit.

Bezos knew this. He believed that writing a four-page memo was a lot harder than cranking out a twenty-slide PowerPoint.[24] But that's the point. Writing forces deeper thinking, clearer logic, and stronger arguments.

It's the ultimate systems-thinking hack. Do the hard thinking up front in writing and you get fewer misunderstandings, fewer meetings, and a whole lot less bullshit.

Default to Public Channels or Get Buried in Digital Debris

Information silos are the kryptonite of asynchronous work. When crucial updates and decisions get buried in the depths of private messages and email chains or sprawled across fragmented communication tools, employees are forced into grueling digital search-and-rescue missions just to find the information they need.

That's why at the social media management company Buffer, employees are encouraged to "default to public channels." Unless there's a valid reason for privacy (such as legal or HR matters), every message should be visible to the entire team. It's one of Buffer's 10 Slack Agreements—a master class in establishing clear, straightforward communication rules.[25]

Sourcegraph takes a similar stance. Slack channels are public by default, with rare exceptions for sensitive topics like recruiting and manager communication. Employees are coached to push for transparency: "If you receive a DM that should be shared in a public channel, ask that person to re-send the message with a broader audience."[26] And if someone wants to make a Slack channel private, they need sign-off from both their manager and IT. That built-in guardrail adds just enough friction to discourage secrecy and reinforce transparency as the default.

When information flows freely—open, accessible, and easy to find—teams don't waste time digging through digital debris. They can self-serve what they need, bypass the digital dumpster dives, and get back to the real work.

UPGRADE 3: DESIGN FOR DISTANCE

During the pandemic, I met Astrid, a remote worker based in Portland, about six hundred miles from her company's San Francisco headquarters. She felt invisible, constantly treated as an afterthought. Key conversations happened without her. Critical updates never reached her inbox. Most days she was left piecing together scraps of information, wondering what she'd missed and why she kept getting left out.

On a Zoom call, I noticed a picture of the Golden Gate Bridge behind her. When I asked about it, Astrid explained it wasn't just decor. She'd put it there intentionally, as a quiet signal to her colleagues, and maybe even to herself, that she was still part of the team. That picture was her makeshift bridge. It was a desperate attempt to close the chasm that remote work had carved between her and her coworkers.

Astrid's struggle isn't unique. In 2020, professors Melissa Valentine (Stanford University), Justin Berg (University of Michigan), Katy DeCelles (University of Toronto), and I interviewed fifty-nine remote workers from companies that had been mostly in-office before the pandemic and largely returned to the office after.[27] The remote employees had eerily similar stories. They felt like second-class citizens: the last to speak in meetings, the first to be forgotten. Their voices were drowned out by the people physically in the room.

Distance is the ultimate stress test for any communication system. When your team is scattered across floors, offices, cities, continents, or time zones, small cracks turn into gaping communication holes. That's because physical distance breeds psychological distance. When someone's out of sight, they're often out of mind. Just because you *can* reach someone doesn't mean you will.

Erin Bradner, now director of strategic foresight at Autodesk, and Gloria Mark tested the effect of distance on collaboration in a clever study.[28] They paired participants up for a set of tasks and told some that their partner was in the same city, in Irvine, California, while others were told their partner was across the country in Boston. In reality, everyone was in the same building, in adjacent rooms.

Bradner and Mark found that participants who believed their partner was "far away" were less cooperative, more deceptive, and harder to persuade, even though the physical distance was the same.

Distance (even the imagined kind) clogs your communication pipes.

Piling on more meetings won't fix it. The real fix is to think like a systems designer. You need to build clear, intentional communication pipes that keep information flowing, no matter how far apart your team is.

Blame the Design, Not the Hybrid

During the pandemic, hybrid work became the media's favorite punching bag:

- "What Companies Are Getting 'Wrong' About Hybrid Work"[29] (*The Wall Street Journal*)
- "The Permanently Imperfect Reality of Hybrid Work"[30] (BBC)
- "Why Hybrid Work Can Become Toxic"[31] (*Harvard Business Review*)

And yet, here we are. According to research by Nick Bloom, 80 percent of US companies now offer some form of remote work.[32] So why do hybrid meetings still crash and burn with remarkable consistency?

Because most companies still treat them like an afterthought. They slap a Zoom link onto the calendar invite, label it "remote-friendly," and move on. Yet as Michael Arena puts it, "proximity matters, but intentionality trumps proximity."[33]

Hybrid meetings don't fail because some folks are in the room while others are on a screen. They fail because no one designed them to bridge the distance gap.

Fight the Gravitational Pull Toward the Room

Every hybrid meeting has an invisible "center of gravity" where attention, influence, and conversation naturally cluster. And unless you design your meetings with that in mind, gravity almost always pulls toward the physical room. In-room participants enjoy a home-field advantage. They read the subtle body language, trade side comments, and bond over pre- and post-meeting small talk. Meanwhile, remote attendees orbit like neglected satellites, waving their virtual hands while the conversation races past.

To fix this, you need to actively fight the gravitational pull toward the physical room. Start by giving remote participants the first word. The first person to speak in a meeting sets the tone. Psychologists call this the *primacy effect*: We naturally give more weight to that first voice. And more often than not, that voice comes from someone in the physical room, reinforcing their influence. But when remote participants speak first, it flips the dynamic. It signals they're not passive observers—they're full participants.

Make Remote Participants Visible Even When They're Not in the Room

Another way to shift the gravitational pull is to give remote participants a "physical twin": a tangible presence in the physical room that signals, "I'm here, even if you can't see me."

Sacha Connor did that when she left Clorox's Oakland headquarters to work remotely. Instead of fading into the background, she had her teammates post a photo of herself imprinted with her phone number in their offices and cubicles. By distributing these physical twins, Connor made sure she stayed visible, even from a distance.

Jeff Bezos used a similar strategy at Amazon. He kept an empty chair in meetings to symbolize the customer. In hybrid meetings, an empty chair for remote employees can serve the same purpose. It's a visual reminder that they're still here, even if you can't see them.

Another way to shift the center of gravity is to assign an in-room "buddy" to be the remote attendees' advocate—someone who watches for their virtual hand raises, brings them into the conversation, and makes sure their voice doesn't get drowned out by the in-room chatter.

Jackie, a remote worker I spoke with during the pandemic, could have used a buddy. She described the exhausting mental calculus of being the lone Zoom square in a room of fifteen people: "I felt like I had to have something really important to say if I was to halt the conversation and get everyone's attention." A buddy relieves that pressure, ensuring remote participants have a voice, without making them feel like they need to "earn" the right to speak.

And if you want to get really creative, take inspiration from researchers at Tsinghua University who invented the SNOTBOX.[34] This delightfully weird robot inflates a balloon from its front surface (mimicking a snot bubble swelling while someone's asleep) whenever a remote participant hasn't spoken for a while. It's a playful but effective nudge to include everyone in the room.

You don't need a snot-snorting robot to balance the center of gravity in hybrid meetings (though it's mighty tempting). Whether it's a photo, an empty chair, or a buddy, these strategies ensure that remote participants aren't just floating in the digital ether. They're active, valued voices in the conversation.

Design Your Meeting Room Like Everyone Has a Front-Row Seat

Most meeting rooms aren't physically designed for hybrid collaboration. Remote participants often end up with the worst seat in the house, forced to stare at the backs of people's heads and squint to read their facial expressions. Meanwhile, their own faces balloon to cartoonish proportions on the screen, making them hyper-visible and hyper-invisible at the same time.

To help remote workers feel like part of the conversation, ditch the medieval "head-of-the-table" layout. Instead, aim for what Tori Paulman, vice president analyst at Gartner, calls "sitcom style." Think of your favorite sitcom: The audience wraps around the stage so they always get a clear view of the action. That's how hybrid meetings should feel. Remote participants should get a front-row seat, not a nosebleed view where they're stuck piecing together the plot.

Start by placing the main screen along the long side of the table (not at the end) so remote attendees can see everyone. That way they're not stuck looking at the sides of heads or a lineup of hairlines staring the other way. Or take a cue from companies like Microsoft, Airbnb, and Zoom and use a U-shaped table. It naturally orients everyone toward the screen so remote participants become part of the conversation. More round table, less fly-on-the-wall. Matt Hempey, a principal program manager at Microsoft, explains, "What creates a great hybrid experience is not necessarily the technology as much as just the way everyone is facing. If people are facing each other in the room, they're not focused on the people that are there remotely."[35]

But hybrid meeting equity isn't just about where people sit. It's about making sure every communication tool in the meeting works for everyone. Take physical whiteboards. For remote attendees, the writing might as well be blurry hieroglyphics. Swap them for digital whiteboards like Miro or Mural so everyone can see and contribute, no matter where they're sitting.

The same applies to printed handouts or physical worksheets. While in-office employees flip through materials and take notes, remote attendees sit empty-handed, waiting for someone to remember to send them a digital copy, if they get one at all. IDEO executive director Leah Marcus recommends that all materials be mirrored in a digital format to keep everyone on the same page—literally.[36]

A hybrid meeting should feel like one meeting. Not an alpha version for the in-office crowd and a buggy beta for remote participants. If you don't design for inclusion, you're designing for exclusion.

Your HQ Time Zone Isn't the Center of the Universe

When teams stretch across time zones, communication can become a high-stakes game of broken telephone.

A strong async culture is your best defense against miscommunication. When decisions are documented, writing is clear, and information is easy to find, teams can pass the baton across time zones without fumbling it. Everything we've covered in this chapter—strong written communication, smart async norms, intentional communication—helps keep communication flowing smoothly across distances. For example, don't assign deadlines with vague hand-wavy phrases like "end of day." That means nothing when your team spans time zones. Whose day? Which clock? Be specific: "by 5 p.m. PST this Thursday."

When live meetings are necessary, avoid the lazy habit of scheduling for headquarters' convenience. Too often, global teammates are left sacrificing sleep, missing family dinners, or scraping by on caffeine and quiet resentment. Share the inconvenience. If the Singapore team took the 6 a.m. call last week, let HQ take the evening hit next time. It sends the message that everyone's time matters.

Always record live meetings so that teammates can catch up on their own clock. And whatever you do, don't schedule a critical meeting for Friday afternoon US time (Saturday morning in the Asia-Pacific region). Nobody wants to review quarterly KPIs over their weekend coffee. Or worse, while nursing a hangover.

Don't Let Meeting Format Be a Coin Toss

You can't always control where a meeting happens. But when you can, think like a systems designer. Don't leave it to chance. Your job is to match the meeting format to the kind of communication flow it needs to support. Two key factors should guide your decision:

1. **EMOTIONAL INTENSITY.** The more your meeting hinges on reading, expressing, or managing emotions, the more it benefits from being face-to-face. In-person meetings give you the full emotional spectrum, from body language and tone shifts to the eye roll that says it all.

2. **COST.** In-person meetings are expensive. There's the travel bill, the calendar Tetris, the commute grind, and the energy drain of too much face time. And if you're stuck in a room full of jerks (more on them in chapter 5), add a surcharge for your sanity. The higher the cost—financial, logistical, or emotional—the stronger the case for keeping it virtual.

	HIGH COST TO MEET IN PERSON	LOW COST TO MEET IN PERSON
HIGH EMOTIONAL INTENSITY	Try to meet in person whenever feasible	Always aim to meet in person
LOW EMOTIONAL INTENSITY	Lean toward meeting virtually	Lean toward in-person if feasible

When emotional intensity runs high, in-person meetings are often your best bet. Relationship-building, persuasion, onboarding, feedback, and mentoring are emotional tightropes that hinge on trust, empathy, and the kind of human connection that's hard to replicate through a screen (no matter how many emojis you toss into the chat).

But if the emotional stakes are lower—approvals, routine decisions, project updates—go virtual. Just make sure the content passes the 4D-CEO Test.

Now, here's where the anti-remote crowd gets it wrong: Strong relationships don't need daily face time. Once trust is built in person, it's surprisingly "sticky." You don't need to re-earn it every day or week during in-person meetings. Based on her research, Stanford professor Pamela Hinds posits that in-person site visits every nine to twelve months are typically enough to maintain a personal connection.[37] Atlassian's data backs that up: Their employees report that the bonds formed during site visits can last four to five months.[38]

What about brainstorming? Should that happen in person? It certainly *feels* like it should. The word conjures up images of Post-its, and teams huddled together around whiteboards. Indeed, Melanie Brucks, a professor at Columbia Business School, and Jonathan Levav, a professor at Stanford's Graduate School of Business, found that videoconferencing groups generate fewer creative ideas than in-person groups.[39] Why? Because communicating virtually narrows your visual field. You focus tightly on the screen and filter out the surrounding environment. That limits *cognitive wandering*: those unexpected mental detours triggered by sights, sounds, and movements in our environment that fuel fresh associations and creative thinking.

But in-person brainstorming isn't always necessary. Brucks and Levav also found that while virtual groups generated fewer ideas, they didn't find any evidence that virtual groups were worse at selecting which ideas to pursue—and found some preliminary evidence that they might be even more effective. The reason? Less cognitive wandering means people stay more focused, making it easier to critically evaluate ideas without getting pulled off track.

So if you're generating ideas, in person might be best. But if you're selecting, sharpening, and stress-testing the best ones, virtual can be just as effective. And it might even give you an edge.

Brainwriting Beats Brainstorming

Just because brainstorming works better in person doesn't mean everyone should do it together. Study after study shows that people generate more—and often better—ideas when they brainstorm solo before the group gets involved.[40] While collective brainstorming can create a contagious "yes, and . . ." energy that fuels creativity, it can also choke the communication flow. Loudmouths dominate the room. Overthinkers freeze under pressure. And groupthink takes over as people nod along instead of speaking up.

That's where *brainwriting* comes in. Everyone writes down their ideas independently and silently before sharing them with the group. Then the team builds on them, refines them, and pushes them further. Every idea gets a fighting chance—before groupthink, hierarchy, or the loudest voice in the room takes over.

Northwestern professor Leigh Thompson's research has found that brainwriting groups generate 20 percent more ideas and 42 percent more original ones compared to traditional brainstorming groups.[41] In fact, Thompson says she's not aware of a single published study where face-to-face brainstorming outperformed brainwriting.[42]

Build Trust with Systems, Not Surveillance

Trust is the grease that keeps communication flowing, especially across distances. Without it, your entire communication system seizes up. People stop sharing ideas, second-guess each other, and start hoarding information.

In a physical office, trust builds naturally through visibility. You see someone typing furiously at their desk, and you assume they're working—even if they're secretly shopping Cyber Monday deals. But remote work strips away that visibility, and trust often evaporates along with it.

During the pandemic, that trust gap grew into a gaping chasm. Many companies panicked and reached for surveillance tools. As professors Mark Mortensen of INSEAD and Heidi Gardner of Harvard have documented,[43] as the pandemic unfolded, Hubstaff, a time-tracking app, quadrupled its UK customer base.[44] Sneek, which snaps webcam shots of employees throughout the day, saw a tenfold increase in sales.[45] Even Zoom briefly flirted with an Orwellian "attentiveness score," where a tattletale clock icon popped up next to your name if Zoom wasn't your active app window for more than thirty seconds.

But more surveillance won't fix a trust problem. Systems thinking will. You need to design a communication system that builds trust by design, instead of Big Brother breathing down everyone's neck.

Daniel McAllister, a professor of management at the National University of Singapore, breaks trust into two types:[46]

- **AFFECTIVE TRUST ("TRUST OF THE HEART").** This is emotional trust. It's the kind that grows through shared experiences, candid conversations, and genuine empathy. It forms when people feel seen, heard, and supported.

- **COGNITIVE TRUST ("TRUST OF THE HEAD").** This is rational trust, based on a colleague's competence and reliability. It's grounded in observable actions: showing up, delivering quality work, and following through on commitments.

Harvard Business School professor Tsedal Neeley emphasizes that cognitive trust is especially important for distributed teams.[47] While affective trust takes time and emotional closeness to build, cognitive trust tends to form more quickly. It's built on evidence: someone delivers consistently, so you trust they will again.

A baseline of both cognitive and emotional trust is essential for building what researchers call *swift trust*: a temporary form of trust that forms quickly when team members don't have a shared history of working together but need to rely on each other anyway. Swift trust allows teams to hit the ground running, trusting one another based on early signs of competence and good intent. That speed and flexibility are especially critical in distributed teams, where members often start with lower levels of familiarity, sometimes connected by nothing more than a single awkward virtual icebreaker.

So, how do you build cognitive trust when you can't swing by someone's desk or catch up in the hallway? Make work visible. Use project boards and dashboards so everyone knows who's doing what and by when. Dedicate meeting time to sharing wins, insights, and expertise. And when someone excels in a project, don't let it fade into the digital void. Celebrate with a Slack shout-out. Flood the Zoom chat with emojis. These aren't just feel-good gestures. They're trust-building currency in a world where you can't peek over a cubicle wall or dish out hallway high-fives.

Grease the Social Gears

When teams are spread across distances, communication can become cold, transactional, and full of awkward pleasantries. That's why you need what Paul Leonardi calls *social lubrication*. In his study of a telecom company in Peru, Leonardi found that employees with strong personal bonds communicated more quickly and more directly. They didn't need to wade through unnecessary formalities or filler. They could get straight to the point.[48]

At Basecamp, that social lubrication is built through optional virtual social prompts every few weeks. Employees are asked to respond to questions like "What's inspiring you lately?" or "What did you do this weekend?"[49] These tiny moments "grease the social gears," as Basecamp puts it, because "when we know each other a little better, we work a little better together."[50]

Buffer takes it further with its three-buddy onboarding system. Every new hire is assigned three different buddies to help them integrate.[51] In addition to a "role buddy" who helps them navigate their job and a "culture buddy" who explains the company's norms, they're assigned a "mastermind buddy": someone who shares a personal interest, like a mutual love of hiking or Marvel movies.

Meanwhile, at visual collaboration company InVision,* a Slack bot called Donut randomly paired employees for virtual meetings, creating unexpected personal connections that wouldn't happen otherwise.[52] One Donut pairing led two employees to discover they both had a family tradition of lime-green Jell-O salads. Swapping their grandmothers' recipes led to a deeper connection—and stronger communication pipes.

---

* InVision shut down its services in 2024 after a multi-year run as a leader in digital collaboration.

Neeley suggests that remote employees proactively share personal quirks and habits, a process researchers call "self-disclosure."[53] In a physical office, you'd notice that Dave always has the latest sci-fi novel on his desk or that Karen is religious about her 3 p.m. Diet Coke ritual. But when your team is spread across distance, you have to engineer opportunities to share personal details like these. Otherwise, the social gears rust and the whole machine starts to grind.

Another way to grease the social gears is with off-sites and site visits—but only if they're intentionally designed. In one study, Pamela Hinds and Catherine Cramton, a professor at George Mason University, found that site visits (where remote employees visit a real company office) built stronger, more lasting connections than off-sites in places like generic hotel ballrooms.[54] Why? Because people see each other in their natural habitat. They get a feel for how their teammates really work: their quirks, routines, and unspoken norms. That context builds trust. After site visits, employees communicated more frequently and were more likely to share personal information and discuss difficult topics.

For fully remote teams with no offices to visit, well-designed off-sites can also build these strong connections. In one study, Harvard professor Raj Choudhury studied a 281-person off-site where employees immediately sorted themselves into silos: marketers with marketers, engineers with engineers—the high school cafeteria effect.[55] But something unexpected broke the pattern: taxi rides. Employees who shared airport rides had spontaneous cross-team conversations that sparked new relationships.

Don't leave social grease to chance. Design for it. Pair people from different teams for travel, activities, or shared sessions. Mix up seating. Build space for unstructured interactions. When it's intentional, these aren't just morale boosters. They're system upgrades that rewire your communication flow after the meeting room empties.

YOU CAN'T SCHEDULE YOUR WAY
OUT OF A BAD SYSTEM

W. Edwards Deming, the legendary systems-thinking expert, once said, "A bad system will beat a good person every time."[56] The same applies to meetings. A broken system will sink even the best-run meeting.

High-performing teams don't just design better meetings. They build better systems around them. They don't slap meetings over every problem like it's workplace duct tape. Instead, they design for flow: communication that reaches the right people at the right time, without overwhelming everyone. In that kind of system, meetings become the last resort, not the first reflex.

If meetings are clogging your communication, the answer isn't to add more. Fix the system, and you'll fix the flow.

PRINCIPLE 5

Engagement: Prioritize User-Centric Design

In 2008 Steve Jobs stormed into a meeting after MobileMe, Apple's much-hyped cloud service, flopped spectacularly.[1] He cut straight to the kill shot: "Can anyone tell me what MobileMe is supposed to do?"

One brave soul answered. Jobs listened, then erupted, "So why the f*** doesn't it do that?"

For the next thirty brutal minutes, he tore into the team. He told them they'd "tarnished Apple's reputation." And that they "should hate each other for having let each other down." By the time he was done, he'd fired the team leader and left the rest of the room deflated.

STOP SHIPPING BAD MEETINGS

You don't need Jobs's volcanic temper to kill engagement in a meeting. Most meetings die slower deaths. Irrelevant updates sneak in. One person hijacks the agenda. Someone says "synergy" for the fifth time. Attention fizzles. Engagement flatlines. Before you know it, your meeting is running like MobileMe: a buggy, unstable product that nobody wants to use.

Great meetings are designed like great products: They put "users"—attendees—at the center. That's Meeting Design Principle 5: user-centric design.

No halfway-decent product team would ship something that frustrates users, puts them to sleep, or solves a problem nobody has. Yet meetings do exactly that, every day.

Want to know if your meeting is user-centric? Start with ROTI (return on time invested) from chapter 2. Did attendees feel their time was well invested? If not, your meeting wasn't designed for them. It was likely designed for *you.*

Here's another litmus test: Who leaves the meeting feeling most satisfied? Research by Steven Rogelberg shows it's usually one of two people:[2]

- **THE MEETING ORGANIZER:** They checked a box and felt productive, even if nothing was accomplished.

- **THE PERSON WHO TALKED THE MOST:** They basked in the sound of their own voice echoing across the room, even if they didn't say anything useful.

And here's the ultimate red flag: People lie to escape your meetings. In research my team led at Asana, 45 percent of knowledge workers admitted to faking excuses, sometimes flat-out lying, to avoid meetings.[3] If your attendees are crafting alibis to avoid your meetings, they aren't helping them—they're bleeding them dry.

THE FOUR ENERGY-SUCKING MEETING BUGS

Why do so many meetings drain the life out of attendees? Because they're crawling with bugs—energy-sapping, culture-rotting bugs that suck the life out of the room. There are four especially gnarly offenders:

ENERGY-SUCKING BUG 1: POWER MOVES. Leaders, often without realizing it, dominate the mic and steer the conversation, relegating everyone else to glorified seat-fillers.

ENERGY-SUCKING BUG 2: LATENESS. Someone struts in ten minutes late, clutches their coffee, and tosses a breezy "Sorry, busy morning" like a Get Out of Jail Free card. The meeting's momentum screeches to a halt.

ENERGY-SUCKING BUG 3: JARGON. Buzzwords, acronyms, and corporate word salad choke meetings with a thick linguistic smog. Half the room squints in confusion. The other half nods along, pretending they understand.

ENERGY-SUCKING BUG 4: BOREDOM. A sleepy agenda. A dull meeting room. All the energy of a DMV waiting room. Engagement evaporates, and people begin fantasizing about being anywhere else.

These bugs don't just wreck one meeting. They infect your entire culture. People stop preparing. Stop contributing. And stop caring. Before you know it, the apathy oozes across your company and your culture starts to decay.

ENERGY-SUCKING BUG 1: POWER MOVES

In 2007, Ford was on life support. The company had just posted a $12.7 billion loss, the worst in its 103-year history.[4] Its market share had tanked 25 percent since 1990, and behind closed doors, meetings had turned into a theater of false confidence and carefully crafted half-truths.[5]

Then came Alan Mulally. When he took over as CEO, he zeroed in on meetings as ground zero for Ford's dysfunction. He knew meetings are where culture gets built. And Ford's culture was broken.

Mulally's first target was his weekly Thursday 7 a.m. management meetings, where he introduced a traffic-light system:

- **GREEN:** Everything is on track.
- **YELLOW:** Issues need attention.
- **RED:** Critical problems require immediate action.

At the first traffic-light meeting, attendees marked nearly every project green, with just a few scattered yellows.[6] Mulally didn't buy it. "How," he asked, "can everything be green when we're losing billions of dollars?"[7] He sent his team back to try again.

The following week, the room lit up with red lights. When the first red light appeared, "Mulally erupted in applause," recounts Deborah Ancona, a professor of leadership at MIT.[8]

Why did his team hold back at first? Because leaders cast long, intimidating shadows. Employees defaulted to self-censorship, feeding Mulally what they thought he wanted to hear, not what he needed to know.

But Mulally's applause sent a clear message: Meetings weren't a stage for performative optimism. They were a place for honesty. If you weren't prepared to be transparent, you didn't belong in the meeting.

The Three Toxic Power Moves

Mulally's influence at Ford was a textbook *power move*: when a leader's power (intentional or not) warps how people participate, speak up, and share ideas. Mulally managed to disarm his power, but most leaders aren't that self-aware.

Meetings are breeding grounds for three highly toxic power moves:

- **AMPLIFICATION:** The boss speaks, and suddenly it's gospel. People start self-censoring, sugarcoating bad news, and swallowing their dissenting opinions.

- **INCOMPETENCE:** When a leader can't run a meeting, it drains the room's energy. People leave annoyed and wondering why they bothered to show up.

- **JERK BEHAVIOR:** Bullies, interrupters, and blowhards hijack the room. Collaboration isn't just stifled—it's publicly executed.

These power moves reduce meetings to lifeless, performative rituals where the people who hold the most power call the shots and everyone else plays defense.

But it doesn't have to be this way. Design your meetings to defang these power moves, and you'll create a space where people speak up, push back, and bring bolder and better ideas to the table.

Amplification: When Power Overpowers

Jade Rubick, former VP of engineering at New Relic, remembers the exact moment he became "brilliant."[9] It wasn't because of a sudden surge in IQ or creativity. It was his promotion to senior director, accompanied by a glowing speech in front of his peers.

Overnight, everything changed. In meetings, people went out of their way to praise his ideas. "Person after person would go out of their way to say why my suggestion was the 'right approach,'" Rubick recalls. "All of a sudden, my ideas were BRILLIANT . . . All of a sudden, I was a different person, a Very Important Person."

What Rubick experienced was a classic case of what Professor Adam Galinsky calls *amplification*[10]: the invisible megaphone leaders inherit when they step into a position of power. A passing comment becomes a marching order. An offhand suggestion rockets to the top of the team's priority list. A poorly timed yawn during your presentation plunges you into a spiral of self-doubt: "They hate this. They hate me." Instead of focusing on the work, people start decoding every glance, sigh, or eyebrow twitch as part of a high-stakes game of corporate charades.

Amplification distorts everything. Even humor. Research has shown that when leaders crack jokes, employees often feel pressured to laugh. Not because it's funny, but to kiss up to their higher-ups.[11] Researchers call this *surface acting*. Meetings fill with forced chuckles, and suddenly cringy dad jokes can land like they're headlining a Netflix comedy special.

Retired four-star general Stanley McChrystal compares amplification to a dinosaur's tail.[12] Picture a brontosaurus: Its tiny head makes decisions, while its massive tail swings wildly behind it, flattening everything in its path. The higher you climb up the org chart, the bigger your tail—and the more collateral damage you leave behind.

Even punctuation isn't safe. At Amazon, Jeff Bezos was known to forward customer complaints to his team with a single "?"[13] That lone punctuation mark launched teams into a frenzy, scrambling to fix the issue like their jobs depended on it.

According to Galinsky, certain types of communication are especially susceptible to amplification. The most obvious? Plain old talking. A leader's words, even the offhanded ones, carry outsized weight and can land like royal decrees. Say something like "We might want to improve onboarding," and suddenly Carol in HR is pulling all-nighters, buried under drafts of a new employee manual. That's not what you meant—but it's what people heard.

When amplification takes over meetings, people start filtering their ideas or stop sharing them altogether. They nod along like bobble-heads and, before long, the room turns into an echo chamber—parrots squawking back the leader's words instead of expressing their own.

Dial Down the Talking

How do you stop your dinosaur tail from flattening the room? First, leaders need to acknowledge the gravitational pull of their words. Then, they need to ease off the megaphone and dial down their talking.

Research shows that high-performing teams share airtime more equally.[14] In a perfect world, leaders would recognize that and adjust accordingly. But self-awareness isn't always their strong suit. And the more power they hold, the less likely anyone is to tell them they're hogging the mic.

If you're dealing with a leader who can't stop steamrolling the room, there are ways to take back the room. At one organization, team members came up with a creative solution: a miniature stuffed horse.[15] "If someone is too long-winded, anyone can toss the horse in front of that person as a signal to 'stop beating a dead horse,'" one team member explained.

Now, chucking stuffed animals at your coworkers—especially the powerful ones—is probably a career-limiting move. But the spirit of the idea is sound: Find a way to flag the airtime hogs.

Fortunately, technology offers a safer option. Back in the late 2000s, MIT's Sandy Pentland and his lab introduced the *meeting mediator*: a smartphone app paired with sensors that tracked who talked and for how long.[16] It displayed a virtual meeting table with a floating ball that drifted toward the biggest talker—a quiet nudge to share the floor.

Today, tools like Fireflies.AI and Equal track metrics like talk-to-listen ratios and flag monologues. Some even analyze gender dynamics, surfacing when women and nonbinary participants are getting drowned out.

Another way to stop people from hijacking the conversation is to get them to speak last. At Pixar, cofounder Ed Catmull understood the risks of speaking first. In brainstorming meetings, he deliberately held back his input until the end so his team could explore ideas without the gravitational pull of his amplified words.[17] Catmull understood what many leaders overlook: New ideas are fragile. As he put it, they need "protection" from getting pancaked by heavy-handed forces like a leader's amplification.[18]

That's also why Catmull struck a deal with Steve Jobs when Jobs was CEO of Pixar. They agreed that Jobs would sit out of Pixar's legendary Braintrust meeting, where senior creatives critiqued early-stage films. As Catmull put it, Jobs's "bigger-than-life presence would make it harder to be candid."[19]

It turns out that leaders aren't always the best judges of creative ideas anyway. Justin Berg, a professor at the University of Michigan, conducted a study with circus professionals and found that managers were consistently worse than peers at spotting which acts audiences would like.[20] They undervalued bold, novel ideas and clung to safe, conventional ones.

If you're a leader and can't keep your dinosaur tail from swinging, try speaking last. Or consider sitting out altogether.

Use a Pulse Check

Another way to prevent power dynamics from steamrolling honest feedback is by running what Coda calls a *pulse check*.[21] Before the meeting, everyone submits anonymous feedback on a specific topic, decision, or proposal. As Shishir Mehrotra, founder of Coda and CEO of Grammarly, puts it, "When you go around the room, you inevitably expose your power structure. Once the boss weighs in, all opinions after that are contrasted with that one. A private pulse check allows everyone to express their opinion at once."[22]

Own the Meeting Like It's a Product

Sometimes balancing airtime takes a designated referee. That's what Piyush Gupta put in place when he took over as CEO of Singapore's DBS Bank in 2009. At the time, DBS was struggling. Customer service ratings were in the gutter. And so was employee morale.[23]

The dysfunction wasn't only showing up in dismal customer service—it was festering in meetings. A company-wide survey found that only 40 percent of employees felt they had an "equal share of voice" in meetings.[24]

To fix this, Gupta's team introduced a new role: the Meeting Owner. Think of it as a product owner in software development: someone responsible for ensuring that the final product delivers real value to customers. Similarly, the Meeting Owner is responsible for ensuring that every meeting provides value. Their job is to set a clear agenda, keep discussions on track, and cut off airtime hogs before they derail the conversation.

And it worked. With Meeting Owners and new norms in place, DBS pulled its meetings out of the mud. The percentage of employees who felt they had an equal share of voice in meetings jumped from 40 percent to 90 percent, a 125 percent improvement. By 2019, *Harvard Business Review* named DBS one of the top twenty business transformations of the decade,[25] an impressive turnaround for a bank that once made its own employees cringe.

Don't Amplify Ambiguity

We've all been there: Your boss drops a cryptic meeting invite on your calendar and your brain immediately spirals. Am I in trouble? Is this about that thing I said in Slack? Am I getting fired? Amplification kicks in, and that vague invite snowballs into employees' worst-case scenarios.

That happened at Mailchimp when CEO Ben Chestnut scheduled his first large all-staff meeting. The company had gone a whole year without one (yikes!) and by then, it had outgrown its usual meeting space.[26] Chestnut decided to move the meeting to the customer support area, temporarily shutting it down. But he didn't explain why.

Employees panicked. Without context, they filled in the blanks themselves. Is customer support being laid off?

This kind of ambiguity is the second type of communication that Galinsky says is prone to amplification. When leaders say or do something vague, employees fill in the blanks—often with their own worst fears.

I've been there. Early in my career, I spotted a mysterious entry on my boss's public calendar: "RH desk move." My stomach dropped, and my brain started to assemble a crime scene:

- RH = Rebecca Hinds = Me
- Desk move = Fired

I spent the night mentally packing up my desk, imagining any possible offense that could have landed me on the chopping block. The next morning, my stomach churning, I asked my boss about it. It turns out, "RH" stood for Restoration Hardware, and "desk move" referred to her buying new furniture for her kids. I had lost an entire night's sleep over her interior decorating project.

Galinsky's advice for leaders prone to amplification is simple: Be transparent. A quick message like "Hey, I need to see you later—it's nothing to worry about" can save your team from hours of anxiety.

And if your calendar is public, don't leave room for speculation. Instead of "Desk move," clarify with "Desk move (picking up kids' furniture)." Trust me, your team is watching your calendar if it's public, and they're overanalyzing every entry, especially the vague ones. Don't give their imaginations room to fill in the blanks. Because they'll assume they're the blanks.

Incompetence: The Accidental Power Move

Some of the most destructive power moves aren't malicious. They're the result of sheer incompetence, which is amplified by a leader's position of power. It's like handing a megaphone to someone who doesn't know how to use it. They shout into the wrong end, and the whole room winces at the ear-splitting feedback.

Leaders who don't know how to effectively design and deploy meetings end up scheduling them for every problem, real or imagined. According to Neil Vyner, VP of growth and go to market at Worklytics, just 5 percent of employees schedule 60 percent of all meetings. These serial schedulers tend to be the most powerful people in the company (or their assistants acting on their behalf).

New managers are some of the worst offenders. They're promoted because they excelled in their previous roles, not because they know how to facilitate productive discussions, navigate hairy decisions, or avoid letting their new dinosaur tail knock over their team's ideas. They're handed a packed calendar of high-stakes meetings and a megaphone, but no user manual.

It's a classic case of the Peter Principle, the phenomenon whereby people keep getting promoted until they land in a role that they're utterly unqualified for.[27] And then, once they reach this level of incompetence, they stay there, armed with a bigger paycheck, a fancier title, and more meetings to drive into a ditch. Research by University of Reading professor Ben Laker and colleagues found that new managers schedule nearly one-third (29 percent) more meetings than experienced ones.[28]

Meanwhile, their employees watch their boss bumble through bad meetings and assume, "Well, I guess this is how it's done." Inefficiency gets institutionalized, and before long, the entire team is trapped in a cycle of toxic meeting mediocrity. Or worse, full-blown dysfunction.

One-on-Ones Aren't for You, Boss

Incompetent managers often treat one-on-ones as *their* meeting—a chance to download updates, deliver monologues, or check a box. But that's not how they should be treated. As Ben Horowitz puts it, "The key to a good one-on-one meeting is the understanding that it is the employee's meeting rather than the manager's meeting."[29] A leader's job is to create space for whatever employees need to move their work forward, whether it's advice, a pitch, or just a chance to vent.

According to research by Gallup, just one meaningful one-on-one meeting each week does more to build high-performance relationships than any other leadership activity—and meetings as short as fifteen minutes are enough to make a difference.[30]

Amplification isn't just about what you say. It's also about what you don't say or do. According to Galinsky, silence is the third form of communication most susceptible to amplification (along with talking and ambiguity). One of the loudest silences? When a leader cancels a meeting without explanation. Employees don't usually assume you're busy. They assume you don't care or that they did something wrong.

Be transparent. Explain why you're rescheduling. Then, reschedule immediately. If you don't prioritize your people, don't be surprised when they stop prioritizing the work.

Stop Hosting Meetings Just to Spoon-feed the Boss

One of the most common—and costly—signs of incompetence is the boss briefing: a meeting held not to collaborate or solve problems, but to spoon-feed status updates to a leader who can't be bothered to check the project tracker.

If you just need updates from your team, don't drag them into a hostage situation. Ask for a written summary or a short video update instead. That's what Atlassian CEO Mike Cannon-Brookes does. He sometimes watches twenty-four Loom videos a week to eliminate status meetings and rescue his team from hours of mind-numbing recaps.[31]

The same goes for updates that you're pushing out to your team. Skip the meeting and record a quick video instead. Film it from a real-life backdrop: a home office with kids barging in, or post-run and still dripping with sweat. That kind of raw, unfiltered communication hits differently. It satisfies the TikTok generation's appetite for authenticity and transparency.[32] Cannon-Brookes does this, too, recording a handful of Looms every week and sending them to staff members. It's part of a shift that helped Atlassian obliterate nearly half a million meetings in a single year.[33]

Before you schedule any meeting, run it through the 4D-CEO Test: Is the purpose to debate, discuss, decide, or develop? If not, it has no business taking up valuable real estate on your team's calendar.

Want to Lead a Team? Learn to Lead a Meeting First

Business schools teach leaders to dissect financial statements, craft visionary strategies, and navigate high-stakes negotiations. But meeting management? It's the neglected stepchild of leadership training—overlooked, undervalued, and brushed aside. Only about 20 percent of leaders have ever been trained on how to run an effective meeting, according to Steven Rogelberg.[34] And yet meetings are where the real action happens. They're where those financial statements are reviewed and challenged, strategies are pressure-tested, and negotiations come to resolution or stall out.

Organizations (and business schools) need to stop treating meeting training as an afterthought—some remedial skill beneath them. Before a leader is handed a packed calendar of meetings, they should prove they can run one without wasting everyone's time.

Make meeting competency a prerequisite for promotion. If someone can't lead a room, why trust them to lead a team?

Jerk Behavior: When the Boss Is the Bully

Unlike amplification or incompetence, jerk behavior isn't an accidental or inevitable side effect of holding a position of power. It's a deliberate abuse of it. And unfortunately, it's disturbingly common. Research by Simon Croom, a professor at the University of San Diego, found that 12 percent of corporate senior leaders exhibit psychopathic traits, up to twelve times the rate found in the general population.[35] Yikes.

Jerk behavior—interrupting, nitpicking, steamrolling, humiliating, or straight-up bullying—sucks the oxygen out of the meeting. And the damage doesn't stay neatly contained at the top. It spreads. Employees who can't push back against a jerk boss don't just absorb the blow, they pass it along to the next person in line. Sure enough, supervisors who report to abusive bosses are more likely to engage in abusive behavior themselves.[36]

Shine a Light on Jerk Behavior

Sometimes, the fastest way to shut down jerk behavior is to bring it into the light. Set up an anonymous feedback form so employees can report toxic behavior without fearing retaliation. But that's just step one. Don't let feedback languish in a forgotten Google Doc. Act on it. Prove you're serious about creating a jerk-free culture. Because doing nothing is worse than not asking for feedback in the first place. It sends a clear message: "We're going to pretend that your voice matters, but it really doesn't."

And that's just another form of jerk behavior.

Add MOJO to Your Meetings

When DBS introduced the Meeting Owner (MO) role, they didn't stop there. They added a sidekick: the Joyful Observer (JO). Together, they became the dynamic duo behind Meeting MOJO, the bank's internal initiative to improve meetings.

While the MO ran the agenda and kept the meeting on track, the JO (appointed by the MO) acted as the meeting's referee. Their job was to call out inappropriate or power-poisoned behavior and ensure everyone had a chance to speak. The JO might say, "I haven't heard anybody challenging anything that's been said."[37]

Try assigning a JO in your meetings, especially if there's a known jerk present in the room. At DBS, their MOJO initiative saved half a million hours of employee time. When you cut jerk behaviors like ego-driven monologues, interruptions, and one-upmanship, the time savings pile up fast.

When All Else Fails, Protect Yourself
Some jerks are beyond redemption. If you're stuck with one of these un-fixable types, your best move is self-preservation. Don't let their toxicity take up space in your head. Or on your calendar.

Start by limiting your exposure to them. Avoid meetings with them if you can. If that's not an option, move the conversation to email or chat to contain their toxicity behind a digital firewall. This will also generate a handy digital paper trail if you need to file a formal report with HR.

And whatever you do, don't feed the beast. Jerks thrive on attention, so starve them of yours. Keep your responses short, flat, and factual. The less entertaining you are as a target, the faster they'll lose interest. Your goal isn't to win them over. It's to bore them into submission.

ENERGY-SUCKING BUG 2: LATENESS

Lateness is the second meeting bug that drains engagement from your meetings.

Marissa Mayer, former CEO of Yahoo, was notorious for being late. Once, she showed up nearly two hours late to a dinner meeting with top executives from Mondelez and Chobani.[38] Her excuse? She'd been taking a nap.

While most of us don't pull off time heists that blatant, lateness is still a rampant issue. How bad is it? Research by University of Utah professor Joseph Allen and his colleagues found that 44 percent to 55 percent of meetings start late because at least one attendee doesn't arrive on time.[39] The damage goes beyond wasted minutes. It also infects creativity. Allen and Rogelberg's research found that late-starting meetings generate fewer ideas, and the ones they do generate are less innovative.[40]

In other words, lateness doesn't just waste minutes. It can waste the whole meeting.

Stop the Clock on Lateness

The fix for lateness starts at the top. When leaders treat meeting start times like loose suggestions, it gives everyone else permission to do the same. But when the boss shows up on time, it sends a different message: This meeting matters. Your time matters. Our work matters.

At Sourcegraph, leaders don't shrug off lateness as a few harmless minutes. They see it for what it is—a slow leak in the meeting's energy, pace, and purpose. That's why they've set a no-nonsense rule: "If the meeting's leader is not present at the precise start time (and hasn't proactively mentioned they are late), everyone should leave the call and switch to other work."[41]

It's a built-in accountability system. If you can't respect the meeting or the people in it enough to show up on time, you don't get to hold it.

Put a Price on Punctuality

Sometimes leading by example isn't enough. Chronic latecomers (the ones who treat 9 a.m. like it comes with a ten-minute grace period) need stronger incentives to show up on time.

Some teams handle tardiness by turning it into public accountability. Show up late to the Daily Scrum (the term for agile teams' short, daily stand-up meetings) and you might find yourself wearing a rubber chicken around your neck as a penalty.[42] Other teams go straight for the jugular: the wallet. Productivity expert Melissa Gratias suggests dealing with lateness using a "tardiness jar."[43] Show up late? Drop some cash in the jar. Venture capital firm Andreessen Horowitz upped the ante even more: Partners pay ten dollars for every minute they're late to founder meetings.[44]

If you want a subtler approach, Alexander Kjerulf, the chief happiness officer at the Denmark-based consulting company Woohoo, uses visual accountability.[45] Each participant gets a glass with their name on it. Show up on time? Drop in a green marble. Show up late? Drop in a red one. Kjerulf explains, "After a month or so of meetings, you may find that some people's glasses tend heavily towards red marbles, making it very visible who's habitually late." He calls this color-coded punctuality record "remarkably effective."

Penalties should be a last resort, but sometimes a little sting is what it takes to jolt people into change. Meeting time is a shared resource, not a personal indulgence. Waste it and you'll pay one way or another, whether in dollars or dignity.

ENERGY-SUCKING BUG 3: JARGON

When Warren Buffett drafts his famous shareholder letters, he starts with "Dear Doris and Bertie."[46] Why? Those are his sisters' names, and they're not business professionals. Writing to them forces Buffett to keep his language clear and jargon-free. (He deletes the "Dear X" salutation before sending, but the rest stays plainspoken.)

More meetings need that mindset. Jargon is the third big meeting bug that drains engagement. Too often, meetings collapse under the crushing weight of acronyms, clichés, and linguistic monstrosities. It's especially problematic in cross-functional meetings, where each team speaks a different dialect of corporate jargon:

- HR says "human capital optimization" instead of "hiring better people";
- engineering discusses "refactoring the codebase" instead of "cleaning up the code"; and
- sales utters "pipeline optimization" instead of "getting better sales leads."

Like jerk behavior and lateness, jargon is contagious. Before long, everyone's "circling back" and "touching base" in feeble attempts to sound smarter. Research by Adam Galinsky found that jargon works like a "fancy title, a conspicuously displayed trophy, or an expensive, branded watch."[47] It's verbal peacocking—a way for people to signal their status and show off without saying anything meaningful. When people lack confidence in what they're saying, they wrap it in jargon like a security blanket. But it doesn't make them sound smarter. It makes them harder to trust.

In 2020, Ohio State communications professor Hillary Shulman put jargon to the test. She gave 650 participants articles to read on topics like self-driving cars and politics.[48] Some were written in plain English, while others were laced with jargon. Even when the jargon-heavy versions included explanations, readers still found them more challenging to understand, less engaging, and—worst of all—less credible.

Jargon doesn't just confuse people. It alienates them. It draws a line between the insiders who spew it like they're getting paid by the syllable and everyone else stuck translating the nonsense. Even worse, it breeds distrust. When people can't understand you, they usually don't think it's their fault. They assume you're hiding something or bullshitting.

Blocklist the Buzzwords

If jargon has infiltrated your meetings, it's time for a detox. Create a jargon blocklist: a running list of overused, confusing, or meaningless phrases that drain the energy from conversations. Round up the worst offenders and substitute them with plain, no-nonsense language.

Don't forget those atrocious acronyms. If "PoC" means "proof of concept" to engineering but "point of contact" to marketing, your meeting will turn into a linguistic obstacle course. Same with "PR." It's a press release to marketing, a pull request to engineering, and "please rescue me" to everyone else trying to keep up.

Make the blocklist impossible to ignore. Pin it to Slack. Slap it on every agenda. Bake it into new-hire onboarding. When a new buzzword elbows its way in, stop it cold. Flag it and banish it before it multiplies.

Tax the Jargon

In 2020, American Express had a wake-up call: Their jargon wasn't just confusing customers—it was driving them away. So they made a shift. As VP of sales Kevin Lowe explained, they stopped talking about "financial services" and started talking about what customers cared about: "money."[49]

As AmEx scrubbed the jargon from its customer messaging, it realized the rot ran deeper. It had infected their internal communications, too. Their solution? A jargon jar. Every time someone spewed jargon, they had to pay up, and the money was funneled into a happy hour fund. Their rule of thumb: Speak clearly enough that a ninth grader can understand you.[50]

Sometimes the jargon gets so thick that you need a shock to the system—like a jargon jar—to snap people back into plain English. But over the long term, it's better to build a culture that rewards clarity. Normalize calling out confusing language when you hear it. Celebrate the people who say things plainly. Give out a "No Bullshit Award" for the clearest communicator each quarter.

Your end goal shouldn't be to police how people talk. It should be to build a culture where people care more about being understood than sounding smart.

ENERGY-SUCKING BUG 4: BOREDOM

When Paul Ketley, a project manager from New Jersey, feels his eyelids drooping in a meeting, he deploys an unconventional survival tactic.[51] He imagines being trapped under earthquake rubble, gasping for air. The sheer panic jolts him awake—just in time to nod along and fake interest in yet another mind-numbing meeting.

If your meetings are so dull that employees resort to apocalyptic daydreams to stay awake, you have a serious problem. That problem is boredom, the fourth meeting bug that kills engagement.

Boredom is a workplace epidemic. A 2023 survey found that nearly half (46 percent) of working adults in the US said they experienced boredom at least three days of the workweek.[52] And meetings are among the biggest repeat offenders.

York University psychology professor John Eastwood explains that boredom isn't about having nothing to do. It's about not having anything worth paying attention to. What boredom really signals is an "unengaged mind": your brain's way of telling you that it's craving to be engaged, but nothing is working.[53]

Boredom can stem from both internal sources (like someone's inability to pay attention) and external ones.[54] In meetings, there are two common external culprits:

- **THE CONTENT.** The agenda is flat. The discussion is dull, irrelevant, or gives people nothing to engage with—no reason to care, contribute, or stay awake.

- **THE ENVIRONMENT.** The external meeting environment is lifeless. Sterile, windowless rooms colored like day-old oatmeal drain the energy from the room, and the people in it.

If you want people to stay engaged, you need to fix both. Start by making your meeting content worth people's attention.

The Content: Make Your Meeting Work Showing Up For

When the content is dull or irrelevant, people tune out—mentally if not physically. To keep them engaged, create an agenda they actually care about.

Use the Dory Method to Crowdsource Your Agenda

Named after the lovable but forgetful fish from *Finding Nemo* (the one who keeps asking the same questions over and over), the Dory Method turns traditional agenda planning upside down. Rather than the meeting organizer force-feeding the agenda to the room, it gives attendees a voice.

First popularized at Google and later used at companies like Coda and Glean, here's how it works: Before the meeting, attendees submit their most pressing questions or topics.[55] Then the team votes. The most upvoted items rise to the top. It's survival of the fittest for your agenda, with the meeting organizer making the final call. (Agenda items should still follow a verb-noun structure, like "Answer customer escalation concerns" or "Decide on Q2 hiring priorities.")

Like its fishy namesake, the Dory method promotes curiosity, questions, and active involvement in designing the agenda. When people help shape the agenda, they show up with skin in the game, ready to engage, contribute, and move work forward.

Dory doesn't just surface the most relevant agenda items. It puts them in the right order. Psychology professors Glenn Littlepage and Julie Poole found that agenda items listed early get most of the airtime, even if they aren't the most important.[56] The Dory Method flips that bias on its head. It ensures the top agenda items are chosen by the group and reflect what matters most to them—not just to the organizer or whoever submitted their agenda item first.

Use the Five-Point Strategy for One-on-Ones

Designing a relevant agenda is just as important for one-on-ones as for team meetings, but the playbooks look different. To make one-on-ones count, borrow legendary football-turned-executive coach Bill Campbell's Five-Point strategy.[57]

It works like this: Both the manager and the employee come prepared with five topics they want to discuss. The meeting kicks off with the overlapping topics that show up on both lists. If there's no overlap, that's a red flag. It means you're out of sync, and getting back in sync just became agenda item number one.

Once you've tackled the shared topics, Campbell suggested focusing on four critical areas:

- **PERFORMANCE:** Are they delivering on their core job responsibilities?

- **PEER RELATIONSHIPS:** Are they collaborating effectively with their colleagues?

- **LEADERSHIP:** How are they managing, mentoring, or leading others?

- **INNOVATION:** Are they pushing boundaries and driving new ideas?

In *The Trillion Dollar Coach*, Eric Schmidt (one of Campbell's many mentees, along with icons like Steve Jobs and Larry Page), summed up Campbell's leadership philosophy in a single line: A great leader is someone who "gives energy, not one who takes it away."[58] That should be the bar.

One-on-ones should leave employees more energized than when they walked in. If they don't, it's not leadership. It's just micromanagement, jerk behavior, or plain old incompetence dressed up as a recurring calendar invite.

Designing One-on-Ones That Accelerate Your Career

Jade Bonacolta rocketed up the ranks in her career at LinkedIn, snagging five promotions in six and a half years. She attributes much of that success to how she ran her one-on-ones. Before each meeting, she sent a pre-read to her manager that kept the conversation focused, strategic, and centered on her growth.[59] Here's her formula:

- **THREE WINS FROM THE PAST WEEK**, along with supporting metrics and positive feedback she'd received. This kept her manager informed and quietly stocked up ammunition for her next promotion push.

- **THREE PRIORITIES FOR NEXT WEEK**. This signaled leadership. She wasn't waiting for direction—she was already thinking ahead and taking ownership.

- **ONE NEW IDEA FOR THE TEAM**. She proactively proposed solutions to improve her team's operations. And then, when she followed through on these, she became the obvious choice for more responsibility.

A one-on-one meeting is never boring when it's catapulting your career forward.

Set Your Meetings Up for Success with a POWER Start

Another way to keep your meetings from turning into irrelevant calendar litter is to run a POWER Start. Initially developed by the Agile Coaching Institute, it's a five-part litmus test to keep your meeting user-centric.[60]

- **PURPOSE ("P")**: What's the purpose of the meeting? What problem are you trying to solve, and does it require a meeting (use the 4D-CEO Test)?

- **OUTCOMES ("O")**: What does success look like? If you can't picture the finish line, don't drag people to the starting line.

- **WHAT'S IN IT FOR ME? ("W")**: Why should attendees care? What will make them feel this was time well invested, not just another calendar tax?

- **ENGAGEMENT ("E")**: How will you keep participants engaged and motivated throughout the meeting? Use the strategies from this chapter.

- **ROLES AND RESPONSIBILITIES ("R")**: Who's responsible for what in the meeting? Everyone in the room should know why they're there and what they're expected to contribute.

If you can't answer one or more of these, your meeting isn't ready to be added to anyone's calendar.

The Environment: Make Your Meeting Room Worth Walking Into

It's not just *what* happens in the meeting that matters. It's *where* it happens. The environment is the second big culprit behind boring meetings.

If your meetings always take place in the same beige, windowless, personality-free conference room, your brain gets the memo: "Nothing interesting is going to happen here." That's when boredom sinks its claws in and drains the energy from the room.

To fight off environment-induced boredom, upgrade your meeting space. Add natural light, plants, and a jolt of color. This isn't just decor.

It's brain fuel. When these elements are used to enrich the environment, they trigger dopamine, the brain's natural wake-up call. Instead of slipping into low-power mode, your brain perks up and thinks, "Wait, this might actually be worth paying attention to."

Plants: The Green Antidote to Boring Meetings

In 2020, Masahiro Toyoda and his team at the University of Hyogo in Japan studied the impact of "plant breaks."[61] They asked sixty-three participants to take short, three-minute breaks during the workday to simply look at or care for small plants. After four weeks of taking these plant breaks, 27 percent of participants experienced a significant decrease in their pulse rate, and employees who had reported high levels of anxiety reported lower levels.

An environment enriched with plants does more than calm us down. It can also boost productivity. In a large study across office buildings in the UK and the Netherlands, psychologist Craig Knight and colleagues compared "lean" (plant-free) offices with "green" (plant-filled) ones.[62] Employees in the greener spaces felt more engaged, more connected to their workplace, and were 15 percent more productive.

There's a biological explanation for that. For our ancestors, greenery signaled survival: food, water, and safety. Over centuries, we developed biophilia, literally, a "love of life." That same wiring is still at work today. Your brain sees greenery and thinks, "This is a place worth paying attention to."

Amazon has taken biophilia to the extreme with the Spheres: three massive glass domes at its Seattle headquarters packed with over forty thousand plants from thirty countries. Instead of pouring money into free coffee or subsidized lunches (Amazon employees pay full price in the cafeteria), the company bet on botany.[63] They even hired a full-time head horticulturist, Ben Eiben, to curate plants that thrive in a human-friendly climate.[64] Inside the Spheres, meeting spaces accommodate up to eight hundred people.[65] They're filled with tables, benches, and private nooks, all surrounded by boredom-busting greenery. As Eiben puts it, "You feel a little bit more creative if you're removing yourself from all of the human implements and you're just out in nature."[66]

Of course, plants aren't a silver bullet for better meetings. But they're affordable and low-maintenance, and, as Toyoda's research found, even a few well-placed succulents or a leafy plant in a meeting room can help prevent your meeting from turning into a sensory dead zone.

Color: The Cure for Beige Thinking

In 2022, Adobe launched Lab 82, an "employee experience experimentation engine" named after the company's founding year (1982).[67] According to Eric Kline, Adobe's global workplace services director, the goal was to design "the best possible future way to collaborate," and that included rethinking how meeting rooms were designed.[68]

One of the lab's initiatives explored the impact of color psychology on collaboration.[69] At Adobe's San Jose campus, they used color to strategically shape how people felt and behaved in different meeting spaces.[70] Social hubs and large all-staff meeting rooms were painted orange—the color of warmth and energy (like fire)—to spark community, connection, and conversation.[71] Collaboration rooms were colored green (like plants), evoking growth, harmony, and teamwork. And focus areas were painted blue (like sky or water)—colors that calm the brain and promote deep, distraction-free work.

You don't need a high-tech lab or lofty renovation budget to tap into the benefits of color. It's one of the cheapest, fastest ways to shift the energy of a room. A bold accent wall, a vibrant piece of artwork, or even just swapping out lifeless gray chairs for something with a pop of color can help the space feel less like a visual punishment and more like a place where people want to think and collaborate.

Light: Let There Be Light

Natural light is another powerful antidote to boredom, and it's also hard-wired into our biology. Morning sunlight triggers your brain to produce serotonin, the mood-boosting chemical that keeps us engaged and alert. As the day goes on, natural light keeps our energy levels steady and wards off the midafternoon crash.

Yet too many meeting rooms feel like interrogation cells: blinds clamped shut, harsh fluorescent lights beaming overhead, and creativity wilting in the artificial gloom.

Dr. Alan Hedge, an environmental design expert at Cornell University, and Danny Nou, a UX product strategy lead at global healthcare company Abbott, studied hundreds of office workers across North America and found that employees who worked in spaces with smart glass technology (windows that automatically optimize daylight) reported 63 percent fewer headaches and a 56 percent drop in drowsiness compared to those stuck in blind-drawn, artificially lit rooms.[72] When our meeting spaces align with basic biological needs—like exposure to daylight—our bodies feel better and our brains wake up.

So, let the sunshine in. Open the blinds. Use meeting rooms with real windows. Or ditch the meeting room entirely and take your meeting outside.

Walking: Move Your Body, Unblock Your Brain

In 2012, LinkedIn's then CEO Jeff Weiner was tired of being cooped up inside all day.[73] A colleague suggested walking meetings, something he'd started doing out of sheer necessity when LinkedIn's Mountain View offices ran out of available conference rooms. Weiner gave it a shot. One walk turned into two. Then three. Soon, he was hooked. "I'll take walking 1:1s over office meetings any day," he declared.

Walking floods your system with endorphins, kicking your brain into a more relaxed, free-flowing state. You're moving, scanning your surroundings, and letting your thoughts wander. In one study, Stanford researchers Marily Oppezzo and Daniel Schwartz found that over 80 percent of participants generated more creative ideas when walking compared to sitting still.[74]

Walking meetings can also flatten hierarchies. There's no head-of-the-table seating to signal who's in charge. Instead, people stand side by side, walking and talking as equals. As LinkedIn's VP of engineering, Igor Perisic, explained, seated desk meetings feel like a trip to the principal's office, while walking meetings feel like real collaboration.[75]

But not every meeting belongs on foot. Oppezzo and Schwartz's research found that walking boosts *divergent thinking*: the creative thinking you need when brainstorming, exploring ideas, and thinking big. It's like your brain, freed from the confines of the fluorescent-lit conference room, suddenly remembers how to think outside the box.

Walking, however, is less useful for *convergent thinking*: analyzing data, making decisions, or narrowing ideas down to a single solution. One possible reason is that it eats up mental bandwidth. Your brain's busy juggling your steps, your stride, and whatever's lurking in your peripheral vision. That extra cognitive load can make it more challenging to zero in and filter out uncommon ideas. Walking unlocks loose, free-flowing creative ideas—but it stumbles when it's time for precision and sharp focus.

Food: The Original Collaboration Tool

When all else fails, there's one surefire way to inject energy into a boring meeting: food.

Sharing food isn't just about satisfying hunger—it's about building trust and connection. Our ancestors didn't gather around the fire just to stay warm and fill their bellies. They swapped stories, built trust, and formed strong social bonds. Evolutionary psychologist Robin Dunbar compares sharing meals to primates grooming each other (without the awkward sniffing and belly rubs).[76] It's hardwired into us.

In a 2015 study, Cornell management professor Kevin Kniffin discovered that firefighter platoons who ate meals together did more than just bond. They performed better under pressure. Some firefighters even ate two dinners (one at home and another at the firehouse) because they knew those shared meals weren't just about food. They built the kind of trust that matters when things are literally on fire.[77]

At the Work Innovation Lab, I periodically hosted "candy labs" during team meetings. Before the meetings, participants submitted their favorite themed candies and I stocked up. One time it was childhood favorites, another it was Halloween-inspired. The moment attendees walked in, their faces lit up. They buzzed with energy as they built custom candy bags, swapping stories about road trips powered by Skittles or turf wars over the last Reese's. Suddenly the meeting wasn't just another calendar block. It was personal. It was delightful. And it was worth remembering.

As former New York City mayor Mike Bloomberg put it, "Food can help build relationships and encourage communication. Families know that. So do communities and religious institutions. Why should businesses be different?"[78]

Design for Delight

Keeping boredom out of your meetings isn't enough. They should spark delight. Every meeting needs at least one moment of it: that magical combination of surprise and joy. Delight is at the core of great product experiences. Disney nails it with hidden Mickeys and other characters that appear out of nowhere at its theme parks. According to research by McKinsey, companies that prioritize delight, not just satisfaction (which doesn't require an element of surprise), see significant boosts in customer loyalty.[79]

The same principle applies to meetings. It might be a horse dressed as a unicorn joining a Zoom call or a fully costumed Santa appearing at a pre-holiday team meeting (I've organized both). But it doesn't have to be elaborate. It can be as simple as a surprise snack, a playlist with team favorites to kick off a meeting, or an unexpected shout-out that brightens someone's day.

Why does it work? Because surprise snaps people to attention and joy makes it stick. That's the powerful chemistry of delight. Together, they make meetings more memorable and turn reluctant seat-fillers into people who want to show up.

THE IRON RULE OF MEETINGS:
RESPECT ATTENDEES' TIME MORE THAN YOURS

A great meeting is like a five-star product: designed for the user. It's something that people want to engage with. It grabs attention. It delights.

But when meetings ignore their users, they turn into time-sucking chores. If you find yourself trapped in one, invoke the Law of Two Feet from chapter 3, or use one of the scripts from chapter 1 and push back. Don't let someone else's bad design gobble up your workday.

In his book *Writing Without Bullshit*, Josh Bernoff proposes what he calls the *iron imperative* for writing: "Treat your audience's time as more valuable than your own."[80] That's not just great writing advice. It's an iron rule for your meetings, too. When you treat your attendees' time as more valuable than your own, you start designing five-star experiences that people want to be part of.

PRINCIPLE 6

Timing: Get Your Meetings in Rhythm

In 2012 Donna Morris, Adobe's senior vice president of HR, boarded a flight to India with a problem gnawing at her: Adobe was bleeding top talent.[1] And she had a strong suspicion about why.

She suspected the culprit was Adobe's annual performance review process. It was a once-a-year slog completely out of sync with how real work happened. Managers fell into the "recency" trap, grading employees based on what happened during the past few weeks or months and overlooking the rest of the year. High performers felt shortchanged when their year-long achievements were lost in the shuffle. And like clockwork, the same cycle played out every February: biased reviews landed, frustration spiked, and top talent started polishing their résumés.

Shortly after arriving in India, Morris sat down for a scheduled interview with India's *Economic Times*. One question caught her off guard: "What could you do that would be disruptive in HR?" Jet-lagged and running on instinct, she replied, "We plan to abolish the annual performance review format." By the next morning, it was headline news: "Adobe Systems set to scrap annual appraisals, to rely on regular feedback to reward staff."[2]

There was no turning back. Morris and her team sprang into action. In just nine months, they replaced the clunky, outdated review process with quarterly "check-ins": regular performance meetings between managers and employees, synced with Adobe's quarterly objectives and key results (OKR) cycle, internally called "Goals and Expectations."[3] Instead of an annual judgment day, feedback became part of the natural, ongoing rhythm of work.

In 2014 I visited Adobe's San Jose headquarters with Stanford professors Bob Sutton and Huggy Rao to talk with executives about the impact of their performance review overhaul. Morris and CEO Shantanu Narayen told us that employees were embracing the new system. Engagement was climbing, and by 2016, voluntary attrition had plummeted by 30 percent.[4]

By aligning performance reviews with the natural rhythm of work, Adobe didn't just fix a broken system. They gave it rhythm. And they gave it purpose.

THE POWER OF RHYTHM

Rhythm is built into our biology. Our circadian rhythms tell us when to wake up and when to fall asleep. Our heart rates speed up when we're stressed and slow down when we're calm. Even our brains pulse with rhythm: Fast brain waves help us focus, while slower ones unlock creativity.

The best products don't fight your natural rhythm. They sync with it. Think about a Fitbit. It doesn't just count your steps. It gives you a nudge when you've started to become a desk potato. That tiny vibration shifts your behavior. Suddenly you're taking the stairs and racking up an extra thousand steps a day without even thinking about it.

Now imagine if your meetings operated the same way. Instead of crashing into your day like an unwanted pop-up ad, they'd show up at just the right moments, pushing work forward instead of stomping all over it. That's the power of rhythm: Meeting Design Principle 6.

THE THREE RHYTHMS THAT KEEP YOUR MEETINGS IN SYNC

If your meetings feel more like interruptions than progress, they're probably out of sync with the natural rhythm of your work. The solution? Sync them with the three core rhythms of work, each one tied to a different layer of focus.

RHYTHM 1: STRATEGIC* RHYTHM. This is your big-picture rhythm. It's where your organization sets direction, prioritizes what matters most, and turns strategy into coordinated action. These meetings include annual planning, quarterly business reviews, leadership off-sites, and performance check-ins. They ensure that everyone, from the C-suite to the front lines, is rowing in the same direction and hitting goals, not just talking about them.

RHYTHM 2: TACTICAL RHYTHM. This is the rhythm that turns strategy into execution. It includes the meetings that drive projects from start to finish: project kickoffs, midpoint check-ins, and

---

* *Strategy* is one of those workplace words that gets tossed around so often it starts to lose meaning. In this chapter, strategy meetings are those designed to align long-term priorities, goals, and actions.

postmortems. They clear roadblocks, keep work on track, and ensure that minor issues don't snowball into bigger ones.

RHYTHM 3: OPERATIONAL RHYTHM. This is the daily rhythm of work. It includes daily huddles, weekly check-ins, and the intentional pauses that help teams unblock work, keep up the momentum, and avoid getting overwhelmed by calendar quicksand.

Each rhythm plays a critical role in how work gets done and your meetings should move to the same beat. Let's start by getting your strategic rhythm right—so that your strategy meetings don't just churn out lofty, feel-good ideas, but deliver tangible, measurable results.

RHYTHM 1: STRATEGIC RHYTHM— ALIGN YOUR MEETINGS WITH YOUR GOAL-SETTING RHYTHM

How often should you hold strategy meetings to set direction, align priorities, and reset goals? There's no one-size-fits-all answer. The key is to sync your strategic meeting rhythm with your organization's goal-setting rhythm. That way, your meetings support the work, not just circle around it.

Take YouTube. After Google acquired it in 2006, YouTube inherited Google's thirteen-week OKR cycle. Every quarter, they would set new goals. But according to Shishir Mehrotra, YouTube's head of product and engineering at the time, the process felt "awkward" and "too short for our big aspirations."[5] The cycle moved so fast that teams were still knee-deep in the last set of goals when the next round started.

So they slowed things down. Instead of cranking through four goal-setting cycles a year, YouTube switched to a twice-yearly cadence, carving out dedicated strategy weeks at the start of each half. That gave teams enough breathing room to do the work before jumping back onto the planning hamster wheel.

Meanwhile, BuildDirect, a Vancouver-based home improvement product company, faced the opposite problem. Its ninety-day strategy cycle felt agonizingly slow.[6] When I visited the company in 2014 with Bob Sutton, CEO Jeff Booth told us that "ninety days felt like an eternity."

And so they did the opposite of YouTube. They sped things up. They scrapped the ninety-day cycle in favor of sixty-day sprints—short enough to stay agile, but long enough to make real progress. At the end of each cycle, they built in "white space" periods for off-site meetings to reflect and recalibrate before diving into the next sprint.

Your strategic rhythm should match the pace of how work gets done. If you're resetting goals so often that no one has time to execute, slow down. But if your team is moving like it's stuck in molasses and can't keep up with internal or external changes, pick up the pace.

Kick Off Strategy Meetings with Truth, Not Theater

Too many strategy meetings devolve into what I call *strategy theater*. Out come the glossy slides, dramatic pitches, and grand vision statements. Everyone applauds for the big reveal, but when the curtain falls, no one knows what they're supposed to do next.

To avoid this, your strategy meetings need a backbone: a clear "source of truth"[7] that aligns everyone around key priorities and their measurable results. Without that anchor, your strategy splinters. People begin chasing personal projects dressed up as priorities, and everyone walks away with their own definition of success.

At HashiCorp, senior leaders avoided this by creating a "company scorecard" during their annual strategy off-site that became the company's source of truth for the year.[8] It was used during quarterly reviews and weekly leadership syncs, keeping teams focused on "what [they] decided was important earlier in the year—not on this week's shiny distraction," says former chief of staff Kevin Fishner.

Salesforce takes a similar approach with V2MOM. It sounds like a robot from Star Wars, but it's their battle-tested system for keeping strategy aligned at every level. V2MOM stands for:

- **VISION:** What do you want to achieve (your goals)?
- **VALUES:** What's important to you?
- **METHODS:** How do you achieve it?
- **OBSTACLES:** What's preventing you from being successful?
- **MEASURES:** How do you know you have achieved it?

Salesforce CEO Marc Benioff created V2MOM after a frustrating stint at Oracle. When Benioff asked CEO Larry Ellison about Oracle's five-year plan, Ellison shrugged and said, "We don't have a five-year plan, we barely have a six-month plan."[9] Even that so-called "plan" was just a budget, Benioff recalls. Determined to do better, he built V2MOM.

Whether you use OKRs, a scorecard, or V2MOM, the framework doesn't matter as much as the purpose it serves: to keep everyone marching in the same direction. When you kick off a strategy meeting, make that "source of truth" impossible to overlook. Project it on the screen, add it to the agenda, print it as a handout, pin it on a digital whiteboard. Whatever it takes. No one should walk into the meeting—or out of it—unclear about what matters most or how success will be measured.

Strategy Meetings Without Rhythm Are Just Wishful Thinking

A great strategy without regular check-in meetings is like a New Year's resolution. It's full of good intentions, but likely to fizzle out by February. Without a steady rhythm of accountability, strategy becomes a dusty pile of goals no one remembers. It needs a consistent cadence of meetings to stay alive, stay useful, and drive results. And as we've seen, that cadence should match the natural pace of your work. As Fishner explained, without a built-in cadence—whether it's business reviews or weekly leadership syncs—employees stop caring. "The effort to actually create the goals was a waste of time," he warns. "OKRs slowly die because no one looks at them anymore."[10]

When people stop paying attention to your strategy, it starts to fade. Then it splinters into different interpretations. Before long, the CEO has one version, sales has another, and marketing has something else entirely. Even the intern has their own version.

Embed Strategy in Meetings or Watch It Disappear

Your strategy is worthless without alignment across your entire organization. As HubSpot CEO Yamini Rangan tells her team, "Alignment eats strategy for lunch."[11]

At Salesforce, V2MOM is embedded at every level. It starts at the top with Benioff setting the company-wide V2MOM. Then, like Russian nesting dolls, each department, team, and individual creates their own version that ladders up to the top.

And it's not stashed away in a corporate SharePoint folder. Every V2MOM is publicly available on Chatter, Salesforce's internal social network, so that anyone can access and reference them anytime. Employees don't just hear about strategy at an annual kickoff. It shows up in meetings, decisions, and daily work. As Benioff puts it, "V2MOM is the glue that binds us together."[12]

This is where most companies faceplant. Strategy gets hyped at the kickoff, paraded around in quarterly business reviews, and then left to gather dust in a slide deck somewhere. Employees hear about it once, nod along, and then go back to work with no idea how their day-to-day connects. They don't see the strategy in action. And they definitely don't see themselves in it.

According to the 2024 State of Work Innovation report, only 42 percent of knowledge workers know how their work connects to their company's bigger goals.[13] That's why teams get buried in "alignment" meetings. No one knows what they're aligning to, so they schedule meeting after meeting trying to reverse-engineer clarity that should've been there from the start.

When people can't see how their work fits into the bigger picture, they stop caring. They just go through the motions. Not to make progress toward a goal, but to make it to 5 p.m.

Kick Off Strategy Meetings with "Fresh-Start" Energy

When it's time to roll out a new strategy, don't just drop it in a memo or slap it onto a PowerPoint. You need a kickoff meeting that does more than inform your employees of the strategy. It should make them sit up, lean in, and feel like they're part of something bigger. It needs to feel like a movement.

Your strategy has a much better chance of winning employees' hearts and minds if you roll it out during a natural reset moment. It taps into what Wharton professor Katy Milkman calls the *fresh-start effect*. These "temporal landmarks" (like a new year, a new quarter, or even just a Monday) act as psychological reset buttons.[14] Milkman's research shows that people are more motivated to commit to change when they feel they're starting fresh. It's why people are 33 percent more likely to hit the gym on the first day of the month than on any random day.[15] And it's why reminders to save for retirement are more effective when they're sent right after someone's birthday—their own personal New Year's Day.

Timing is key. Strategy kickoffs should sync with your organization's natural rhythm. The start of the fiscal year is often ideal because it aligns with goals, budgets, and beginning-of-the-year momentum.

But even the best fresh-start energy can fade quickly. As Milkman puts it, "You need to keep motivating people. And keep looking for opportunities to grab their attention and give them the sense of empowerment they need to succeed."[16] In other words, strategy can't be a one-and-done event. It needs a steady heartbeat of fresh starts. Whether you refresh goals every sixty days, quarterly, or semiannually, each cycle should begin with a strategy booster shot—a kickoff meeting that doesn't just realign your team but also jolts them awake.

Because strategy isn't only about setting direction. It's about sustaining it.

Turn Strategy Meetings into Storytelling Moments

If you want your strategy to stick, it needs to hit harder than a list of bullet-point objectives rattled off during the kickoff meeting. It should lodge in employees' minds and stay there long after the meeting ends.

Most employees won't rally around a list of company goals—

they rally around stories. At BuildDirect, that story was their Flooring Manifesto. Let's be honest: Flooring (one of BuildDirect's flagship products) isn't exactly thrilling. But the company found a way to make it personal. Here's an excerpt from the Manifesto: "[Flooring] is the first thing your feet touch in the morning and the last thing they leave before you fall into bed at night . . . It's where babies sit as they marvel at banging pots and pans. Where stubborn toddlers stomp their feet. Where aspiring, young ballerinas twirl . . . Flooring matters."[17]

Suddenly, flooring was more than a product. It was the stage for life's most cherished moments.

Every company needs its version of a Flooring Manifesto. When employees see the bigger picture behind their work, they don't just follow your strategy. They own it.

RHYTHM 2: TACTICAL RHYTHM— ALIGN YOUR MEETINGS WITH YOUR PROJECT RHYTHM

Thomas Edison is credited with saying, "Strategy without execution is hallucination."[18] These hallucinations show up in meetings all the time. Leaders get drunk on their slide decks, crank out vision statements, churn out two-by-two frameworks, and toss around buzzwords like confetti, assuming the execution will somehow take care of itself.

It won't. Without a strong execution rhythm, strategy stays stuck in the clouds while teams flail on the ground, hopelessly trying to turn lofty vision into tangible results. That's where your second meeting rhythm comes in: your tactical rhythm.

Whereas strategy meetings should sync with your fiscal calendar, tactical meetings should sync with the real engine of execution: projects.

Every major project needs three essential pit stop meetings:

KICKOFF MEETING. Rally your team around the project's purpose. Everyone should walk out knowing what they're doing, why it matters, and how success will be measured.

MIDPOINT CHECK-IN. Pause at the halfway mark and take a brutally honest look at how things are going. What's working? What's not? Where do you need to pivot before it's too late?

POSTMORTEM. Once the project is complete, don't just move on. Take time to celebrate the wins, confront the missteps, and extract those hard-earned lessons so you don't trip over the same mistakes next time.

Tactical meetings shouldn't be places to relitigate your strategy. They should focus squarely on execution. But it's easy to skid off course. One minute, you're nailing down the final details for next week's product launch. The next, someone's pitching a full rebrand as an "AI-first" company.

When strategy hijacks a tactical meeting, don't hand over the keys. Pull over. Park it in the parking lot from chapter 3 and save it for the next strategy meeting.

Project Kickoff Meetings: Light a Fire or Lose Your Team

Your project kickoff is your first critical pit stop. Get it right, and your team will hit the ground running, energized and aligned. Blow it, and the wheels start wobbling. Nobody knows who's doing what, why it matters, or where they're headed. Soon, people start prioritizing other projects. And before long, you're buried in spin-off meetings, re-explaining priorities, clarifying roles, and watching deadlines slip while your budget bleeds out.

Start with the "why." Kickoff meetings bring a natural fresh-start energy. Don't waste it. This is your shot to make the project feel real, urgent, and impossible to ignore. As Apple's Ken Segall puts it, "New projects should consume their participants from the get-go."[19] If your team isn't hooked from the start, good luck keeping them engaged when the real work begins.

Always anchor the project to your organization's source of truth, whether that's V2MOM, OKRs, or whatever acronym holds your strategy together. But don't stop there. Just like with strategy kickoffs, if you want to light a fire under your team, you need a story that makes people care. If people don't feel the weight of the problem they're solving—or the impact of solving it—the project will turn into another task. Another box to check. Another tab to close. And eventually, another priority to forget.

At Amazon, every project begins with a story, not just a spec sheet. Before building anything, teams use a method called *working backward*. They write a press release and an FAQ as if the project has already launched.[20] It spells out the problem, the solution, and the impact. It even includes a hypothetical customer testimonial from a delighted user. The logic is simple: If you can't clearly explain why a project matters before you begin, you probably shouldn't build it. (The same goes for meetings. If you can't explain why a meeting deserves to happen, you shouldn't schedule it.)

Sacha Connor knew how important this "why" was while leading the launch of new marketing programs and product innovation at Clorox. When her team gathered to kick off the launch of a new marketing strategy for Brita water filters, she didn't just discuss features. She made her team feel the impact. She calculated how many plastic bottles they could eliminate if they achieved their annual sales goal for Brita filters. Suddenly, her team wasn't just selling water filters. They were on a mission to help save the planet. At the start of each project meeting, she regrounded the team in that mission.

Your kickoff meeting isn't just a box to check. It's a battle for your team's mindshare. You want your project to be the one that sticks—the one that elbows its way to the front of their brains long after they leave the meeting.

Why does this matter so much? Because today's workers are caught in a nonstop tug-of-war over priorities. According to research by the Institute for Corporate Productivity (i4cp), the number one dysfunction teams face is *priority overload*: too many competing priorities yanking people in too many different directions.[21] Between 2015 and 2020, the average number of teams an employee belonged to doubled, which meant even more competing priorities from more stakeholders.[22] If your kickoff doesn't punch through the noise and make your project stand out, it'll get buried under the growing pile of other priorities.

Build a Real Team Agreement and Live By It

Every project kickoff should include a *team agreement* (sometimes called a *team contract* or *team charter*). But only 28 percent of companies create them.[23] And when they do create one, it's usually just a glorified FAQ document—a lifeless list of meeting schedules, preferred communication tools, and working hours. That's not a real team agreement. It's a box-checking illusion, a way to look like a team without doing the messy and difficult work of acting like one.

A real team agreement answers the big, thorny, existential questions first:

WHAT'S OUR PURPOSE? Why do we exist as a team, and what are we here to achieve?

WHAT ROLES ARE WE PLAYING? Who's responsible for what, and where do our responsibilities start and stop?

WHAT VALUES DO WE SHARE? What principles will guide how we make decisions, collaborate, and handle conflict?

One of my favorite ways to clarify these questions is an exercise from Mural.[24] Ask each team member to respond to this prompt: "Your project is a huge success and gets media attention. What would be the one headline and hero image that reflects the project's outcome?"

This Amazon-style working backward exercise forces people to ditch vague mission statements and get concrete. Their answers will reveal what success looks like to them. Is it a game-changing product? A loyal user base? A splashy front-page story that makes your competitors sweat? It'll also reveal what your team values most. Innovation? Customer love? Industry bragging rights?

Once your team is aligned on the bigger picture, then and only then should you zoom in and define the operational details of your team agreement:

HOW DO WE COMMUNICATE? Define your team's working hours (when people are generally expected to be online), the tools you'll use to communicate, and where different types of conversations should happen (for example, in Slack, shared documents, or email). Make sure your team's tool norms align with your company-wide standards (see chapter 4), but leave room for team-specific tools and practices.

HOW DO WE MAKE DECISIONS? Choose a default decision-making framework like RACI.* That way, you'll spend less time debating how to decide, and more time actually deciding.

HOW DO WE DISAGREE? Conflict is a feature, not a bug, of high-performing teams. But you need rules for handling it productively, like Disagree and Commit. Try banning "drive-by objections." At Okta, chief development officer Sagnik Nandy had a simple rule: "You cannot say NO without either proposing something new or endorsing another alternative."[25] Don't like an idea? Fine. Step up with a better one—or step aside.

HOW DO WE MEASURE SUCCESS? Define what success looks like and anchor it to your organization's source of truth. If success metrics aren't clear, your team will default to chasing busywork instead of real impact.

---

* RACI is a useful decision-making framework for clarifying roles and responsibilities in projects or processes. The acronym stands for *Responsible* (the person doing the work), *Accountable* (the person ultimately answerable for the outcome), *Consulted* (the people whose input is needed), and *Informed* (the people who need to be kept in the loop).

Don't let your team agreement become a decorative PDF that gets filed away and forgotten. Revisit it at every major project pit stop (kick-offs, midpoints, and postmortems) to make sure it's still relevant and working as intended. In between these pit stops, Sacha Connor, who now runs Virtual Work Insider (which teaches teams at companies like Sephora, Under Armour, and Toyota the skills to work more effectively across distance), suggests appointing a *team effectiveness lead*. This person is responsible for making sure the team sticks to its commitments and keeps the agreement up to date. Their own performance is measured, in part, on how well they do that.

Use a Premortem to Save Your Project Before It Implodes

Nail your project kickoff, and your team will be buzzing with fresh-start energy, ready to charge ahead. But that same enthusiasm can also make them vulnerable to what psychologists call the *planning fallacy*.

Coined by Daniel Kahneman and Amos Tversky in 1979, the planning fallacy describes our brain's tendency to underestimate how long, expensive, or complicated things will be.[26] Deadlines slip. Budgets balloon. Before you know it, your project is behind schedule and over budget, and you're left wondering why it costs more than a Marvel movie.

You can prevent this reality distortion field by running a premortem at your project kickoff. Instead of just envisioning success (as we covered in previous exercises), flip the script and imagine worst-case scenarios. Ask your team, "It's six months from now, and this project failed. What went wrong?" Brainstorm every possible failure, from minor hiccups to full-blown catastrophes.

Research shows that mentally time-traveling to a future failure and reverse-engineering what led to it (what researchers call *prospective hindsight*) improves risk forecasting by up to 30 percent.[27] That's why companies like Square, PayPal, Sequoia Capital, and even NASA incorporate premortems as standard practice. They know that the best way to prevent failure is to look it in the eye before it shows up.

Shreyas Doshi, who has led high-stakes projects at Stripe, Twitter, Google, and Yahoo, uses premortems to combat what he calls the "preventable problem paradox."[28] Organizations love a hero story. They celebrate the employee who swoops in at the last second to put out a fire, but they hardly acknowledge the one who made sure the fire never started in the first place.

Premortems make problem prevention just as visible—and valuable—as problem-solving. Because the best projects aren't the ones that were saved at the eleventh hour. They're the ones that never needed saving in the first place.

Midpoint Meetings: Don't Sleep Through Your Team's Wake-Up Call

The second pit stop in your project's tactical rhythm is the midpoint.

Every project has a natural rhythm. At the start, it's messy. Ideas are flying, experiments are running, and mistakes are piling up as your team stumbles to find its footing. Then, smack in the middle of the project—at the halfway point—reality hits. That's when your team collectively realizes, "Oh crap, we actually have to deliver this thing."

Psychologist Connie Gersick calls this the *midpoint transition*.[29] Her research has found that the halfway point, whether it's a seven-day project or a six-month-long one, acts like a built-in alarm clock. It's the moment the clock flips—when the time that's left shrinks smaller than the time that's past. And that jolts everyone awake to the reality that time is running out.

Too many leaders coast through the midpoint like it's just another

Tuesday. But ignore it, and you miss your shot to course-correct before it's too late.

Name the Elephants, Toss the Dead Fish, Purge the Vomit

Aside from the project kickoff, the midpoint meeting is your best chance to strip away wishful thinking and get brutally honest about what it'll take to cross the finish line. That's where Airbnb's brilliant framework comes in: elephants, dead fish, and vomit.[30] It's gross. And that's why it works.

Set up a safe space—whether it's a Slack channel, an anonymous form, or a dedicated time in your meeting—where your team can air out issues before they jeopardize your project's success:

ELEPHANTS. These are the big, obvious problems everyone sees but no one wants to confront, like that overhyped feature that's clearly doomed, but nobody wants to challenge it because the big boss pitched it. It's the classic "elephant in the room."

DEAD FISH. These are the unresolved issues from earlier in the project that are stinking up meetings and other communication, like the customer research you conveniently ignored because it suggested your target audience doesn't want what you've spent eighteen months building.

VOMIT. These are the pent-up frustrations your team has been silently stewing over, like festering team conflicts, scope creep, or recurring miscommunications. It's messy, but once it's cleared out, everyone feels lighter.

The midpoint is your last real shot to fix these issues. Elephants will only grow bigger. Dead fish will only decay further. And vomit? Well, if you don't let it out now, it will explode all over your project at the most inconvenient moment.

So grab the mop, the shovel, and possibly a hazmat suit. If you don't clean up the mess now, you'll be wading through it at the end of the project. And by then, it'll reek. And your project will be part of the stench.

Postmortems: The Meetings That Save Your Future Projects

When a project wraps up, your instinct is to jump directly into the next thing. But companies like Google, Pixar, and Etsy know better. They hit "Pause" and make time for a postmortem.

A postmortem meeting (also known as a debrief, retrospective, or after-action review) should happen within two weeks of wrapping up a project, before selective amnesia kicks in and hard-earned mistakes are swept under the rug.

Postmortems shouldn't feel like courtroom interrogations. If people think they're about to get grilled, blamed, or thrown under the bus, they'll sugarcoat the truth—or avoid it entirely. And that's how you guarantee a repeat performance of the same mistakes.

If you want postmortems to teach you something, failure has to feel safe. Expected, even. Harvard professor Amy Edmondson discovered this while studying medical teams at two Boston hospitals.[31] She expected the best teams would report the fewest errors. Instead, they reported more—not because they made more mistakes, but because they weren't afraid to talk about them. They knew they wouldn't be punished for speaking up.

Creating that type of environment isn't easy, even at a company like Pixar where failure is considered part of the creative process. In their early postmortems, like during the first one after *A Bug's Life*, teams were honest about what went wrong.[32] But over time, that honesty faded. Why? Because when things get uncomfortable, people naturally look for ways to sidestep things that make them squirm. Over time, instead of tackling the big, hairy issues (like why a story arc didn't land), Pixarians zeroed in on safer, surface-level problems (like the poor lighting in scene five). It let them dodge discomfort—and the real learning that comes with it.

Pixar cofounder Ed Catmull saw what was happening and decided to shake things up. He began experimenting with new postmortem formats to break the routine. In one version, teams were prompted to list five things they would do again and five they wouldn't. Pairing wins with missteps helped take the sting out of failure and made it easier to talk about what really went wrong.

Catmull was protecting against what Jeff Bezos calls the "process as proxy" trap: when teams begin to focus too much on the process, instead of the outcome.[33] As Bezos put it, "The process is not the thing." He pushed his teams to ask, "Do we own the process, or does the process own us?"

That's a question worth asking about every meeting, especially the uncomfortable ones, like postmortems. Are they helping your team learn and grow? Or are they just checking a box and giving you a cozy illusion of productivity?

Celebrate the Right Kind of Failures

To create an environment where teams feel safe in pre- and postmortems, it's not enough to tolerate failure. You need to celebrate the right kind of failure. Not careless mistakes. Not sloppy shortcuts. But bold, well-intentioned experiments that didn't pan out—or even flopped spectacularly.

The best teams don't just acknowledge failure, they mine it for insights. Spotify exemplifies this with *fail-fikas* (Swedish for "coffee breaks") where teams share failure stories over lattes.[34] Eli Lilly has been throwing "failure parties" since the 1990s, raising a toast to their most ambitious flops.[35] Ben & Jerry's built an actual Flavor Graveyard, complete with headstones for their worst misfires. RIP Sugar Plum and Peanut Butter and Jelly.[36]

Google digs even deeper for failures. As part of their Postmortem of the Month and Postmortem Reading Club, teams don't just pick apart their own mistakes. They study the best failures across the company and beyond.[37]

The goal is to normalize failure. Failure isn't something to hide or bury. It's something to learn from, dissect, and—in the best cases—celebrate.

RHYTHM 3: OPERATIONAL RHYTHM—ALIGN YOUR MEETINGS WITH THE RHYTHM OF DAILY WORK

Your strategic rhythm syncs with your goal-setting rhythm.

Your tactical rhythm syncs with your project rhythm.

Your operational rhythm? It syncs with the rhythm of your daily work.

And that daily rhythm is what Dr. Tom Mihaljevic zeroed in on when he took over as CEO of the Cleveland Clinic in 2018. With 77,000 employees spread across hospitals from Ohio to Abu Dhabi, he faced a massive challenge: staying on top of daily operations without getting tangled in the weeds.[38]

"I was bothered by the fact that I didn't know what was happening every single day at the Clinic," Mihaljevic admitted.[39] He needed a system to surface critical issues quickly, without creating a bureaucratic traffic jam for his people.

His solution? A tiered system of fifteen-minute daily huddles designed to escalate urgent issues from the frontline to the CEO within twenty-four hours. It worked like a relay race. The process kicked off with short daily meetings between caregivers and their managers to flag pressing issues. If an issue couldn't be resolved on the spot, it moved up the chain to the next leadership level. This continued through six tiers of meetings, each happening sequentially, until only the most critical matters reached Mihaljevic's desk.

Five years in, Mihaljevic called these huddles "easily, in my opinion, one of the most important instruments that we have at our disposal to run a large integrated healthcare delivery system."[40]

The real engine of the daily huddles is their rhythm. By syncing these daily operational meetings to the fast-paced reality of patient care, the Clinic ensured decisions happened at the speed of care, not the glacial speed of bureaucracy. As Mihaljevic puts it, "The effort to provide uniformity of care . . . starts . . . with the way that we communicate among ourselves and our patients every single day."[41]

Operational Meetings Shouldn't Feel Like Groundhog Day

Daily operational meetings can be essential in high-stakes environments like hospitals. One missed update can mean the difference between saving a life and making a fatal mistake. These meetings are true one-way-door decisions. Once they're made, there's no do-over. They pass the 4D-CEO Test every time.

But for most teams, daily operational meetings are overkill. Zapier CEO Wade Foster learned that from trial and error. He initially assumed that fifteen-minute daily stand-ups would improve visibility and clear roadblocks.[42] But over time, the rhythm felt off. There wasn't enough new information each day to justify dragging everyone into a meeting.

Foster pivoted to weekly huddles, allowing time for updates to accumulate and actually justify a meeting. But something was still off. The meetings failed the 4D-CEO Test. They had devolved into one-way status dumps. "People spent the entire meeting talking at each other about tasks we completed rather than discussing tasks that could drive significant results for the company," Foster recalls.

Something had to change. So Foster took a page from Jeff Bezos's playbook and scrapped the real-time status updates. Instead, weekly huddles started with ten minutes of silent reading. Participants read through everyone's key updates and then each person had five minutes to ask clarifying questions or flag issues. "Since it's time-constrained, team members make sure to ask only pertinent questions and ask their questions in order of importance," Foster explained. If someone needed more than five minutes, that was a red flag. It meant the update wasn't clear enough or the issue needed its own meeting, with a much leaner group.

To keep things human, participants shared their questions and feedback in the order of their birthdays. Whoever's birthday came next went first. This added a little social grease to the system and a moment of delight—people always knew whose birthday was around the corner.

Once you think you've landed on the right cadence for your operational meeting, pressure-test it. Ask yourself: If we canceled the next meeting, would the real work slow down or be at risk? If the answer's no, you're probably meeting too often. Then run it through the 4D-CEO Test: Is the purpose of your meeting to debate, discuss, decide, or develop? If it's just a status update, it flunks the test and doesn't need to happen live.

When in doubt, default to async. Fire off an email. Draft a memo. Post an update in Slack. Record a Loom. If none of those options work, then call a meeting. Put on your systems thinking cap from chapter 4 and remember, meetings should be your last resort, not your first reflex.

High-Performing Teams Communicate in Bursts

A steady cadence of operational meetings can be critical in high-risk environments where real-time coordination can literally save lives.[*] Still, for many teams, especially creative ones or those solving novel problems, a steady drip of communication can do more harm than good. Ideas don't clock in at 9 a.m. Breakthroughs don't magically appear just because there's a recurring Tuesday meeting.

In a 2016 study, professors Anita Williams Woolley and Christoph Riedl analyzed fifty-two teams of software engineers who were tasked with designing an algorithm to optimize medical kits for space missions.[43] They found that the highest-performing teams didn't communicate at a steady pace. Instead, they communicated in bursts: intense, rapid-fire exchanges of ideas and creative riffing, followed by deep, heads-down execution. These bursts might be scheduled (like a daily high-intensity brainstorming session) or spontaneous (triggered when someone hits a wall or has a breakthrough and pulls in their teammates to pressure-test the idea).

---

[*] As Anita Woolley pointed out to me, organizations in high-risk environments also need ad-hoc synchronous check-ins and strong asynchronous communication (like the tools we covered in chapter 4) to ensure critical information is always accessible and teams can tackle issues as they arise, without waiting around for the next scheduled meeting.

But bursts don't magically sync across a team. One person's creative high can crash straight into someone else's deep focus block. High-performing teams don't just communicate in bursts. They coordinate them. Woolley recommends pinpointing when your team's energy naturally spikes—when ideas fly, people jump in, and the whole group sharpens each other's ideas in real time.[44]

These high-voltage moments often happen outside of formal meetings, like during spontaneous Slack threads, hallway conversations, or quick-fire brainstorms when no one's heads down in deep work. There's no universal blueprint. Every team's rhythm is different. Your goal is to identify these natural bursts for your team and protect them as "bursty time."

Bursty time shouldn't take the form of another recurring meeting. It should be a protected window for flexible, real-time collaboration. Depending on the challenge you're tackling, that might mean a rapid-fire Slack exchange, an impromptu whiteboard session, or a fast-paced, ad hoc huddle.

Build Strategic Pauses into Your Operational Rhythm

The burst is only half of the equation.

Just as important as the burst is what comes after. If you don't protect the post-burst window with meeting-free work time, all that creative momentum will fizzle out before it turns into anything real.

That's where strategic meeting pauses come in. They're not just fuel for burstiness—they're a lifeline for any team trying to trade calendar clutter for real, meaningful progress. These pauses aren't about doing nothing. They're about carving out protected time for deep, uninterrupted work. Skip them, and your team will get stuck in a cycle of frantic busywork, always moving, rarely making progress.

When Kevin Kruse was doing research for his book *15 Secrets Successful People Know About Time Management*, he interviewed over two hundred highly successful people, including billionaires, millionaires, and top entrepreneurs. One habit came up again and again: They "themed" their days to minimize context switching and dodge distractions.[45]

Take Jack Dorsey. When juggling CEO duties at both Twitter and Square, he assigned each day a singular focus:

- Monday: Management
- Tuesday: Product, engineering, and design
- Wednesday: Marketing, growth, and communications
- Thursday: Partnership and developers
- Friday: Company and culture
- Saturday: Day off
- Sunday: Strategy and job interviews

On days that started with a *T* (Tuesday and Thursday), Dorsey spent his mornings at Twitter and his afternoons at Square. On non-*T* days, he reversed the routine. This rhythm protected his focus and gave his teams predictability. They knew precisely when they would have his attention, with seven days to get ready before Dorsey's focus cycled back around.

Now, most of us aren't tech moguls with assistants to meticulously choreograph our schedules. The closest we get to "theming" might be remembering Taco Tuesday. But anyone can build strategic pauses into their operational rhythm. There are three main ways to do it:

NO-MEETING DAYS. Declare at least one day a week when meetings are completely off-limits.

NO-MEETING BLOCKS. Carve out a few sacred hours each day or week where meetings are banned.

MEETING BUFFERS. Build five-to-fifteen-minute breaks between meetings so you can reset, recharge, and process what just happened.

These pauses aren't indulgences. They're mental survival tactics. Skip them and your brain turns to mush, worn down by the relentless grind of meeting overload.

No-Meeting Days: Give Your Brain a Full Day to Breathe

In Canva's early days, Jennie Rogerson, the founders' executive assistant, watched their schedules turn into a nightmarish game of Tetris.[46] Meetings were crammed into every available slot, leaving no room for deep, meaningful work. To stop the madness, Jennie introduced Meeting-Free Wednesdays. What started as a survival tactic for the overwhelmed founders worked so well that Canva made it a company-wide policy.

Canva isn't alone. Asana, Facebook, and Shopify have all introduced no-meeting days to give their employees a fighting chance at uninterrupted stretches of deep work. And workers are all for it: Eight out of ten full-time workers want one meeting-free day a week, according to research from videoconferencing company Owl Labs.[47]

Even when your next meeting is hours away, your brain treats it like a mental tripwire. Rutgers University professor Gabriella Tonietto calls this *contracting time*: the way scheduled commitments like meetings and deadlines shrink your perception of how much time is available.[48] Instead of diving into meaningful work, you default to busywork, like checking emails, organizing your computer desktop, or rearranging your physical one. The real problem isn't time. It's that your brain refuses to commit when it knows an interruption is looming ahead.

But do no-meeting days actually work? In one study Benjamin Laker, a professor of leadership at Henley Business School, and his research team found that when organizations implemented one no-meeting day per week, productivity increased by 35 percent. With two no-meeting days, that number jumped to 71 percent.[49]

But the benefits went beyond productivity. Cooperation improved too, jumping 55 percent when companies introduced three no-meeting days per week. Without meetings as a lazy fallback, employees had to be more intentional about how they communicated—and they discovered smarter ways to do it asynchronously. No-meeting days also curbed micromanagement. With fewer meetings to camp out in, managers had fewer opportunities to hover, nitpick, or use meetings as a surveillance tactic. Employee engagement increased as well. When you give people back their autonomy and time, they stop calendar-surfing and start engaging with their work.

According to Laker and team, the sweet spot was three no-meeting days per week—enough to maximize focus time without starving human connection. But if that feels too ambitious for your organization, start with one.

For no-meeting days to work, leaders need to take them seriously. If executives ignore them, everyone else will, too. And whatever you do, don't just shove all your meetings onto the remaining days. That'll throw your team's rhythm even further out of whack. By the time the no-meeting day arrives, your team will be too fried to do anything meaningful with it.

Paul Holbrook, a former managing director in the City of London, has a solution to prevent this: a *meeting budget*.[50] It's a concept similar to what Wade Foster advocated in chapter 1. Instead of letting meetings dictate your calendar, flip the script. Block off time for your actual priorities first—deep work, strategic thinking, personal development. Whatever's left is your meeting budget. And you don't have to spend it all. In fact, you probably shouldn't.

No-Meeting Blocks: Give Deep Work a Fighting Chance

If a full no-meeting day isn't realistic, no-meeting blocks can still protect your team's focus with dedicated windows for deep, distraction-free work, while still leaving room for real-time collaboration.

Dropbox found a sweet spot in 2021 with its Core Collaboration Hours: four-hour windows when meetings typically happen, leaving the rest of the day blissfully meeting-free by default. Instead of meetings scattered across the calendar, employees know exactly when to expect them.

Each region has its own time block to keep teams in sync:

AMERICAS: 12 noon to 4 p.m. Eastern time (9 a.m. to 1 p.m. Pacific)

EUROPE: 10 a.m. to 12 noon and 4 p.m. to 6 p.m. Greenwich Mean Time. Tel Aviv follows Sunday to Thursday, noon to 4 p.m. GMT+2

ASIA-PACIFIC AND JAPAN: 9 a.m. to 1 p.m. GMT+9

These blocks are designed to maximize overlap across time zones. For example, a San Francisco employee's 9–10 a.m. window overlaps with teammates in New York (12–1 p.m. local time) and Dublin

(5–6 p.m. local time), creating a shared hour for real-time collaboration across three continents.

By the end of 2022, 81 percent of Dropbox employees had adopted Core Collaboration Hours.[51] Seventy-two percent of employees reported getting more done, 80 percent felt more effective, and 72 percent said their work-life balance improved. This shift was a significant step toward Dropbox becoming "async by default."[52]

Meeting Buffers: Stop the Back-to-Back Brain Drain

The third type of strategic pause is the meeting buffer: a five- to fifteen-minute break between meetings. Even short breathers like these can mean the difference between showing up sharp for your next meeting or feeling like your brain has been shoved through a mental meat grinder.

In 2021 Microsoft's Human Factors engineering team monitored people's brain activity during two different meeting schedules:[53]

SCHEDULE 1: Four back-to-back thirty-minute meetings with no breaks.

SCHEDULE 2: Four thirty-minute meetings with ten-minute breaks in between.

Without breaks, participants' stress levels spiked and their focus nosedived. But with just ten-minute buffers, stress levels dropped, focus improved, and participants left meetings with their brains more intact.

That fried, foggy state you feel after a meeting is what Brent Reed, Steven Rogelberg, Jon Gray, and I call a *meeting hangover*.[54] In a survey we ran with over five thousand knowledge workers in the US and

UK, workers reported experiencing meeting hangovers after 28 percent of their meetings, and about 90 percent said they experienced meeting hangovers at least occasionally.

And when that hangover hits, your brain enters power-saving mode. You begin to avoid tasks that require serious focus and instead default to low-effort busywork: clearing your inbox, chit-chatting, or mindlessly scrolling through Slack channels.

But meeting hangovers don't just drain productivity—they can also strain your relationships. Nearly half (47 percent) of respondents said post-meeting fatigue negatively impacted their interactions with colleagues. One big reason? Venting.

After a frustrating meeting, and with no time to decompress and clear your head before the next one, you're more likely to offload your frustration onto nearby coworkers. What might feel cathartic in the moment ends up spreading negativity and chipping away at trust.

Buffers are your insurance policy against brain fog and the fallouts of hangovers. If your meeting ends at 10:30, don't schedule the next one at 10:30. Block off 10:30 to 10:35 or 10:30 to 10:45 as a pause.

Use the break wisely. Grab a coffee, meditate, stretch, or go for a quick walk. And if you need to vent, do what I call *fix-it venting*: vent with the goal of diagnosing the problem and finding a solution. According to our research, that's much more productive than "feel-it" venting, when you just complain about the meeting to get it off your chest.

If you're concerned that blocking off a break on your public calendar will make you look lazy or uncommitted, rebrand it. Call it a "strategic pause." It sounds official and important (because it is) and may even inspire your coworkers to do the same.

STOP SCHEDULING MEETINGS.
START TIMING THEM TO THE RHYTHM OF WORK

In 1992 researchers Deborah Ancona and Chee-Leong Chong introduced a concept to the business world called *entrainment*.[55] Borrowed
from biology, it describes how systems, like the human body, function
more effectively when they sync with natural rhythms, like sleep cycles
or daylight. The same is true for meetings.

When meetings align with your organization's natural rhythm—goal
cycles, project timelines, daily operations—things click. Strategy turns
into execution. Decisions turn into progress. Meetings stop being a place
to talk about the work and become a place to actually do the work.

But when meetings are out of sync, it's like trying to build a product with parts arriving out of order. You slap on last-minute fixes, force
mismatched components to fit, and end up with a Frankenstein of a
product—bloated, clunky, and barely functional.

Well-timed meetings work like well-designed products. Everything
fits. They're intuitive and built to drive results. The best products make
life easier. The best meetings make work easier. Get the rhythm right,
and meetings stop dragging you down and start pushing you forward.

PRINCIPLE 7

Technology: Innovate and Iterate

In the summer of 2021, I logged into another weekly Zoom team meeting with a group of scientists from a US government lab. For months, I had been shadowing their meetings, observing them wrestle with the transition to hybrid work during the pandemic.

The team leader kicked things off with a blunt confession about a recent hybrid meeting with senior leaders at the organization. "We had a dumpster fire of a meeting on Monday," he said, shaking his head. "Even in this fancy room, it was broken. People on the phone couldn't hear anything, and we had to have people get up and stand underneath the microphones."

He wasn't exaggerating. I'd witnessed that dumpster fire. It started with remote participants straining to decipher the muffled voices in the room. Then, trying to fix the mess, someone hauled out a stand-up mic and plopped it in the middle of the floor like it was open mic night— except the mic was entirely out of the camera's view. Remote attendees were left playing an unwinnable game of Where's Waldo? trying to match disembodied voices to the figures drifting in and out of the frame.

Frustrated, the team leader sighed, "Our building is a marvel of modern technology from the 1960s." This was one of the most advanced scientific labs in the country, but only a few conference rooms across the sprawling campus had fully functional audio-visual setups, and those were hoarded like prime real estate. The rest were disasters—filled with crackling mics, frozen cameras, and other temperamental tech.

You've probably experienced this nightmare. When your meeting technology feels like it belongs in a museum, your productivity gets fossilized alongside it. The antidote is Meeting Design Principle 7: Innovate your meeting technology.

THREE RULES FOR INNOVATING YOUR MEETING TECHNOLOGY

Innovating your meeting technology isn't about chasing the latest gadgets or cramming AI into every corner. It's about unlocking the benefits of new ways of working—like hybrid work and AI-powered workflows—without smothering your team with distractions or needless complexity.

To innovate your meeting technology without turning your meetings into a tech circus, follow these three rules:

RULE 1: GET YOUR MVP RIGHT. Effective hybrid and remote meetings start with the basics. If people can't hear or see each other clearly, nothing else matters.

RULE 2: ADOPT "CALM" TECHNOLOGY. Your meeting technology shouldn't scream for attention. It should quietly do its job, unobtrusively support the meeting, and amplify the best of both humans and technology.

RULE 3: RELENTLESSLY PROTOTYPE WITH ARTIFICIAL INTELLIGENCE. Treat your meetings like a product in beta, constantly improving. Nothing's more important to prototype right now than AI. Figure out what role AI should play in your meetings. And then keep testing, adjusting, and upgrading.

Let's start by fixing the tech foundation of your meetings.

RULE 1: GET YOUR MVP RIGHT

In product development, the MVP (minimum viable product) is the simplest version of a product that effectively solves a problem. When it comes to technology, your meeting MVP is made up of two building blocks: audio and video. But that doesn't just mean keeping both turned on. It means using them intentionally.

If They Can't Hear You, They Won't Trust You

You've polished your slides, nailed your pitch, and maybe even donned your lucky underwear. Then it happens: "Can you hear me?" "Wait, there's an echo." "Hello? Are you frozen?"

In seconds, your well-planned meeting nosedives into an impromptu IT support group.

Poor audio isn't just a nuisance. It can undermine your credibility. Researchers have shown that when sound quality degrades, listeners don't just find the content harder to follow. They rate the speakers as less intelligent, less likable, and less credible.[1]

Clear audio is easy for your brain to process. But when sound glitches, your brain needs to work overtime. And it hates that. Before long, you're not just annoyed. You're questioning the speaker's credibility, thinking, "If this were really important, it wouldn't be this hard to hear."

Researchers call this *processing fluency*: how easily our brains process and absorb information. It's why eBay sellers with hard-to-pronounce names attract fewer buyers,[2] and why workout plans written in simple fonts like Arial seem more achievable than ones in fancy fonts like Brush Script.[3] Make your audience work too hard to hear you, and they'll stop trying. Or worse, they'll stop believing you.

To fix bad audio, begin by taking control of your environment. Shut the windows, find a quiet room, and surround yourself with sound-absorbing allies like curtains, carpets, and cushions. Next, ditch your laptop's built-in mic. Most are positioned near the webcam or under the keyboard—great for picking up sounds from your ceiling fan or the thunderous clatter of your typing, but terrible for capturing your voice. Invest in a headset so your mic is close to your mouth (ideally just a finger or two away[4]) and you'll sound sharper, more professional, and more credible.

Take it as seriously as GitLab does. Headsets (and external mics) are considered "essential item[s] which you will need to ensure you are able to perform your role."[5]

For extra clarity, pair your headset with an AI-powered noise-canceling app like Krisp. Trained on 170 years of audio data, it filters out distractions, from barking dogs to your toddler's impromptu drum solo.[6] It even works in reverse, scrubbing the noise coming from other people's mics, too.

Remember, great audio is a team sport. Follow cofounder and former GitLab CEO Sid Sijbrandij's advice, "Hear nothing, say something."[7] If someone sounds like they're calling from inside a washing machine, don't just wince silently. Speak up and rescue the meeting.

Mute Like a Human

Muting is your first line of defense against distracting background noise. But overuse it, and your meeting will turn lifeless and sterile.

Many meeting organizers dole out the same well-worn piece of advice: "Mute yourself when you're not speaking." It sounds reasonable—until you join a call and see a grid of muted faces, staring blankly like prisoners condemned to solitary confinement in a Zoom box prison.

Fortunately, there's a better way. Priyanka Parker calls it "silent, but unmuted."[8] Keep your mic turned on (unless there's loud background noise) but stay quiet when you're not talking. This preserves those subtle human sounds—giggles, sighs, murmured *mmm-hmm*s—that make conversations feel human.

But this works only up to a point: about twenty-five people. That's how many faces fit in a standard Zoom grid, allowing you to spot who's speaking and identify the culprit whose coffee grinder just joined the call. Cross that threshold, and your meeting becomes an open mic night of coughs, sneezes, and rogue burps.

Still, some meetings with more than twenty-five attendees deserve to be unmuted. At Buffer's All Hands meetings, they kick things off by celebrating wins: both work-related and personal ones, like someone running a marathon (a healthy dose of the social grease from chapter 4).[9] Everyone unmutes, and the screen erupts with cheers, claps, and hollers.

To make muting less clunky and awkward, GitLab encourages its employees to use the Shush app.[10] Instead of fumbling for the mute button, Shush lets you assign a hot key to toggle your mic on and off—no frantic clicks, no delays, no "Am I muted?" panic. It's nicknamed the "cough button" for a reason. It lets you silence sneezes, hiccups, or whatever else your body surprises you with before it crashes your meeting.

Audio Says It. Video Proves It.

Video is the other half of your meeting's MVP. Researchers call video a "richer" form of communication than audio because it gives you more than just words. It adds body language, facial expressions, and subtle reactions that make conversations feel more human.[11] And that matters because in every interaction, your brain is scanning for signals: Can I trust this person? Are they paying attention? Are they nodding along, or secretly hating my idea?

With video, silence comes with context. A nod says, "I'm with you." A raised eyebrow says, "I'm not so sure." These micro-cues can cut through the ambiguity and help build trust before misinterpretations have a chance to take the wheel.

When Video Hurts More Than It Helps

Video can make meetings more human, but it can also suck the life out of them, pixel by pixel.

Keeping your camera on has become the workplace equivalent of "eat your vegetables." It's supposed to be good for you (and often is), but sometimes it feels more like choking down cold, soggy Brussels sprouts.

Forcing people to keep their cameras on can backfire, cranking up Zoom fatigue. In a 2021 study at healthcare services company Broad-Path, University of Georgia professor Kristen Shockley and colleagues randomly assigned employees to attend meetings with their cameras either on or off.[12] Employees reported significantly higher levels of fatigue on days when they were required to keep their cameras on. It wasn't too many meetings that wore people out. It was too much video. The fatigue was especially intense for women and employees newer to the organization, likely because of the extra "self-presentation" pressure to constantly look polished, professional, and camera-ready.

For most employees, turning off their camera isn't a sign of slacking. It's a way to conserve energy and stay focused.

Turning off video has other unexpected upsides, too. The moment someone pops up on screen, our brains get to work, making snap judgments based on age, gender, race, and even what's lurking in their background. A study by researchers at Durham University found that people with bookcases or plants in their virtual backgrounds were rated as more trustworthy and competent than those with more generic backgrounds, like a living room or blank wall.[13]

A boss calling in from a mahogany-lined office with an artfully curated bookshelf oozes authority. Meanwhile, a junior employee dialing in from a cluttered bedroom—or using a blurred background to hide it—gets quietly docked for not looking professional enough.

Turning off video can level the playing field, neutralizing biases and allowing ideas to speak louder than appearances.

That's what Martha, a remote worker I interviewed during the pandemic, discovered. With her "baby face," senior executives often underestimated her expertise. But when she switched to audio-only during some of her meetings, others' perceptions of her changed. Her ideas became the focus, instead of her appearance.

The common assumption that turning your camera on always boosts engagement is a dangerous myth. When the energy is high, people are fully present, and their biases don't interfere, video can help strengthen connections. But when Zoom fatigue sets in, that camera doesn't bring people closer. It often just turns your meeting into a high-definition energy drain.

The Gender Tax of Zoom Fatigue

Zoom fatigue isn't gender neutral. In one study, University of Gothenburg professor Géraldine Fauville and her colleagues found that women were more than twice as likely as men to feel drained after video calls: About 14 percent of female participants reported feeling "very" or "extremely" tired, compared to less than 6 percent of men.[14]

A key culprit is what Fauville and team call *mirror anxiety*: the nagging self-consciousness triggered by having to stare at your own face. For many women, video meetings become two meetings at once: one with their colleagues, and another with their own hypercritical reflection. That's why, for women especially, it's important to build meeting cultures that value substance, not stage presence.

Don't Turn Video into a Loyalty Test

Despite the downsides of a camera-on culture, the pressure to stay visible is relentless. According to a survey conducted by Wakefield Research, 93 percent of US executives said that "employees who turn their cameras off on virtual calls are generally less engaged in their work." And 92 percent said, "Employees that frequently go on mute or don't go on camera probably don't have a long future with our company."[15] When the screen goes dark, executives make biased judgments:

- 43 percent think you're scrolling the internet
- 40 percent think you're texting
- 40 percent think you're multitasking

It's no wonder "cameras on" feels less like a choice and more like an unspoken rule. And one that carries real career consequences.

Employees get the message loud and clear. A 2023 Korn Ferry survey found that 76 percent of workers said they believed people who leave cameras off in meetings are "looked upon negatively," and 60 percent said choosing to go off-camera during meetings is a "career-minimizing move."[16] That's a whole lot of pressure—and job security—riding on a single button.

To break this cycle of camera-based paranoia, leaders need to stop treating video as a loyalty test and start setting clear expectations. One way to do that is by labeling meetings:

(AUDIO RECOMMENDED). Use this label for emotionally low-stakes meetings, where no one needs to read facial expressions, manage sensitive topics, or build deep connection. But still run it through the 4D-CEO Test first. If it doesn't deserve to be a meeting, don't make it one.

(VIDEO RECOMMENDED). Use this label for emotionally high-stakes meetings, like ones that involve mentoring, team building, delivering tough feedback, or resolving conflict. If people need to read, express, or manage emotions, it's better to turn the camera on and show up like a full human, not just a disembodied voice. Here's a gut check: If you're nervous about how your message might land, it probably deserves your face, not just your voice.

Labeling meetings like this allows people to step off the virtual stage and conserve their energy for meetings where video adds real value. Even with clear guidelines, employees should have the final say.

Zoom fatigue, personal distractions, or just having a bad day are all valid reasons to hit "video off." Remember, turning off the camera isn't a sign of slacking. It's more often a sign of self-preservation. Take a cue from GitLab, which tells its employees, "Do not feel forced to have your video on; use your best judgment." Trust your team.

And remember: If video is the only thing keeping people engaged, the problem isn't the camera. It's probably your meeting.

The Visibility Tax of Remote Work

In hybrid meetings (where some participants are physically present while others join remotely), it's tempting for remote workers to turn off their cameras to avoid appearing as a large floating head on the conference screen. However, this disappearing act can have negative consequences.

People remember what they see. Psychologists call this *visibility bias*, our brain's lazy shortcut that defaults to remembering the people and things that are most visible. In the workplace, that means the faces people see most often are the ones that come to mind when it's time to hand out new projects, stretch assignments, or promotions.

If you're remote, you're already missing out on the career-boosting optics of the physical office: the hallway run-ins, coffee chats, or just being visible at your desk. Keeping your camera on is one way to re-create that visibility. It ensures that your face is tied to the work being discussed. Turn it off, and you risk fading into the digital wallpaper, coming across as disengaged, uncommitted—or, worse—invisible.

RULE 2: EMBRACE CALM TECHNOLOGY

In 2021 Texas lawyer Rod Ponton became an accidental meme when his face turned into a wide-eyed animated kitten during a Zoom court hearing.[17] Trapped behind a Zoom filter he couldn't disable, he stuttered, "I don't know how to remove it," while his assistant scrambled to fix the situation. Desperate to salvage his credibility, he reassured the judge, "I'm here live. I'm not a cat." But the damage was done. He had become an internet punchline.

I witnessed a similar tech fiasco during a high-stakes budget review meeting in 2024. Apple had just rolled out 3D reactions on Zoom. In the middle of the meeting, an executive held up two fingers to signal "two." But Zoom misread it as a peace sign, triggering a confetti explosion across the screen as she solemnly announced budget cuts.

Technology should work *for* you, not against you. That's the crux of calm technology.[18]

Pioneered in the 1990s by Mark Weiser and John Seely Brown at Xerox PARC (the legendary lab that gave us Ethernet, word processing, and laser printing), calm technology refers to technology that does its job so well that you barely notice it's there. Amber Case, a calm technology expert, gives the example of a tea kettle.[19] Most of the time, the kettle sits quietly, unobtrusively, blending into the background. But when it's ready, it whistles, just loudly enough to grab your attention, without demanding it.

The opposite of calm technology? Meeting links that make you feel like you're hacking into the Pentagon—wrestling with passwords, verification codes, and plug-ins just to get inside. Or PowerPoints so jam-packed with flying text and spinning animations that they leave you seasick by slide three. And, of course, Zoom filters that turn you into an animated kitten.

The Two Calm Tech Principles That Save Your Meetings

How can you determine if your meeting technology is truly calm? Case outlines several principles, but when it comes to meetings, two matter most:

1. **TECHNOLOGY SHOULD REQUIRE THE SMALLEST POSSIBLE AMOUNT OF ATTENTION.** Meeting technology shouldn't steal your focus. It should step in when necessary and fade away when it has done its job.

2. **TECHNOLOGY SHOULD AMPLIFY THE BEST OF TECHNOLOGY AND THE BEST OF HUMANITY.** Meeting technology should handle the grunt work—capturing notes, scheduling, crunching data—so you can focus on what humans do best: thinking critically, being creative, building relationships, and inspiring your team.

Before jumping on the latest AI meeting assistant, Zoom upgrade, or shiny new collaboration app, ask yourself: Does it deliver on these principles? If not, it's not calm.

Escape Zoom Fatigue and Take Your Brain Back

How do Zoom and other video platforms like Webex and Microsoft Teams measure up against calm principles? Not great.

The worst offense? They demand too much of your attention. Zoom's default gallery view—the *Brady Bunch* grid of floating heads—turns meetings into a nonstop staring contest. Stanford professor Jeremy Bailenson has explained why it's so exhausting. In the physical world, if someone's face is inches from yours—like it appears on Zoom—your brain assumes one of two things is about to happen: They're either going to kiss you or punch you.[20] On Zoom, neither is true, but try convincing your brain of that. It registers that uncomfortable closeness and stays on high alert, unsure whether to pucker up or duck.

Then there's the self-view: Zoom's default setting that forces you to stare at your own face while interacting with others. It's like having a conversation while holding up a mirror. It's not natural. In real life, we don't stare at our own faces while talking to other people. That constant scrutiny takes a toll. It drains your mental battery and leaves you nursing a case of Zoom fatigue.

Zoom fatigue doesn't just wear you down. It wears down your judgment. When your brain's running on fumes, it's easier to nod along than speak up. That's when groupthink tightens its grip.[21] Bad ideas get greenlit. Not because people believe in them, but because no one has the stamina to push back.

In meetings where you need your camera on, make Zoom less draining by dialing down the intensity. Start by using the Hide Self-View feature to remove your face from the screen while keeping it visible to others. Then, back away from the screen. Creating more physical distance between you and the screen creates more mental distance. Try shrinking the Zoom video window, too—so the grid feels less like an interrogation lineup and more like a conversation.

If you're Zooming from home, create a dedicated "meeting zone." Don't let your workspace double as your dining table, couch, or the corner of your unmade bed. Even if space is tight, claim one chair, one corner of a room, or one end of a desk exclusively for video calls to create a mental separation between work and life. Otherwise, your couch becomes a holding pen for the next Zoom meeting, and every meal at your table feels like a working lunch you didn't sign up for.

Stack the Phones, Save the Meeting

Cell phones are the antithesis of calm, especially in meetings. Even when they're face down and silenced, they lead to what researchers call *absent presence*.[22] Your body is in the meeting, but your mind is tethered to your phone, violating the first principle of calm technology: Demand the least possible attention.

If you want better meetings, try banning phones from your meetings altogether. Or take a page from DBS Bank and play Phone Jenga. At DBS, the Joyful Observer can ask everyone to stack their phones in the middle of the table, and no one is allowed to touch the pile until the meeting's over.[23]

PowerPoint: When Simplicity Becomes Stupidity

In 2003 engineers sent NASA senior leadership a bloated twenty-eight-slide PowerPoint deck assessing whether the Columbia space shuttle's tiles had been damaged during launch.[24] The real warnings were buried under layers of technical jargon, sanitized bullet points, and vague corporate language, dulling the risks and creating a deadly false sense of security that led to the tragic loss of seven astronauts.

After the disaster, the Columbia Accident Investigation Board didn't just criticize the engineers. It singled out PowerPoint itself. Their report described it as a "problematic method of technical communication at NASA," pointing out how the slides buried life-or-death warnings under a mountain of corporate fluff and sugar-coated bullet points.[25]

Like Zoom, PowerPoint (and its slideware siblings like Google Slides and Keynote) violates the core principles of calm technology. In the army, junior officers are mockingly called "PowerPoint Rangers" because of the absurd amount of time they spend churning out decks. And the problem certainly isn't confined to the military. Across industries, organizations worship the aesthetics of the slides instead of the thinking behind them. Critical information gets buried under a landslide of bullet points, animations, and bad stock photos. And all that visual pollution muddies our thinking. As four-star Marine Corps general James Mattis, who later served as US Secretary of Defense, put it, "PowerPoint makes us stupid."

PowerPoint also violates the second calm principle: It doesn't amplify human thinking—it flattens it. Meetings turn into dull monologues, where presenters read slides to a room of bored faces. Bullet points don't simplify information—they dumb it down, distort it, and suck the urgency out of what matters most. Just ask NASA. As General H. R. McMaster, who later became national security advisor, warned in 2005 after calling PowerPoint an "internal threat": "Some problems are not bullet-izable."[26]

Kill Slide Bloat with the 10/20/30 Rule

One way to make PowerPoint more calm is to follow venture capitalist Guy Kawasaki's 10/20/30 Rule.

Frustrated by bloated decks crammed with tiny fonts and too many slides, Kawasaki blamed PowerPoint for worsening his Ménière's disease, a condition that causes dizziness and hearing loss.[27] To save his sanity (and possibly his inner ear), he came up with a rule: no more than ten slides, no more than twenty minutes to present them, and no font smaller than thirty points.

Don't Label Your Slides. Headline Them

Another way to make PowerPoint more calm is to rethink your slide titles. Generic titles like "Revenue Growth" or "Customer Feedback" make
your audience work too hard. They're forced to squint at graphs, scan
bullet points, and piece together what you're trying to say. Don't make
them play detective. Instead, make your slide titles do the heavy lifting
with headlines that spell out the takeaway:

- Instead of "Revenue Growth," try "Our Revenue More Than
  Doubled."
- Instead of "Customer Feedback," try "Customer NPS Improved
  by 15 Points This Quarter."

A good title works like a signpost. It keeps your audience on track,
even if they mentally veer off course.

Kill the Live Slide Decks

Slides have a nasty habit of turning meetings into one-way monologues.
That's why at GitLab, cofounder and former CEO Sid Sijbrandij laid
down a blunt rule: If employees wanted to use slides, they had to record
their presentation as a video and share it before the meeting. Live slide
presentations weren't allowed.* The logic was simple: valuable synchronous meeting time should be reserved for real conversations.

By pre-recording presentations, employees could fast-forward
through the irrelevant parts, replay key sections, and focus on what mat-

---

* While it's no longer a strict rule at the company, GitLab still encourages sharing
  slides in advance to boost engagement and make the most of live meeting time.

tered to them. As Sijbrandij put it, "The assumption that the entire presentation is exactly as interesting to everyone and worth watching one time at 1x speed . . . the chances of that are zero."[28]

Ban PowerPoint

If PowerPoint keeps sucking up your team's time and brain cells, it might be time to pull the plug.

In the mid-1990s, Sun Microsystems CEO Scott McNealy discovered that PowerPoint slides were eating up 12.9 gigabytes of space on the company's network.[29] He called PowerPoint a "huge waste of productivity" and banned it outright.

What happened next? Sun Microsystems enjoyed three consecutive record-breaking fiscal quarters. Reflecting on the shift, McNealy claimed that if every company banned PowerPoint, "their earnings would skyrocket."[30]

Over the years, other leaders like Jeff Bezos have followed McNealy's lead by banning slideware in meetings. Less time in slide purgatory means more time for actual thinking. Now that's a bullet point worth remembering.

RULE 3: RELENTLESSLY PROTOTYPE WITH ARTIFICIAL INTELLIGENCE

In 2021 David Shim, former CEO of check-in and location intelligence platform Foursquare, found himself trapped in yet another mind-numbing virtual meeting.[31] As the presenter droned on, Shim's attention drifted. That's when he spotted a flicker of red and white reflected in another participant's glasses: ESPN. Shim recognized it instantly because he'd also been sneaking peeks at game scores on his phone.

That flicker was a wake-up call. If Shim could spot someone tuning out just by catching a screen reflection, while the presenter remained oblivious, imagine what the right technology could do. By the end of 2021, Shim launched Read AI, a productivity startup that uses AI to analyze meetings, emails, and messages, surfacing insights that flag when communication is breaking down, like when attendees start zoning out mid-meeting.

Fast-forward to today and the AI arms race has turned the videoconferencing world upside down. From startups like Read AI to tech giants like Microsoft, everyone's slapping "AI First" stickers on their products. Even Zoom, the poster child for video calls, dropped "Video" from its name in 2024, eager to flaunt its AI glow-up.[32] It's like that friend who suddenly claims they've always loved hockey right after you mention your season tickets.

Every platform wants you to believe that AI is the secret to fixing your meetings. But AI won't save a lousy meeting. As the head of AI at a large multinational retail company once told me, "A fool with a tool is still a fool." AI can help, but it can't replace the hard work of running better meetings. That responsibility—along with using the seven Meeting Design Principles—is yours.

The Three Roles for AI in Your Meetings

Before inviting AI into your meetings, ask yourself: "What job do I need it to do?"

AI can play three key roles in meetings:

- **AUTOMATE:** AI can manage meeting scheduling, note-taking, and summaries so that you can focus your attention on the people in the room.

- **ADVISE:** AI can surface real-time insights before, during, and after meetings, nudging you to make better decisions about your meetings.

- **PARTICIPATE:** AI can show up as a participant, joining meetings, steering the conversation back on course, and politely flagging the person who thinks the meeting is their TED Talk audition.

Don't adopt AI just to hop on the hype train. If it's not solving a real problem and playing an intentional role, it's just another pointless participant taking up space and bleeding attention.

AI to Automate: Let AI Handle the Meeting Busywork

Meetings come with a mountain of soul-sucking grunt work: scheduling, note-taking, chasing down action items. Let AI automate the drudgery so your team can focus on what matters most: the conversation and the people in the room. That's how you amplify the best of both humans and machines.

Stop Playing Calendar Roulette

Uber can summon a car in seconds, dating apps can find your soulmate in minutes, and Netflix knows your next binge before you do. But scheduling a meeting with even two people still feels like a logistical nightmare. And it's not just the first round of scheduling that's painful. More than half (55 percent) of people end up rescheduling or canceling meetings at least 30 percent of the time, according to data from Reclaim.AI.[33] That kicks off another round of inbox Ping-Pong, flinging new time slots into the void and hoping the scheduling gods show mercy.

According to the software company Boomerang, when people use its Suggest Times feature (which lets them propose multiple meeting slot options), their best shot of securing a time that everyone agrees on comes after offering seven to fourteen options.[34] At that point, you're not scheduling. You're spinning the calendar roulette wheel and hoping it doesn't land on "double-booked."

AI solutions like Clockwise and Reclaim can automate this drudgery. Just type, "Find time for a meeting with Joe," and let the bots do the wrangling. They'll even honor your no-meeting days and strategic pauses from chapter 6. It's like having a super-accommodating personal assistant, minus the judgmental side-eye when you reschedule for the third time.

Stop Taking Notes. Start Paying Attention

At their best, AI transcription tools are the epitome of calm technology—quietly capturing everything in the background so you can stay focused on the conversation. Tools such as Zoom's AI Companion and Otter.ai can tag speakers, log decisions, and make every word instantly searchable. As Alan Lepofsky, chief marketing officer at Mobeus Spacecloud, put it, "I'd rather people be looking up at the camera, engaged in conversation, than scrambling to write."[35]

But transcripts don't just help you stay engaged during meetings. They also give you a more accurate replay of what happened, slicing through the fog of fuzzy memories and vague commitments. Instead of "Wait, didn't we say . . ." or "I thought you meant . . . ," you get a more objective record of what really happened. When transcripts are shared after the meeting, they wipe out second-guessing, memory lapses, creative interpretations, and participants' conveniently selective hearing. Everyone's working from the same source of truth. And that makes it a lot harder to rewrite history.

But you need to be vigilant. Always get consent before you hit record. Ask Alex Bilzerian. In 2024 an AI transcription tool dutifully transcribed his meeting with investors—then kept recording after he hung up.[36] Hours of the investors' private post-meeting conversations were transcribed and later emailed to Bilzerian. Trust imploded. And so did the deal.

Before you turn your meeting into a searchable database, confirm who has consented and what's being recorded. And make sure your AI knows when to leave the room.

Turn Talk into Action

We've all been in those meetings. Everyone nods along enthusiastically, commitments are made, and then nothing happens. "Susan will create the deck," but no deadline is set. "Joe, loop back on that next week!" Joe nods enthusiastically, already forgetting what he just agreed to.

AI can step in as the adult supervision that many meetings desperately need. Tools like Microsoft Copilot and Zoom can automatically flag action items, assign tasks with deadlines, and track follow-ups without relying on human memory. For recurring meetings, Read AI can keep a running log of open action items and carry it over to the next meeting's agenda, so nothing gets lost or forgotten. It even tracks whether action items are completed, pulling information from meetings, emails, and messages to make the determination.

AI to Advise: Your Intelligent Meeting Coach

Automation is great for offloading grunt work, but it won't fix the deeper dysfunctions that bog down your meetings. That's where AI can level up even more, not just as a glorified task manager, but as a trusted advisor, nudging you toward better meetings—before, during, and after the meeting.

Pre-Meeting Insights: Read the Room Before You Enter It

Before joining a meeting, AI can gather intel, flag pitfalls, and help you show up prepared. Tech executive Ephraim Allon built his meeting prep workflow using Relay.app, a platform for building AI agents.[37] When a meeting lands on his calendar, AI gets to work, pulling LinkedIn bios, background summaries, and even predicting the meeting's purpose so Allon shows up ready to go.

But sometimes Allon's AI digs a little too deep, surfacing attendees' wedding registries, or the price someone paid for their house. Suddenly, you could be left wondering if that $3,000 espresso machine on their registry means your in-office coffee is about to feel embarrassingly inadequate.

Beyond gathering intel, AI can help you design better meetings. Upload your meeting agenda or paste meeting transcripts (with consent), along with your notes from this book, and ask AI to flag anything that violates the seven Meeting Design Principles. It can catch hollow agenda items that lack verb-noun combinations (from chapter 3), call out slides that breach the 10/20/30 Rule from earlier in this chapter, or even expose those bloated invite lists packed with people who haven't unmuted since 2025.

AI can also help you dodge cultural land mines. During an "AI Friction Bot Challenge" I helped lead with Stanford's design school (also known as the Stanford d.school) lecturers Perry Klebahn and Kathryn Velcich, one group of Stanford students pitched a "cross-cultural bot" designed to help teams bridge cultural divides and avoid cultural faux pas.[38] Imagine it saying, "In Greece, avoid a thumbs-up. It's the equivalent of flipping someone off." Or "In Japan, don't hand out business cards like you're dealing poker. Exchange them with two hands if you're able and treat them with respect."

You don't need a specialized bot for this. Input attendee details into ChatGPT and ask, "What cultural norms should I be aware of for attendees from [specific countries]?" You'll learn, for example, that Germans deliver feedback like they design their cars—precise and efficient. Americans, meanwhile, are fluent in the "compliment sandwich," layering criticism between enough praise that a German might wonder why there's so much bread. Understanding these cultural quirks is how you build trust, earn respect, and avoid torpedoing your meeting with an accidental insult.

Try hosting your own AI design challenge. Rally your team to brainstorm how AI can make your meetings more productive and less of a collective endurance test.

Insights During the Meeting: Your Meeting Play-by-Play

AI can also serve up insights in real time during your meetings. Missed the first five minutes? Zoned out mid-slide? Need clarification on what's been said before weighing in? AI can instantly summarize key points and clear up the confusion, sparing you from the awkwardness of asking someone to repeat what they just said.

Real-time AI insights don't just help you get up to speed during the meeting. Read AI can analyze speaking pace, tone, and sentiment, flagging when the room's energy starts to sag—long before attendees start checking ESPN. That allows leaders to pivot in the moment, before engagement flatlines.

Machine learning algorithms, a core component of many AI systems, can also dissect deeper collaboration patterns. Between 2015 and 2017 researchers Katharina Lix, Amir Goldberg, Sameer Srivastava, and Melissa Valentine from Stanford University and the University of California, Berkeley analyzed over 800,000 Slack messages from 117 software development teams at Gigster, a software development platform.[39]

They measured "discursive diversity": how much teams varied their communication styles during different phases of work.

The results were striking: the top-performing teams adjusted their communication to match the task at hand. During brainstorming, their conversations were diverse, full of different ideas and perspectives. But when it came time to execute, their discursive diversity dropped as they aligned, coordinated, and focused on getting things done.

We're not quite at this level of sophistication yet, but AI-powered meeting tools are catching up fast. It won't be long before your meeting bot can say something like "You're still brainstorming, but your team's already starting to converge on an idea. Keep the ideas flowing a little longer."

Post-Meeting Insights: Let the Bots Spill the Tea

When the meeting ends, AI doesn't just clock out. It keeps working, analyzing what happened in the meeting and how to improve the next one. It can flag who hijacked the conversation, measure engagement levels, and extract key themes, takeaways, and decisions.

Even if your meeting platform doesn't have these features built in, you can still upload meeting transcripts (with consent) and ask, "What decisions were made?" or "What action items am I responsible for?" If transcripts are shared (and they should be by default), you can even ask about meetings you didn't attend. Wondering if Jackie from marketing threw shade while you were on vacation? AI can flag that, too.

AI also helps eliminate tribal knowledge: insights locked away in someone's notebook, private messages, or leaky memory. David Shim shared an example from a major tech company where five hundred product managers each handled about five customer calls a week, totaling over 2,500 meetings a year. In the past, all those insights were scattered, buried, or lost. Now, AI extracts key takeaways, identifies trends, and delivers summaries to stakeholders in minutes.

The real holy grail of post-meeting AI insights isn't searching for information. It's *discovering* it. Imagine logging in on Monday to an AI-generated highlight reel of the previous week's key moments, including relevant insights from meetings you didn't even attend. Marketing teams can instantly see which features wowed customers in demos. Sales teams can discover common customer objections bubbling up in sales calls so they can adjust their pitches. Instead of digging for information, AI can drop it in your lap. Fresh, relevant, and ready to act on.

AI to Participate: Give Bots a Seat at the Table

The biggest leap for AI in meetings is graduating from automating drudgery and nudging with insights to taking a seat at the table as a full-fledged participant.

Skip the Meeting, Send a Bot

Tools like Microsoft Teams and Read AI let you send a bot when you're double-booked, on vacation, or too emotionally drained for another status update meeting. And the bots are multiplying: In over 20 percent of Read AI meetings, at least one attendee sends their AI bot instead of attending themselves, according to Shim. It can be quite tempting. Unlike humans, bots don't zone out, roll their eyes, or burn out. They don't even need a coffee break.

But these digital stand-ins aren't just digital wallflowers that capture key points, summarize discussions, and log action items with cold-blooded efficiency. Some can dig up historical context, analyze data in real time, or flag when someone tries to weasel their way out of a past decision. Others can pick up where your skills fall short. Zoom CEO Eric Yuan predicts that the future of meetings will revolve around "digital twins": AI-powered clones of humans.[40] One might be your cutthroat deal closer. Another, your pitch-perfect presenter who wows clients without breaking a sweat.

That future is already taking shape. In 2025 Otter.ai CEO Sam Liang revealed that he'd built an AI bot trained on thousands of his meetings, complete with a synthetic voice that sounds just like him. The bot was built to handle about 90 percent of the straightforward issues that arise in meetings, freeing Liang to focus on higher-stakes work. He plans to sell these digital doppelgängers to other CEOs, promising them more time for strategy and less time slogging through meeting muck.[41]

Sometimes sending an AI bot to your meeting is an obvious choice. You're double-booked and need someone to cover the meeting and contribute your expertise. Or you're on vacation and want a summary waiting when you return. Or the meeting is in another language, and you need real-time translation to keep up or contribute.

But in many cases, the decision to send a robot or show up yourself isn't clear-cut. This is where ROTI (return on time invested) comes back into play. Ask yourself: "Will I get a higher return from being present in the room, or from sending a bot and using that hour elsewhere?"

And don't just think about the short term. Sure, sending a bot instead of showing up yourself might save you an hour today, but what's the cleanup cost tomorrow? When a bot can't match your judgment, empathy, or ability to steer a high-stakes conversation back on track, you risk spending twice as long cleaning up misunderstandings or explaining why your bot smiled and nodded along to a terrible idea.

Sending a bot doesn't signal, "I'm efficient." It signals, "This wasn't worth my time." One hour saved today isn't worth two tomorrow untangling the mess. Or repairing the dent in your reputation.

The more a meeting passes the 4D-CEO Test with flying colors, the more important it is to show up yourself. Complex and emotionally charged conversations still need a human brain and a human pulse.

Bots are notoriously bad at reading the room and handling black swan events.[42] And if the meeting involves a one-way-door decision, it's too risky to outsource to a bot with zero accountability.

Bots That Moderate: The Ruthless Meeting Referees

In 2024 MIT professor Ethan Mollick challenged an AI avatar to moderate "the most stereotypical corporate Zoom meeting ever."[43] The bot rose to the challenge, kicking things off with the classic "Hey, are you on mute?" It went on to hit all the corporate clichés, asking if Mollick had anything to add to the agenda and if he'd heard the latest updates from marketing.

But AI moderators aren't just glorified meeting emcees making small talk and clicking through slides. They can monitor keywords, tone, and participation, nudging participants back to the agenda, prompting quieter voices to speak up, and flagging unproductive tangents before they hijack your meeting.

The first AI-powered moderator I tested was Stanford's Online Deliberation Platform. In 2022, I tried it with a group of executives, including one notorious for steamrolling every meeting. Each person had forty-five seconds to speak before the bot automatically muted their mic. When his time ran out, the bot cut his mic in mid-sentence. He sat there, stunned—a volcano in a suit—mouth flapping, words gone, rage simmering. Meanwhile, everyone else finally had their turn to speak, freed by the bot's ruthless fairness.

AI moderation doesn't stop at turn-taking. On the Deliberation Platform, every statement is assigned a "toxicity score."[44] If the toxicity score crosses a certain threshold, the bot polls the group to determine whether the speaker has said something offensive. If the majority agrees, the offender's mic is muted for a timeout. Separately, the platform also keeps track of who's staying silent and gently nudges quieter participants to speak up and even out the conversation.

AI moderators are promising, but they're not a magic bullet for bad meetings. The key is to experiment, collect feedback, and track the metrics that matter (from chapter 2). Are people contributing more equally? Is the ROTI climbing? Or is the bot just another piece of red tape, enforcing rules while engagement stays just as stale as before?

AI That Makes Dissent Safer and Decisions Smarter

One of AI's most underrated strengths in meetings is contributing different or dissenting ideas. Speaking up can feel risky, especially when you're challenging the boss or questioning the group's direction when everyone else is eagerly nodding along.

But AI doesn't generally care about politics, pecking orders, or whose idea it's about to kneecap. It can lob criticism at your pet idea without flinching. And it can do that right now. Mid-meeting, you can ask Microsoft Copilot, "Challenge this idea. What might we be missing?" Seconds later, it will be flagging risks, poking holes, and raising counterpoints without sugarcoating or tiptoeing.

Even when AI doesn't directly contribute a solution in a meeting, it can improve how decisions get made. Soohwan Lee, a PhD candidate at the Ulsan National Institute of Science and Technology, and colleagues developed a large language model–powered devil's advocate that was trained to ask thoughtful questions during discussions, like "Could the option currently favored by the group be too conservative? Have you considered alternatives?"[45] Lee and colleagues found that the AI helped foster a more inclusive atmosphere where human participants felt safer voicing dissenting views. That psychological safety led to better decisions and attendees felt more satisfied with both the process and the outcome.

Sometimes, AI's greatest strength isn't what it says. It's what it makes others brave enough to say.

The Limits of AI: When the Buzz Hits the Fan

Incorporating AI into your meetings shouldn't be a "set it and forget it" solution. It requires vigilance, a healthy dose of skepticism, and a clear understanding of what AI should and shouldn't do.

Take AI transcripts. They can seem harmless—until they aren't. One wrong move and you're knee-deep in compliance issues, legal liabilities, and a workforce that feels spied on. Make sure you understand data privacy regulations like the General Data Protection Regulation* and how they're evolving. What's compliant today might lead to a lawsuit tomorrow.

Then there's what management professor Tim Hannigan calls *bot-shit*[46]: "made-up, inaccurate, and untruthful chatbot content that humans uncritically use for tasks."[47] It's the robotic version of human BS, and it can cause just as much collateral damage.

Consider Lisa, the AI scheduling assistant that Paul Leonardi told me about. Lisa was supposed to eliminate the hassle of scheduling meetings. Just CC her on a scheduling email, and she'd handle the rest. But things went sideways when Rahul, one of Lisa's users, gave her control over his calendar. One of Rahul's colleagues, Noah, just wanted to set up a simple meeting with Rahul. Instead, Lisa kept "optimizing" the meeting location—so many times that Noah racked up hundreds of dollars in cab fares and wasted hours ping-ponging across town. Noah wasn't mad at Lisa. He was furious at Rahul for trusting it.

As Leonardi explains in his book *Digital Exhaustion*, when a human assistant screws up on a scheduling or other task, they share the blame.[48] But when AI screws up, the blame doesn't land on the bot—it lands

---

* The GDPR is a data privacy law enacted by the European Union in 2018. It governs how organizations collect, store, and use personal data of EU residents.

squarely on you. You're the one who appears incompetent for trusting it. That's why you might want to keep AI out of sensitive or confidential discussions. The stakes are high, and if things go sideways, you'll be the one eating the fallout.

As bots infiltrate more of our meetings, they risk making everything more robotic and soulless. Marketing director Colin Dougherty experienced this when he logged into a meeting in 2023, only to realize he was the only human present. Every other participant was an AI bot. "It felt super dystopian," he said.[49]

Often the problem isn't how accurate or reliable the AI is. It's how people perceive it. Harvard professor Raj Choudhury and his colleagues tested this by building an AI twin of Zapier CEO Wade Foster called the "Wade Bot." It was trained on years of Foster's actual communication.[50] Employees were asked to guess whether responses came from the real Wade or his AI twin. They guessed correctly only 59 percent of the time, not much better than a coin flip.

But that wasn't the biggest takeaway. It was this: When employees thought a response came from the Wade Bot—even when it didn't—they rated it as less helpful. Why? Because people don't just want answers. They want connection. No matter how advanced AI gets, in many cases, people still want to know they're talking to a real person.

Don't forget that second principle of calm technology. Meeting technology should amplify the best of humanity, not just the best of technology. Before you start packing your meetings with bots, ask yourself: If AI can replace most people in the room, does the meeting need to happen?

Probably not. If a meeting runs just fine without humans, it shouldn't be a meeting. It should be an email or an update in your work management system. Use AI to improve meetings that matter, not to avoid showing up yourself or to keep holding meetings that never should've existed in the first place.

When you roll out AI for meetings, take a page from Toyota's *kaizen* philosophy, Japanese for "continuous improvement."[51] At Toyota, everyone from the factory floor to the C-suite is expected to call out inefficiencies and suggest ways to fix them. Bring that same mindset to your meetings. Challenge your team to pitch one AI meeting tech upgrade per quarter. Then ask for honest ROTI feedback: Did it help? Did it make meetings better? Or just shinier?

Bring AI into Your Meetings Without Starting a Revolt

New technology rarely fails because it can't do the job. It fails because humans resist change. AI in meetings is no different. Roll it out the wrong way, and your team will push back on principle. Not because the technology is broken, but because the rollout is.

Be upfront and transparent. Don't make people guess why AI suddenly showed up in their meeting. Tell your team exactly why AI is in the room. What will it do? How will it help—not replace—the people in the room?

If AI feels like a threat, people will resist it. At one global retail giant I studied, employees initially pushed back against AI, seeing it as a threat. The term *artificial intelligence* can stoke that fear. It suggests something unnatural that competes with human intelligence rather than supports it.

So leaders rebranded it as "amplified intelligence." That slight, one-word pivot reframed AI—from replacing human skills to a tool that augments them. It changed how employees felt about the technology and made them more open to using it. Evernote took a similar approach, dubbing it "augmented intelligence," a shift that "landed well with customers," says Joshua Zerkel, former director of global community and training.

Whatever you do, don't put your meetings on AI autopilot. That's how you fall into the *automation paradox*: the more sophisticated AI gets, the more likely we are to let our guard down, exactly when we need it most.[52] The more powerful the AI, the more critical your human judgment becomes. And when something goes wrong, it won't be the bot that takes the blame. It'll be you.

Roll out AI with intention, not wishful thinking, and even the biggest skeptics will warm up. Because while the technology will keep changing and evolving, one thing won't: When used wisely, AI can help you design your best meeting ever.

THE SIMPLE MEETING
DESIGN USER MANUAL

Design Your Best Meeting Ever

During World War II, meetings were used as weapons of sabotage. The OSS instructed citizens in enemy territory to use them to bog down productivity, drain morale, and derail decision-making. Fast-forward to today, and meetings still feel like weapons of mass distraction and dysfunction. Only now, the sabotage isn't deliberate. It's just the byproduct of bad design.

If you want better meetings, start thinking like a product designer. Great meetings, like great products, don't happen by accident. They need thoughtful design, rigorous testing, and relentless optimization.

Designing better meetings isn't just the organizer's job. Everyone in the room is a codesigner. If a meeting is derailing, dragging, or just plain dead on arrival, speak up. Propose improvements. Call out what's broken. Your time—and everyone else's—is too valuable to waste on a broken product.

To put these principles to work, use the Simple Meeting Design User Manual in this final chapter. Think of it as your evergreen bite-sized blueprint for designing your best meeting ever. Unlike the wartime *Simple Sabotage Field Manual*, which taught people how to tank productivity, this one is built to rescue it. It breaks down all seven principles and arms you with strategies from this book that you can start using right away.

Make it part of your team's daily operating system. Print it and post it in your meeting rooms. Create digital versions for remote and hybrid meetings. Include it in onboarding guides and team playbooks. When everyone knows the principles, they stop being passive victims or bystanders of bad meetings and start becoming active designers of better ones.

THE SIMPLE MEETING DESIGN USER MANUAL

Meetings are your most important product. Design them as if they are.

Principle 1
Volume: Cut Your Meeting Debt

Meetings pile up like technical debt—quietly draining time, energy, and sanity. Use these five steps to wipe out your meeting debt:

STEP 1: LAUNCH A CALENDAR CLEANSE. Delete your recurring meetings for forty-eight hours and rebuild your calendar from the ground up.

STEP 2: EQUIP EMPLOYEES TO DEFEND THEIR TIME. Give your team the tools—and permission—to say no to meetings.

STEP 3: BUILD A MEETING DEBT REPOSITORY. Create a place where employees can flag bloated or broken meetings. And make sure leaders act on it.

STEP 4: ADD GUARDRAILS TO PREVENT MEETING DEBT. Use speed bumps, gatekeepers, and blocks to stop bad meetings before they hit the calendar.

STEP 5: COMMIT TO REGULAR MAINTENANCE. Hold recurring Meeting Doomsdays—and reward the people who don't let the clutter creep back in.

Principle 2
Measurement: Choose the Right Metrics

You can't fix what you don't measure. And you also can't fix what you measure badly. Stick to these four mantras for meaningful meeting measurement:

MANTRA 1: AVOID MISLEADING METRICS. Watch out for four misleading metrics: sentiment, self-ratings, cost, and time saved. They're easy to track. And easy to misinterpret.

MANTRA 2: USE RETURN ON TIME INVESTED (ROTI). ROTI is your most brutally honest—and most reliable—metric for assessing whether a meeting was effective.

MANTRA 3: MEASURE WHAT MATTERS. Use meeting analytics to move past surface metrics and dissect what's really going on. Start with time in meetings, airtime, multitasking, punctuality, and attendance.

MANTRA 4: BEWARE METRICS AS TARGETS. When a metric becomes a target, it stops driving progress. People start gaming the system instead of fixing the meeting.

Principle 3
Structure: Become a Meeting Minimalist

Apply the Rule of Halves and other minimalist strategies to cut the clutter from your meetings across four key dimensions: agenda, duration, attendees, and frequency.

> **DIMENSION 1: AGENDA.** Every agenda item should have a job to do. Give it one by converting it into a verb-noun combination, like "Decide budget," "Finalize draft messaging," or "Align on Q2 plan."

> **DIMENSION 2: LENGTH.** Beware Parkinson's Law: Your meeting will expand to fill the time you give it. So set tight time limits and stick to them.

> **DIMENSION 3: ATTENDEES.** Follow the Rule of Eight: no more than eight attendees. Only invite stakeholders, not spectators.

> **DIMENSION 4: FREQUENCY.** Eliminate meetings that happen too often, especially "meetings about the meetings." Prevent zombie meetings by giving each one an expiry date. Use the Disagree and Commit rule to shut down spin-off meetings—and make sure the real decision-makers are in the room.

Principle 4
Flow: Apply Systems Thinking

Broken meetings are often the result of broken communication outside of the meeting. Use these three upgrades to improve the flow—before, during, and after the meeting:

UPGRADE 1: STANDARDIZE YOUR COMMUNICATION TOOLS. Pick a core communication tech stack and stick to it. Then, standardize what justifies a live meeting with the 4D-CEO Test: meet only to discuss, decide, debate, or develop, and only if the topic is complex, emotionally intense, or involves a one-way door.

UPGRADE 2: DEFAULT TO ASYNCHRONOUS COMMUNICATION. Meetings should be your last resort, not your first. Build a system where work moves forward without needing real-time conversations.

UPGRADE 3: DESIGN FOR DISTANCE. Don't just design for the people in the room. Make sure your communication system works for everyone, everywhere.

Principle 5
Engagement: Prioritize User-Centric Design

Meetings should serve the people in the room—not just the person who scheduled them. Start by squashing these four energy-sucking bugs:

ENERGY-SUCKING BUG 1: POWER MOVES. Don't let volume, title, or ego run your meeting. When one person dominates, everyone else checks out.

ENERGY-SUCKING BUG 2: LATENESS. Start on time. End on time. Respect for people starts with respect for the clock.

ENERGY-SUCKING BUG 3: JARGON. Jargon doesn't make you sound smart. It just makes your message harder to understand and easier to ignore. Speak like a smart ninth grader. Ditch the buzzwords and gobbledygook.

ENERGY-SUCKING BUG 4. Boredom. Beige rooms breed beige ideas. Add plants, color, light, movement, or food. And make sure every meeting has at least one moment of delight.

Principle 6
Timing: Get Your Meetings in Rhythm

The best meetings sync with the natural flow of work—not interrupt it. Align your meetings to three key rhythms:

RHYTHM 1: STRATEGIC RHYTHM. Sync your strategy meetings with your company's goal-setting cycles and anchor them to a single source of truth.

RHYTHM 2: TACTICAL RHYTHM. Align your tactical meetings with key project milestones: premortems, midpoint check-ins, and postmortems.

RHYTHM 3: OPERATIONAL RHYTHM. Match operational meetings like daily huddles to the rhythm of your day-to-day work. Protect deep work with strategic meeting pauses: no-meeting days, blocks, and buffers.

Principle 7
Technology: Innovate and Iterate

Treat your meetings like a product in beta that needs constant upgrading and refining. Stick to these rules:

RULE 1: GET YOUR MVP RIGHT. Prioritize clear audio and video quality before piling on extra features.

RULE 2: EMBRACE CALM TECHNOLOGY. When adding new technology to your meetings, follow two calm principles. First, it should require minimal effort to use. Second, it should amplify the best of both humans and technology.

RULE 3: RELENTLESSLY PROTOTYPE WITH ARTIFICIAL INTELLIGENCE. Use AI to handle the grunt work, surface real-time insights, and (sometimes) attend meetings for you. But never run a meeting on AI autopilot.

You have the blueprint. Now go design your best meeting ever.

CONCLUSION

Design Your Meetings Like a Product or Pay the Price

In a 2013 TED Talk, Paola Antonelli, senior curator at the Museum of Modern Art, said, "Design is . . . everything that is around us in our life."[1]

We celebrate great design in architecture, apps, and everyday consumer products—things that have been intentionally designed to function well and make life easier. But when was the last time you or anyone else raved about the design of a meeting?

Antonelli went further, explaining, "People think that design is styling. Design is not style. It's not about giving shape to the shell and not giving a damn about the guts."

Yet that's how most meetings work. They're all shell: a calendar invite, maybe a vague agenda. The guts of the meeting—the structure, the purpose, the outcomes, the parts that really matter—get neglected. Does the meeting drive decisions? Solve real problems? Create momentum? Get things done? Too often, the answer is no.

Right now, most meetings feel like a tax on our time. But what if they gave you time back by creating clarity, alignment, and momentum for real work? What if meetings didn't get in the way of great work, but made it possible?

That's the opportunity in front of you. Meetings are your most powerful product for driving success—for your team, your organization, and yourself. But like any great product, they require deliberate design, constant iteration, and the guts to rethink everything.

So be bold. Experiment. Ditch what doesn't work. Fix what's broken. Treat every meeting like a product in beta. Prototype, test, refine, repeat until it earns its spot on the calendar.

That's how you'll design your best meeting ever. And just like any great product, you won't realize how broken the old version was until you experience the upgrade. And once you do, you won't want to settle for the old way ever again.

ACKNOWLEDGMENTS

This book exists thanks to some wildly smart and kind people, far too many deeply dysfunctional meetings—and that special kind of nausea that sets in when both are trapped in the same room.

To Bob Sutton, your fingerprints are all over this book. You've been a coconspirator in the fight against broken meetings from day one. Getting to play a small part in your wonderful books over the years gave me the tools and the guts I needed to write this one.

I'm grateful to the many people who joined me on some wild and wonderful adventures to fix broken meetings. Steven Rogelberg, your work has been a north star, proving that science can make meetings suck less. Rob Cross, Michael Arena, and Greg Pryor, thank you for showing me that the science of collaboration doesn't have to be dry or abstract. Your work has shaped so much of how I think about teamwork, collaboration, and what it takes to design better meetings.

To my other coauthors and collaborators in the quest for smarter collaboration and better meetings: Steven Li, Brent Reed, Jon Gray, Huggy Rao, Katy DeCelles, Melissa Valentine, Perry Klebahn, Kathryn Velcich, Tim Bowman, Paul Leonardi, and Federico Torreti, thank you for helping me more deeply understand how teams really work, warts, quirks, status games, and all.

Steph Hess and Joshua Zerkel, thank you for giving me the space to chase bold ideas about fixing dysfunctional collaboration. You believed in me and never flinched when my ideas got a little weird—instead, you encouraged me to chase them.

To my teammates at the Work Innovation Lab—Anna James, Mark Hoffman, Cambria Naslund, Andre Na, and Jessica Shi—thank you for showing me what world-class teamwork looks like. You've inspired so much of how I think about meetings and their design. Thank you also to Jake Cerf and Rena Fallstrom for your support and encouragement in the final mile.

I'm deeply grateful to several authors I've long admired who took the time to point me in the right direction. Adam Grant, thank you for your endless kindness and brilliance. Over the years, you opened doors, shared wisdom, and gave this work a platform long before it had a book to live in. Nir Eyal, thank you for your thoughtful advice and steady guidance. I still keep circling back to it.

Thank you to the fabulous team at Simon & Schuster, especially Kimberly Meilun, my brilliant editor. I'm forever grateful that you gave me the perfect mix of creative freedom and just enough structure to bring this book to life.

I'm endlessly grateful to the team at United Talent Agency, especially Sarah Fuentes and Christy Fletcher. Thank you for guiding me through the wild ride of being a first-time author.

Thank you to the countless people who gave me a window into your meeting habits—and let me poke holes and occasionally lob obnoxious questions at your brilliant strategies: Francesca Gentile, Sacha Conner, Ashley Waxman, Elise Keith, Rajiv Pant, Jake Knapp, Jade Bonacolta, Alexander Kjerulf, Shishir Mehrotra and the team at Grammarly, Sid

Sijbrandij and the team at Gitlab, Wade Foster and the team at Zapier, and many others.

This book is much wiser because of the brilliant minds who lent their time and expertise to strengthen the research powering it: Tori Paulman, Amy Edmondson, Anita Williams Woolley, Randall Rollinson, Norbert Schwarz, Justin Berg, Hillary Shulman, Gabrielle Adams, Allen Bluedorn, Sameer Srivastava, Raj Choudhury, David Shim, Neil Vyner, Nick Bloom, Benjamin Laker, Andrew Knight, Laurie Santos, Leidy Klotz, John Eastwood, Kevin Kniffin, Alan Hedge, Soohwan Lee, Neil MacLaren, Lodewijk Gelauff, Hancheng Cao, Craig Knight, Michael Impink, Jen Rhymer, Jonathan Levav, Daniel McAllister, Tsedal Neeley, Pam Hinds, Amber Case, Carrie Goucher, Marily Oppezzo, Daniel Schwartz, and many others.

To my parents, family, and Carlos, thank you for tolerating the endless dinner-table dissections of broken meetings and the "final" manuscript read that somehow birthed twenty more. You endured the secondhand dysfunction that came with writing this book—but never stopped cheering me on.

And to you, dear reader, I wrote this book for you. Anyone can become a great meeting designer, and now it's your turn. Keep pushing for better meetings. Go design your best one ever. You've earned it.

NOTES

INTRODUCTION HOW MEETINGS TURNED INTO WEAPONS OF MASS DYSFUNCTION

1. *Simple Sabotage Field Manual—Strategic Services Field Manual No. 3* (Washington, DC: Office of Strategic Services, 1944), https://www.cia.gov /static/5c875f3ec660e092cf893f60b4a288df/SimpleSabotage.pdf
2. *Simple Sabotage Field Manual.*
3. Randall Rollinson, "Strategic Management After World War II," LBL Strategies, February 19, 2024, https://www.lblstrategies.com/strategic-manage ment-after-world-war-ii/
4. Neil Fligstein, *The Transformation of Corporate Control* (Cambridge, MA: Harvard University Press, 1990).
5. Leslie A. Perlow, Constance Noonan Hadley, and Eunice Eun, "Stop the Meeting Madness," *Harvard Business Review*, July/August 2017, https:// hbr.org/2017/07/stop-the-meeting-madness
6. Steven G. Rogelberg, Cliff Scott, and John Kello, "The Science and Fiction of Meetings," *MIT Sloan Management Review*, January 1, 2007, https:// sloanreview.mit.edu/article/the-science-and-fiction-of-meetings/
7. Elise Keith, "How Many Meetings Are There per Day in 2022? (And Should You Care?)," Lucid Meetings, https://blog.lucidmeetings.com/blog/how -many-meetings-are-there-per-day-in-2022/
8. Elise Keith, "55 Million: A Fresh Look at the Number, Effectiveness, and Cost of Meetings in the U.S.," Lucid Meetings, updated September 3, 2022, https://blog.lucidmeetings.com/blog/fresh-look-number-effectiveness -cost-meetings-in-us/

9. Jen Howard, "Clarizen Survey: Workers Consider Status Meetings a Productivity-Killing Waste of Time," Clarizen press release, April 19, 2019, https://web.archive.org/web/20190419222945/https://www.clarizen.com/press-release/clarizen-survey-workers-consider-status-meetings-a-productivity-killing-waste-of-time/

10. Evan DeFilippis et al., "The Impact of COVID-19 on Digital Communication Patterns," *Humanities and Social Sciences Communications* 9 (2022): 180, https://www.nature.com/articles/s41599-022-01190-9

11. Rebecca Hinds, "The Rise of Unproductive Meetings—and the Hangovers They Leave," Asana, April 8, 2025, https://asana.com/inside-asana/unproductive-meetings

12. Rebecca Hinds and Bob Sutton, "Dropbox's Secret for Saving Time in Meetings," *Inc.*, May 11, 2015, https://www.inc.com/rebecca-hinds-and-bob-sutton/dropbox-secret-for-saving-time-in-meetings.html

13. Rebecca Hinds, "Meetings Are Broken: It's Time for a Meeting Doomsday," *Inc.*, April 26, 2022, https://www.inc.com/rebecca-hinds/meetings-are-broken-its-time-for-a-meeting-doomsday.html

14. Steven G. Rogelberg et al., "Employee Satisfaction with Meetings: A Contemporary Facet of Job Satisfaction," *Human Resource Management* 49, no. 2 (2010): 149–72, https://doi.org/10.1002/hrm.20339

15. Roy F. Baumeister et al., "Bad Is Stronger Than Good," *Review of General Psychology* 5, no. 4 (2001): 323–70, https://assets.csom.umn.edu/assets/71516.pdf

16. Robert I. Sutton, "Bad Is Stronger Than Good: Why Good Bosses Eliminate the Negative First," *Fast Company,* September 13, 2010, https://www.fastcompany.com/1688622/bad-stronger-good-why-good-bosses-eliminate-negative-first

PRINCIPLE 1 MEETING VOLUME: CUT YOUR MEETING DEBT

1. Rebecca Hinds and Bob Sutton, "Dropbox's Secret for Saving Time in Meetings," *Inc.*, May 11, 2015, https://www.inc.com/rebecca-hinds-and-bob-sutton/dropbox-secret-for-saving-time-in-meetings.html

2. Oliver Pickup, "How to Create a 25% Productivity Hike: Lessons from Shopify's Meetings Purge," *WorkLife*, March 29, 2023, https://www.worklife.news/culture/how-to-create-a-25-productivity-hike-lessons-from-shopifys-meetings-purge/

3. Sarah Jackson, "Why Shopify's CEO Uses 'God Mode' to Delete Meetings from His Employees' Calendars and Stakes His Company Culture on What He Calls a 'Trust Battery,'" *Business Insider*, December 23, 2021, https://

www.businessinsider.com/shopify-ceo-tobi-lutke-god-mode-nix-staff
-meetings-bloomberg-2021-12

4. Brian Elliott, Sheela Subramanian, and Helen Kupp, "Declare 'Calendar Bankruptcy' to Move Beyond Meeting-Driven Culture," *MIT Sloan Management Review*, May 25, 2022, https://sloanreview.mit.edu/article/declare-calendar-bankruptcy-to-move-beyond-meeting-driven-culture/

5. Elliott, Subramanian, and Kupp, "Declare 'Calendar Bankruptcy.'"

6. Rebecca Hinds and Robert I. Sutton, "Meeting Overload Is a Fixable Problem," *Harvard Business Review*, October 28, 2022, https://hbr.org/2022/10/meeting-overload-is-a-fixable-problem

7. Hinds and Sutton, "Meeting Overload Is a Fixable Problem."

8. Daniel Kahneman, *Thinking, Fast and Slow* (New York: Macmillan, 2011).

9. Rebecca Hinds, "Meetings Are Broken: It's Time for a Meeting Doomsday," *Inc.*, April 26, 2022, https://www.inc.com/rebecca-hinds/meetings-are-broken-its-time-for-a-meeting-doomsday.html

10. Rebecca Hinds, Joshua Zerkel, and Bob Sutton, "Fixing Meetings: A Research-Backed Playbook," Asana, https://asana.com/resources/fixing-meetings-playbook

11. Michael I. Norton, Daniel Mochon, and Dan Ariely, "The IKEA Effect: When Labor Leads to Love," *Journal of Consumer Psychology* 22, no. 3 (July 2012): 453–60, https://myscp.onlinelibrary.wiley.com/doi/10.1016/j.jcps.2011.08.002

12. Wayne Baker, "The More You Energize Your Coworkers, the Better Everyone Performs," *Harvard Business Review*, September 15, 2016, https://hbr.org/2016/09/the-energy-you-give-off-at-work-matters

13. Dropbox Team, "Virtual First Toolkit: How to Communicate Effectively," Work in Progress (*blog*), October 13, 2020, https://blog.dropbox.com/topics/work-culture/-virtual-first-toolkit--how-to-communicate-effectively

14. "How to Embrace Asynchronous Communication for Remote Work," *GitLab Handbook*, https://handbook.gitlab.com/handbook/company/culture/all-remote/asynchronous/

15. Robert B. Cialdini, *Influence, New and Expanded: The Psychology of Persuasion* (New York: HarperCollins, 2021).

16. The Cost of Unnecessary Meeting Attendance, Otter.ai, https://public.otter.ai/reports/The_Cost_of_Unnecessary_Meeting_Attendance.pdf

17. Tijs Besieux and Amy C. Edmondson, "How to Improve a Meeting (When You're Not in Charge)," *Harvard Business Review*, March 26, 2024, https://hbr.org/2024/03/how-to-improve-a-meeting-when-youre-not-in-charge

18. The Cost of Unnecessary Meeting Attendance, *Otter.ai*.

19. The Cost of Unnecessary Meeting Attendance, *Otter.ai*.
20. Andy Jassy, "Message from CEO Andy Jassy: Strengthening Our Culture and Teams," *Amazon News*, September 16, 2024, https://www.about amazon.com/news/company-news/ceo-andy-jassy-latest-update-on-amazon -return-to-office-manager-team-ratio
21. Jena McGregor, "This Company Is Canceling All Meetings with More Than Two Employees to Free Up Workers' Time," *Forbes*, January 3, 2023, https:// www.forbes.com/sites/jenamcgregor/2023/01/03/shopify-is-canceling-all -meetings-with-more-than-two-people-from-workers-calendars-and -urging-few-to-be-added-back/
22. Andrea Hsu and Stacey Vanek Smith, "Shopify Deleted 322,000 Hours of Meetings. Should the Rest of Us Be Jealous?," *NPR*, February 15, 2023, https://www.npr.org/2023/02/15/1156804295/shopify-delete-meetings -zoom-virtual-productivity
23. Shannon Shaper, "How Many Interviews Does It Take to Hire a Googler?," *Re:Work* (blog), April 4, 2017, https://web.archive.org/web/20180615111319 /https://rework.withgoogle.com/blog/google-rule-of-four/
24. Shaper, "How Many Interviews Does It Take to Hire a Googler?"
25. Robert I. Sutton and Huggy Rao, "Rid Your Organization of Obstacles That Infuriate Everyone," *Harvard Business Review*, January-February 2024, https://hbr.org/2024/01/rid-your-organization-of-obstacles-that-infuriate -everyone
26. Shaper, "How Many Interviews Does It Take to Hire a Googler?"
27. Josh Braun, "Let's Talk About My Three-Strike Rule in Sales," *LinkedIn*, https://www.linkedin.com/posts/josh-braun_lets-talk-about-my-three -strike-rule-in-activity-7074809587954003969-Syy3
28. Bob Sutton and Huggy Rao, "Make Productivity Easy with These Friction-Busting Mindsets," *Next Big Idea Club*, February 12, 2024, https:// nextbigideaclub.com/magazine/make-productivity-easy-friction-busting -mindsets-bookbite/47951/
29. Erik Samdahl, "Top Employers Are 5.5x More Likely to Reward Collaboration," *Institute for Corporate Productivity blog*, June 22, 2017, https://www .i4cp.com/productivity-blog/top-employers-are-5-5x-more-likely-to -reward-collaboration
30. Stav Ziv, "Shopify Wants You to Be Relentless About Canceling Unnecessary Meetings," *Fast Company, March 19, 2024*, https://www.fastcompany .com/91036624/shopify-most-innovative-companies-2024
31. Hsu and Smith, "Shopify Deleted 322,000 Hours of Meetings."

PRINCIPLE 2 MEASUREMENT: CHOOSE THE RIGHT METRICS

1. Mia Gindis and Matthew Boyle, "Shopify Shames Employees with Cost Calculator for Pointless Meetings," *Bloomberg*, July 12, 2023, https://www.bloomberg.com/news/articles/2023-07-12/shopify-shames-workers-with-a-1-600-price-tag-for-pointless-meetings

2. Cheryl Teh, "There's an Obvious Problem with Shopify's Gimmicky Calculator That Claims to Calculate the True Cost of Meetings," *Business Insider*, July 13, 2023, https://www.businessinsider.com/shopify-gimmicky-calculator-true-cost-meetings-cool-wont-work-2023-7

3. "New Coke: The Most Memorable Marketing Blunder Ever?" Coca-Cola Company, https://www.coca-colacompany.com/about-us/history/new-coke-the-most-memorable-marketing-blunder-ever

4. "New Coke: The Most Memorable Marketing Blunder Ever?" Coca-Cola Company.

5. A. Willem M. Koetsenruijter, "Using Numbers in News Increases Story Credibility," *Newspaper Research Journal* 32, no. 2 (2011): 74–82, https://doi.org/10.1177/073953291103200207

6. Peter High, "Half of All Meetings Are a Waste of Time—Here's How to Improve Them," *Forbes*, November 25, 2019, https://www.forbes.com/sites/peterhigh/2019/11/25/half-of-all-meetings-are-a-waste-of-timeheres-how-to-improve-them/

7. Jane Thier, "Meetings Are a Productivity Killer—And 3 in Every 4 Are Totally Ineffective, According to a New Wide-Ranging Study," *Fortune*, March 21, 2024, https://fortune.com/2024/03/21/meetings-productivity-ineffective-atlassian-report/

8. Steven G. Rogelberg, Cliff Scott, and John Kello, "The Science and Fiction of Meetings," *MIT Sloan Management Review*, January 1, 2007, https://sloanreview.mit.edu/article/the-science-and-fiction-of-meetings/

9. Roy F. Baumeister et al., "Bad Is Stronger Than Good," *Review of General Psychology* 5, no. 4 (2001): 323–70, https://assets.csom.umn.edu/assets/71516.pdf

10. Adam Grant, "I Hate Meetings," *LinkedIn*, https://www.linkedin.com/posts/adammgrant_i-hate-meetings-for-season-6-of-worklife-activity-7064213294407938049-iJvC/

11. Elise Keith, "Adam Grant vs. Mary Poppins: Framing Meetings," *New Rules for Work Labs*, October 20, 2023, https://labs.newrulesforwork.com/p/adam-grant-vs-mary-poppins-framing-meetings

12. Elizabeth A. Krusemark, W. Keith Campbell, and Brett A. Clementz, "Attributions, Deception, and Event-Related Potentials: An Investigation of the

Self-Serving Bias," *Psychophysiology* 45, no. 4 (2008): 511–15, https://doi
.org/10.1111/j.1469-8986.2008.00659.x

13. Tom Goodwin, "These Days It's Harder to Expense a Twix," *LinkedIn*,
https://www.linkedin.com/posts/tomfgoodwin_these-days-its-harder-to
-expense-a-twix-activity-6985331291172839424-YZJt/

14. Michael Mankins, Chris Brahm, and Gregory Caimi, "Your Scarcest Resource," *Harvard Business Review* 92, no. 5 (May 2014): 74–80, 133, https://
hbr.org/2014/05/your-scarcest-resource

15. Warren E. Buffett, Letter to Shareholders of Berkshire Hathaway Inc.,
Berkshire Hathaway, February 27, 2009, https://www.berkshirehathaway
.com/letters/2008ltr.pdf

16. Michael Howard Saul, "Mayor Wants Meetings on the Clock—Literally,"
Wall Street Journal, updated January 26, 2011, https://www.wsj.com
/articles/SB10001424052748704698004576104420112230608

17. Saul, "Mayor Wants Meetings on the Clock—Literally."

18. Belinda Lanks, "Google Ventures' Secret to Productive Meetings: A Timer,"
Bloomberg, June 25, 2014, https://www.bloomberg.com/news/articles
/2014-06-25/how-to-run-a-productive-meeting-the-google-ventures-secret

19. Jake Knapp, "The Time Timer: A Simple Tool for Instantly Better Meetings,"
GV Library, July 14, 2014, https://library.gv.com/the-time-timer-google
-ventures-secret-weapon-for-instantly-better-meetings-53c94faf426b

20. Daniel Kahneman and Amos Tversky, "Prospect Theory: An Analysis of
Decision under Risk," *Econometrica* 47, no. 2 (1979): 263–91, https://www
.jstor.org/stable/1914185

21. Paul M. Leonardi, "COVID-19 and the New Technologies of Organizing:
Digital Exhaust, Digital Footprints, and Artificial Intelligence in the Wake
of Remote Work," *Journal of Management Studies* 58, no. 1 (2021): 249–53,
https://doi.org/10.1111/joms.12648

22. "A Conversation with NVIDIA's Jensen Huang," posted May 21, 2024, by
Stripe, YouTube, 1 hr., 4 min., 49 sec., https://www.youtube.com/watch?v
=8Pfa8kPjUio

23. "12 Meeting Metrics for Efficient & Effective Collaboration," *Worklytics
blog*, April 1, 2024, https://www.worklytics.co/blog/top-12-metrics-for
-effective-meetings

24. Vivek Wadhwa and Alex Salkever, "Could Company 'Productivity Pol-
icies' That Regulate Your Email and Meetings Make You Happier at
Work?" *LinkedIn*, June 29, 2018, https://www.linkedin.com/pulse/could
-company-productivity-policies-regulate-your-email-vivek-wadhwa/

25. Leigh Thompson, "How to Neutralize a Meeting Tyrant," *Fortune*, February 11, 2013, https://fortune.com/2013/02/11/how-to-neutralize-a
-meeting-tyrant/

26. Neil G. MacLaren et al., "Testing the Babble Hypothesis: Speaking Time Predicts Leader Emergence in Small Groups," *Leadership Quarterly* 31, no. 5 (2020): 101409, https://doi.org/10.1016/j.leaqua.2020.101409

27. Anita Williams Woolley et al., "Evidence for a Collective Intelligence Factor in the Performance of Human Groups," *Science* 330, no. 6004 (2010): 686–88, https://doi.org/10.1126/science.1193147

28. Jose Maria Barrero et al., "SWAA October 2023 Updates," *WFH Research website,* October 9, 2023, https://wfhresearch.com/wp-content/uploads/2023/10/WFHResearch_updates_October2023.pdf

29. Kevin P. Madore and Anthony D. Wagner, "Multicosts of Multitasking," *Cerebrum,* April 1, 2019, https://www.ncbi.nlm.nih.gov/pmc/articles/PMC7075496/

30. Steven G. Rogelberg et al., "Lateness to Meetings: Examination of an Unexplored Temporal Phenomenon," *European Journal of Work and Organizational Psychology* 23, no. 3 (2014): 323–41, https://doi.org/10.1080/1359432X.2012.745988

31. Rob Cross et al., "How to Fix Collaboration Overload," *Harvard Business Review, December 9, 2022,* https://hbr.org/2022/12/how-to-fix-collaboration-overload

32. Cross et al., "How to Fix Collaboration Overload."

33. "This Man's Meeting Calculator Adds Up the True Cost of Doing Business," *CBC News,* April 4, 2019, https://www.cbc.ca/news/canada/ottawa/online-calculator-meetings-civil-service-1.5082680

34. "This Man's Meeting Calculator Adds Up the True Cost of Doing Business," *CBC News.*

35. Sean Boots (@sboots), "Ever wonder how much your public sector meetings cost? Shame your enemies. Impress your friends!," *X,* April 13, 2017, https://x.com/sboots/status/852559310014042112

36. Rebecca Hinds et al., *2024 State of Work Innovation Report,* Asana, https://assets.asana.biz/m/7247625de89a76e6/original/State-of-Work-Innovation-2024_Global.pdf

37. William Bruce Cameron, *Informal Sociology: A Casual Introduction to Sociological Thinking* (New York: Random House, 1963).

38. "Team Meeting Rituals & Best Practices—Block Party 2021," posted by Coda, YouTube, 49 min., 9 sec., October 13, 2021, https://www.youtube.com/watch?v=mopICs6CLOM

PRINCIPLE 3 STRUCTURE: BECOME A MEETING MINIMALIST

1. Robert I. Sutton and Huggy Rao, "Organization of Obstacles That Infuriate Everyone," *Harvard Business Review*, January-February 2024, https://

hbr.org/2024/01/rid-your-organization-of-obstacles-that-infuriate
-everyone

2. Leidy Klotz, *Subtract: The Untapped Science of Less* (New York: Flatiron Books, 2021).

3. Rebecca Hinds and Robert I. Sutton, "Meeting Overload Is a Fixable Problem," *Harvard Business Review,* October 28, 2022, https://hbr.org/2022/10 /meeting-overload-is-a-fixable-problem

4. Leidy Klotz and Robert Sutton, "Our To-Do Lists Can't Grow Forever. It's Time to Try Subtraction," *Times Higher Education,* March 24, 2022, https:// www.timeshighereducation.com/blog/our-do-lists-cant-grow-forever-its -time-try-subtraction

5. Steven G. Rogelberg, *The Surprising Science of Meetings: How You Can Lead Your Team to Peak Performance* (New York: Oxford University Press, 2019).

6. C. Northcote Parkinson, *Parkinson's Law* (London: Murray, 1957).

7. Parkinson, *Parkinson's Law.*

8. Dan Pilat and Sekoul Krastev, "Why Do We Focus on Trivial Things," *Decision Lab,* https://thedecisionlab.com/biases/bikeshedding

9. Oren Kaniel, "'Parking Lot' for Effective Meetings," *LinkedIn,* https://www .linkedin.com/posts/orenkaniel_collectivemind-meetingguidelines -productivity-activity-7209504105889771520-csmE

10. Jeff Roth, "Keeping Your Meetings on Track with the 'Parking Lot' Technique," *Idealistic Future* (blog), June 2, 2024, https://idealisticfuture.com/f /keeping-your-meetings-on-track-with-the-parking-lot-technique

11. C. Northcote Parkinson, "Parkinson's Law," *Economist,* November 19, 1955, https://www.economist.com/news/1955/11/19/parkinsons-law

12. Meetingnotes Team, "How to Choose the Right Meeting Cadence for Your Team," MeetingNotes.com blog, April 11, 2024, https://meetingnotes.com /blog/meeting-cadence

13. Claire Cain Miller, "Google's Chief Works to Trim a Bloated Ship," *New York Times,* November 9, 2011, https://www.nytimes.com/2011/11/10 /technology/googles-chief-works-to-trim-a-bloated-ship.html

14. Rajiv Pant, "The Evolution of the 50/25 Meeting Format: Why Starting Late Is the New On-Time," *Rajiv.com* (blog), September 17, 2023, https://rajiv .com/blog/2023/09/17/the-evolution-of-the-50-25-meeting-format-why -starting-late-is-the-new-on-time/

15. Juan Perez, "The Curse of the Ineffective Meeting," *LinkedIn Pulse,* https:// www.linkedin.com/pulse/curse-ineffective-meeting-j-perez/

16. Allen C. Bluedorn, Daniel B. Turban, and Mary Sue Love, "The Effects of Stand-Up and Sit-Down Meeting Formats on Meeting Outcomes," *Journal of Applied Psychology* 84, no. 2 (1999): 277–85, https://doi.org/10.1037 /0021-9010.84.2.277

17. My Say, "Kick the Chair: How Standing Cut Our Meeting Times by 25%," *Forbes*, June 19, 2014, https://www.forbes.com/sites/groupthink/2014/06/19/kick-the-chair-how-standing-cut-our-meeting-times-by-25/

18. Stephanie Vozza, "How 12 Companies Make Meetings Memorable, Effective, and Short," *Fast Company*, June 19, 2015, https://www.fastcompany.com/3048815/how-12-companies-make-meetings-memorable-effective-and-short/

19. Andrew P. Knight and Markus Baer, "Get Up, Stand Up: The Effects of a Non-Sedentary Workspace on Information Elaboration and Group Performance," *Social Psychological and Personality Science* 5, no. 8 (2014): 910–17, https://doi.org/10.1177/1948550614538463

20. Shereen Lehman, "Standing Meetings May Improve Group Productivity," *Reuters*, June 20, 2014, https://www.reuters.com/article/business/healthcare-pharmaceuticals/standing-meetings-may-improve-group-productivity-idUSKBN0EV29U/

21. Laurie Santos, "What's on Your 'Time Confetti' Wish List?" *LinkedIn*, https://www.linkedin.com/posts/laurie-santos_whats-on-your-time-confetti-wish-list-activity-7256983766416375809-lRCK/

22. Santos, "What's on Your 'Time Confetti' Wish List?"

23. Tim Kasser and Kennon M. Sheldon, "Time Affluence as a Path Toward Personal Happiness and Ethical Business Practice: Empirical Evidence from Four Studies," *Journal of Business Ethics* 84, no. S2 (2009): 243–55, https://link.springer.com/article/10.1007/s10551-008-9696-1

24. Alex Diaz, "Better Notes, Better Meetings," *Medium*, February 19, 2017, https://medium.com/@alexdiazproduct/better-notes-better-meetings-6063ddd354fc

25. "Two-Pizza Teams: From Ops to DevOps," in *Public Sector Cloud Transformation: An AWS How-To Guide*, Amazon Web Services, August 31, 2021, https://docs.aws.amazon.com/whitepapers/latest/public-sector-cloud-transformation/two-pizza-teams-from-ops-to-devops.html.

26. Walter Isaacson, Steve Jobs (New York: Simon & Schuster, 2011).

27. Hancheng Cao et al., "Large Scale Analysis of Multitasking Behavior During Remote Meetings," *Proceedings of the 2021 CHI Conference on Human Factors in Computing Systems* (CHI '21), article no. 448, May 7, 2021, https://www.microsoft.com/en-us/research/publication/large-scale-analysis-of-multitasking-behavior-during-remote-meetings/

28. *The Cost of Unnecessary Meeting Attendance*, Otter.ai, https://public.otter.ai/reports/The_Cost_of_Unnecessary_Meeting_Attendance.pdf.

29. Michael C. Mankins and Jenny Davis-Peccoud, *Decision Insights: Decision-Focused Meetings*, Bain & Company, June 7, 2011, https://media.bain.com

/Images/2011-6-7%20Decision%20Insights%209-Decision-focused%20
meetings.pdf

30. Rebecca Hinds and Bob Sutton, "Dropbox's Secret for Saving Time in
Meetings," *Inc.*, May 11, 2015, https://www.inc.com/rebecca-hinds-and
-bob-sutton/dropbox-secret-for-saving-time-in-meetings.html

31. Mankins and Davis-Peccoud, *Decision Insights: Decision-Focused Meetings.*

32. Ken Segall, *Insanely Simple: The Obsession That Drives Apple's Success* (New
York: Portfolio, 2012).

33. Catherine Clifford, "Elon Musk's 6 Productivity Rules, Including Walk Out
of Meetings That Waste Your Time," CNBC, April 18, 2018, https://www
.cnbc.com/2018/04/18/elon-musks-productivity-rules-according-to-tesla
-email.html

34. Jonathan Opp, "Darwin Meets Dilbert: Applying the Law of Two Feet
to Your Next Meeting," Opensource.com, August 30, 2010, https://open
source.com/business/10/8/darwin-meets-dilbert-applying-law-two-feet
-your-next-meeting

35. Hinds and Sutton, "Meeting Overload Is a Fixable Problem."

36. Jessica Stillman, "Warren Buffett's Unusual Approach to Scheduling Meetings," *Inc.*, June 1, 2016, https://www.inc.com/jessica-stillman/warren
-buffett-s-unusual-approach-to-scheduling-meetings.html

37. Zeb Evans, "Don't Cancel Meetings to Be Productive, Cancel One-on-
Ones," *Fast Company*, July 11, 2024, https://www.fastcompany.com/911
53338/dont-cancel-meetings-to-be-productive-cancel-one-on-ones

38. Mankins and Davis-Peccoud, *Decision Insights: Decision-Focused Meetings.*

39. Mankins and Davis-Peccoud, *Decision Insights: Decision-Focused Meetings.*

40. Jeff Bezos, "2016 Letter to Shareholders," *Amazon News*, April 17, 2017,
https://www.aboutamazon.com/news/company-news/2016-letter-to
-shareholders

41. Shishir Mehrotra, "Rituals for Hypergrowth: An Inside Look at How You-
Tube Scaled," *Coda*, https://coda.io/@shishir/rituals-for-hypergrowth-an
-inside-look-at-how-youtube-scaled/bullpen-21

42. Mehrotra, "Rituals for Hypergrowth."

43. Shishir Mehrotra, "The Art of the Multi-Threaded Meeting," *Coda*, https://
coda.io/@shishir/the-art-of-the-multi-threaded-meeting.

44. Drake Baer, "3 Ways Steve Jobs Made Meetings Productive," *World Economic Forum*, December 18, 2014, https://www.weforum.org/stories/2014
/12/3-ways-steve-jobs-made-meetings-productive/.

45. Ken Segall, *Insanely Simple: The Obsession That Drives Apple's Success* (New
York: Portfolio, 2012).

PRINCIPLE 4 FLOW: APPLY SYSTEMS THINKING

1. Alex "Sandy" Pentland, "The New Science of Building Great Teams," *Harvard Business Review,* April 2012, https://hbr.org/2012/04/the-new-science-of-building-great-teams
2. Rebecca Hinds et al., "Are Collaboration Tools Overwhelming Your Team?" *Harvard Business Review,* August 31, 2023, https://hbr.org/2023/08/are-collaboration-tools-overwhelming-your-team
3. Chip Heath and Nancy Staudenmayer, "Coordination Neglect: How Lay Theories of Organizing Complicate Coordination in Organizations," *Research in Organizational Behavior* 22 (2000): 153–91, https://doi.org/10.1016/S0191-3085(00)22005-4
4. Rebecca Hinds et al., *2024 State of Work Innovation Report, Asana,* https://assets.asana.biz/m/7247625de89a76e6/original/State-of-Work-Innovation-2024_Global.pdf
5. Devon Maloney, "Knowledge Sharing Is Caring," *Slack,* December 16, 2019, https://slack.com/blog/collaboration/knowledge-sharing-is-caring
6. "Standard Communication Tools," *How HashiCorp Works,* HashiCorp, October 17, 2019, https://works.hashicorp.com/articles/standard-communication-tools
7. "Standard Communication Tools," *How HashiCorp Works.*
8. "How We Use Slack at Sourcegraph," *Sourcegraph Handbook,* updated April 11, 2024, https://github.com/sourcegraph/handbook/blob/main/content/company-info-and-process/communication/team_chat.md
9. Hinds et al., *2024 State of Work Innovation Report.*
10. Hinds et al., "Are Collaboration Tools Overwhelming Your Team?"
11. Hinds et al., "Are Collaboration Tools Overwhelming Your Team?"
12. Hinds et al., *2024 State of Work Innovation Report.*
13. Jeff Bezos, "2016 Letter to Shareholders," *Amazon News,* April 17, 2017, https://www.aboutamazon.com/news/company-news/2016-letter-to-shareholders
14. Tomas Chamorro-Premuzic, Seymour Adler, and Robert B. (Rob) Kaiser, "What Science Says About Identifying High-Potential Employees," *Harvard Business Review,* October 3, 2017, https://hbr.org/2017/10/what-science-says-about-identifying-high-potential-employees
15. "Most Emails Answered in Just Two Minutes, Study Finds," ABC News, April 13, 2015, https://abcnews.go.com/Health/emails-answered-minutes-study-finds/story?id=30280230
16. Gloria Mark, Daniela Gudith, and Ulrich Klocke, "The Cost of Interrupted Work: More Speed and Stress," *Proceedings of the SIGCHI Conference on*

Human Factors in Computing Systems (2008): 107–10, https://ics.uci.edu/~gmark/chi08-mark.pdf

17. Jen Rhymer, "Location-Independent Organizations: Designing Collaboration Across Space and Time," *Administrative Science Quarterly* 68, no. 1 (2023): 1–40, https://doi.org/10.1177/00018392221129175

18. Pete Abilla, "What I Learned from Jeff Bezos About Sales Management," HireVue blog, July 28, 2015, https://web.archive.org/web/20160202025652/http://blog.hirevue.com/sales/what-i-learned-from-jeff-bezos-about-sales-management

19. Justin Bariso, "Why Intelligent Minds Like Jeff Bezos Embrace the Rule of Writing," *Inc.*, August 29, 2021, https://www.inc.com/justin-bariso/how-to-write-amazon-jeff-bezos-memos-meetings-clear-writing-clear-thinking-rule-of-writing.html

20. Erik Larson, "How Jeff Bezos Uses Faster, Better Decisions to Keep Amazon Innovating," *Forbes*, September 24, 2018, https://www.forbes.com/sites/eriklarson/2018/09/24/how-jeff-bezos-uses-faster-better-decisions-to-keep-amazon-innovating/

21. "GitLab Communication," *GitLab Handbook*, https://handbook.gitlab.com/handbook/communication/

22. Rebecca Hinds et al., *An Executive's Guide to High-Value Collaboration*, Asana, https://brand.asana.biz/images/v1684532864/Business/WIL/the-lab-report-High-value-Collaboration_Final_V4/the-lab-report-High-value-Collaboration_Final_V4.pdf?_i=AA

23. Taylor Locke, "Jeff Bezos: This Is the 'Smartest Thing We Ever Did' at Amazon," *CNBC*, October 14, 2019, https://www.cnbc.com/2019/10/14/jeff-bezos-this-is-the-smartest-thing-we-ever-did-at-amazon.html

24. Ruth Umoh, "Why Jeff Bezos Makes Amazon Execs Read 6-Page Memos at the Start of Each Meeting," *CNBC, April 23, 2018,* https://www.cnbc.com/2018/04/23/what-jeff-bezos-learned-from-requiring-6-page-memos-at-amazon.html

25. Hailley Griffis, "The 10 Slack Agreements of Buffer," *BufferBlog*, May 31, 2017, https://buffer.com/resources/slack-agreements/

26. "How We Use Slack at Sourcegraph," *Sourcegraph Handbook*, updated April 11, 2024, https://github.com/sourcegraph/handbook/blob/main/content/company-info-and-process/communication/team_chat.md

27. Rebecca Hinds, Melissa Valentine, Katherine DeCelles, and Justin M. Berg, "Virtually Even: Status Equalizing in Distributed Organizations," *Organization Science* 0, no. 0 (2025), https://doi.org/10.1287/orsc.2021.15846

28. Erin Bradner and Gloria Mark, "Why Distance Matters: Effects on Cooperation, Persuasion, and Deception," *CSCW '02: Proceedings of the 2002*

ACM Conference on Computer Supported Cooperative Work (2002): 226–35, https://doi.org/10.1145/587078.587110

29. "What Companies Are Getting 'Wrong' About Hybrid Work," *Wall Street Journal,* November 17, 2022, https://partners.wsj.com/industrious/reimag ining-the-office/what-companies-are-getting-wrong-about-hybrid-work/

30. Alex Christian, "The Permanently Imperfect Reality of Hybrid Work," *BBC,* December 11, 2023, https://www.bbc.com/worklife/article/2023 1207-the-permanently-imperfect-reality-of-hybrid-work

31. Mortensen, Mark, "Why Hybrid Work Can Become Toxic," *Harvard Business Review,* July 28, 2023, https://hbr.org/2023/07/why-hybrid-work-can -become-toxic

32. Krysten Crawford, "Study Finds Hybrid Work Benefits Companies and Employees," *Stanford Report,* June 2024, https://news.stanford.edu/stories /2024/06/hybrid-work-is-a-win-win-win-for-companies-workers

33. Elise Keith, "Intentionality Trumps Proximity," *New Rules for Work Labs,* October 4, 2023, https://labs.newrulesforwork.com/p/intentionality -trumps-proximity

34. Siran Ma et al., "Social Bots That Bring a Strong Presence to Remote Participants in Hybrid Meetings," *HRI '23: Proceedings of the 2023 ACM/IEEE International Conference on Human-Robot Interaction* (2023): 853–56, https://doi.org/10.1145/3568294.3580200

35. Alice Twu, "Top 5 Companies Setting Up Hybrid Meeting Rooms Right," *Skedda,* January 8, 2024, https://www.skedda.com/blog/top-5-companies -setting-up-hybrid-meeting-rooms-right

36. Leah Marcus, "3 Tips to Run a Successful Hybrid Workshop," *LinkedIn,* https://www.linkedin.com/pulse/3-tips-run-successful-hybrid-workshop -leah-marcus/

37. Pamela Hinds, "Global Teams Should Have Office Visits, Not Offsites," *Harvard Business Review,* March 3, 2016, https://hbr.org/2016/03/global -teams-should-have-office-visits-not-offsites

38. "Lessons Learned: 1,000 Days of Distributed at Atlassian," *Atlassian Work Life, January 2024,* https://www.atlassian.com/blog/distributed-work /distributed-work-report

39. Melanie S. Brucks and Jonathan Levav, "Virtual Communication Curbs Creative Idea Generation," *Nature* 605, no. 7908 (2022): 108–12, https:// doi.org/10.1038/s41586-022-04643-y

40. Tomas Chamorro-Premuzic, "Why Group Brainstorming Is a Waste of Time," *Harvard Business Review,* March 25, 2015, https://hbr.org/2015/03 /why-group-brainstorming-is-a-waste-of-time

41. Leigh Thompson, *Creative Conspiracy: The New Rules of Breakthrough Collaboration* (Boston: Harvard Business Review Press, 2013).

42. Rebecca Greenfield, "Brainstorming Doesn't Work; Try This Technique Instead," *Fast Company*, July 29, 2014, https://www.fastcompany.com /3033567/brainstorming-doesnt-work-try-this-technique-instead

43. Mark Mortensen and Heidi K. Gardner, "WFH Is Corroding Our Trust in Each Other," *Harvard Business Review*, February 10, 2021, https://hbr.org /2021/02/wfh-is-corroding-our-trust-in-each-other

44. Lora Jones, "I Monitor My Staff with Software That Takes Screenshots," *BBC News*, September 29, 2020, https://www.bbc.com/news/business -54289152

45. Aaron Holmes, "Employees at Home Are Being Photographed Every 5 Minutes by an Always-On Video Service to Ensure They're Actually Working—and the Service Is Seeing a Rapid Expansion Since the Coronavirus Outbreak," *Business Insider*, March 23, 2020, https://www .businessinsider.com/work-from-home-sneek-webcam-picture-5-minutes -monitor-video-2020-3

46. Daniel J. McAllister, "Affect- and Cognition-Based Trust as Foundations for Interpersonal Cooperation in Organizations," *Academy of Management Journal* 38, no. 1 (1995): 24–59, https://www.jstor.org/stable/256727

47. Tsedal Neeley, *Remote Work Revolution: Succeeding from Anywhere* (New York: Harper Business, 2021).

48. Paul M. Leonardi and Samantha R. Meyer, "Social Media as Social Lubricant: How Ambient Awareness Eases Knowledge Transfer," *American Behavioral Scientist* 59, no. 1 (2014): 10–34, https://doi.org/10.1177 /0002764214540509

49. "The 37signals Guide to Internal Communication," *Basecamp*, https:// basecamp.com/guides/how-we-communicate/

50. "The 37signals Guide to Internal Communication."

51. Tat Bellamy Walker, "'Virtual Buddies' Can Help Companies On-Board New Hires When Working Remotely," *Business Insider*, April 24, 2020, https://www.businessinsider.com/buffer-how-to-use-virtual-buddies-to -onboard-remote-employees-2020-4

52. Ben Goldman, Abby Sinnott, and Greg Storey, *Remote Work for Design Teams* (InVision, 2020), https://www.scribd.com/document/455747345 /InVision-RemoteWorkforDesignTeams

53. Kevin J. Delaney, "'Remote Work Revolution' by Tsedal Neeley: Getting Remote Work Right," *Charter*, March 26, 2021, https://www.charterworks .com/remote-work-revolution-by-tsedal-neeley/

54. Pamela J. Hinds and Catherine Durnell Cramton, "Situated Coworker Familiarity: How Site Visits Transform Relationships Among Distributed Workers," *Organization Science* 25, no. 3 (2014): 794–814, https://doi.org /10.1287/orsc.2013.0869

55. Victoria Sevcenko et al., "Office at Offsite: How Temporary Colocation Shapes Communication in an All-Remote Organization," INSEAD Working Paper No. 2024/39/STR/OBH, May 1, 2024, https://sites.insead.edu /facultyresearch/research/doc.cfm?did=72300

56. John Hunter, "A Bad System Will Beat a Good Person Every Time," *W. Edwards Deming Institute,* February 26, 2015, https://deming.org/a-bad -system-will-beat-a-good-person-every-time/

PRINCIPLE 5 ENGAGEMENT: PRIORITIZE USER-CENTRIC DESIGN

1. Jay Yarow, "What It's Like When Steve Jobs Chews You Out for a Product Failure," *Business Insider,* May 7, 2011, https://www.businessinsider.com /steve-jobs-mobileme-failure-2011-5

2. Steven G. Rogelberg, *The Surprising Science of Meetings: How You Can Lead Your Team to Peak Performance* (New York: Oxford University Press, 2019).

3. Rebecca Hinds et al., *2024 State of Work Innovation Report, Asana,* https:// assets.asana.biz/m/7247625de89a76e6/original/State-of-Work-Innovation -2024_Global.pdf

4. "Ford Posts $12.7B Loss in 2006, Worst Ever," *CBS News,* January 25, 2007, https://www.cbsnews.com/news/ford-posts-127b-loss-in-2006-worst -ever/

5. Keith Naughton, "Ford's New CEO Fields Faces Challenges at Company on Roll," *Bloomberg,* May 2, 2014, https://www.bloomberg.com/news/articles /2014-05-02/ford-s-new-ceo-fields-faces-challenges-at-company-on-roll

6. Sarah Miller Caldicott, "Why Ford's Alan Mulally Is an Innovation CEO for the Record Books," *Forbes,* June 25, 2014, https://www.forbes.com/ sites/sarahcaldicott/2014/06/25/why-fords-alan-mulally-is-an-innovation -ceo-for-the-record-books/

7. Scott Eblin, "Five Things Alan Mulally Is Doing to Help Ford Win," *Government Executive,* September 2, 2009, https://www.govexec.com /management/2009/09/five-things-alan-mulally-is-doing-to-help-ford -win/39277/

8. Tom Relihan, "Fixing a Toxic Work Culture: Breaking Down Barriers," *Ideas Made to Matter,* MIT Sloan School of Management, May 29, 2019, https://mitsloan.mit.edu/ideas-made-to-matter/fixing-a-toxic-work -culture-breaking-down-barriers

9. Jade Rubick, "Everyone Lies to Leaders," *Jade Rubick* (blog), June 1, 2021, https://www.rubick.com/everyone-lies-to-leaders/

10. Adam Galinsky, *Inspire: The Universal Path for Leading Yourself and Others* (New York: Harper Business, 2025).

11. Xiaoran Hu et al., "Faking It with the Boss's Jokes? Leader Humor Quantity, Follower Surface Acting, and Power Distance," *Academy of Management Journal* 67, no. 5 (2024): 1175–1206, https://doi.org/10.5465/amj.2022.0195

12. Henry Stewart, *Creating Joy at Work: 501+ Ideas for Creating a Happy, Productive Workplace* (London: Happy Ltd, 2024).

13. Brad Stone, *The Everything Store: Jeff Bezos and the Age of Amazon* (New York: Little, Brown, 2013).

14. Anita Williams Woolley et al., "Evidence for a Collective Intelligence Factor in the Performance of Human Groups," *Science* 330, no. 6004 (2010): 686–88, https://doi.org/10.1126/science.1193147

15. David Maxfield, "What to Do When Coworkers Monopolize Your Meetings," *Crucial Skills* (blog), Crucial Learning, September 5, 2017, https://cruciallearning.com/blog/what-to-do-when-coworkers-monopolize-your-meetings/

16. Joshua Rothman, "Big Data Comes to the Office," *New Yorker*, June 3, 2014, https://www.newyorker.com/books/joshua-rothman/big-data-comes-to-the-office

17. "How the World's Most Creative Teams Consistently Produce 'Magic'—Ed Catmull (Pixar Founder)," posted by 97th Floor, YouTube, 5 min., 37 sec., April 27, 2022, https://www.youtube.com/watch?v=wiIoySsG66U

18. "Spark Creativity with These Tips from Pixar's President," *First Round Review*, https://review.firstround.com/spark-creativity-with-these-tips-from-pixars-president/

19. Ed Catmull, *Creativity, Inc.: Overcoming the Unseen Forces That Stand in the Way of True Inspiration* (New York: Random House, 2014).

20. Justin M. Berg, "Balancing on the Creative Highwire: Forecasting the Success of Novel Ideas in Organizations," *Administrative Science Quarterly* 61, no. 3 (2016): 433–68, https://doi.org/10.1177/0001839216642211

21. Shishir Mehrotra, "Supercharging Decision Making: 14 Ways to Dory/Pulse," *Coda*, https://coda.io/@shishir/dory-pulse

22. Shishir Mehrotra, "Shishir's Guide to Distributed Teams—2. Meetings," *Coda*, https://coda.io/@shishir/guide-to-distributed-teams/2-meetings-3

23. David Kiron and Barbara Spindel, "Redefining Performance Management at DBS Bank," *MIT Sloan Management Review*, March 26, 2019, https://sloanreview.mit.edu/case-study/redefining-performance-management-at-dbs-bank/

24. "How DBS Transformed Its Culture to Become 'The World's Best Bank,'" *Innosight*, https://www.innosight.com/client_impact_story/dbs-bank

25. Scott D. Anthony, Alasdair Trotter, and Evan I. Schwartz, "The Top 20 Business Transformations of the Last Decade," *Harvard Business Re-

view, September 24, 2019, https://hbr.org/2019/09/the-top-20-business -transformations-of-the-last-decade

26. Chris Beier, "MailChimp's CEO Bombed His First-Ever, Big All-Hands Meeting," *Inc.*, December 3, 2018, https://www.inc.com/video/ben -chestnut/mailchimps-ceo-kept-scaring-his-employees-until-he-learned -this.html

27. Laurence J. Peter and Raymond Hull, *The Peter Principle: Why Things Always Go Wrong* (New York: William Morrow and Company, 1969).

28. Benjamin Laker et al., "Dear Manager, You're Holding Too Many Meetings," *Harvard Business Review,* March 9, 2022, https://hbr.org/2022/03 /dear-manager-youre-holding-too-many-meetings

29. Ben Horowitz, "One on One," *Andreessen Horowitz,* August 30, 2012, https://a16z.com/one-on-one/

30. Jim Harter, "In New Workplace, U.S. Employee Engagement Stagnates," *Gallup,* January 5, 2024, https://www.gallup.com/workplace/608675/new -workplace-employee-engagement-stagnates.aspx

31. Tess Bennett, "Atlassian Co-Founders $5B Richer as Cannon-Brookes Answers Doubters," *Australian Financial Review,* November 1, 2024, https:// www.afr.com/technology/atlassian-co-founders-5b-richer-as-cannon -brookes-answers-doubters-20241031-p5kmz0

32. Tracy Francis and Fernanda Hoefel, "'True Gen': Generation Z and Its Implications for Companies," McKinsey & Company, November 12, 2018, https://www.mckinsey.com/industries/consumer-packaged-goods/our -insights/true-gen-generation-z-and-its-implications-for-companies

33. Bennett, "Atlassian Co-Founders $5B Richer."

34. Peter High, "Half of All Meetings Are a Waste of Time—Here's How to Improve Them," *Forbes,* November 25, 2019, https://www.forbes.com/ sites/peterhigh/2019/11/25/half-of-all-meetings-are-a-waste-of-timeheres -how-to-improve-them

35. "USD Professor Simon Croom Pens Fortune Article on Prevalence of Psychopathy in Corporate Leadership," *University of San Diego News Center,* June 10, 2021, https://www.sandiego.edu/news/detail.php?_focus=81705

36. Mary Bardes Mawritz et al., "A Trickle-Down Model of Abusive Supervision," *Personnel Psychology* 65, no. 2 (2012): 325–57, https://doi.org /10.1111/j.1744-6570.2012.01246.x

37. Erik Roth, "The Committed Innovator: A Conversation with DBS's Han Kwee Juan," McKinsey & Company, August 1, 2022, https://www.mckinsey .com/capabilities/strategy-and-corporate-finance/our-insights/the -committed-innovator-a-conversation-with-dbss-han-kwee-juan

38. Jacqueline Whitmore, "Arrive Late to a Big Meeting? How to Recover," *NBC News,* June 24, 2014, https://www.nbcnews.com/id/wbna55496937

39. Joseph A. Allen et al., "The Ubiquity of Meeting Lateness! A Cross-Cultural Investigation of the Small to Moderate Effects of Workplace Meeting Lateness," *Cross-Cultural Research* 55, no. 4 (2021): 351–81, https://doi.org/10.1177/10693971211024193

40. Joseph A. Allen, Nale Lehmann-Willenbrock, and Steven G. Rogelberg, "Let's Get This Meeting Started: Meeting Lateness and Actual Meeting Outcomes," *Journal of Organizational Behavior* 39, no. 8 (2018): 1008–21, https://doi.org/10.1002/job.2276

41. "Communication," *Sourcegraph Handbook,* https://sourcegraph.com/github.com/sourcegraph/handbook@2f4a8affc57038a0bf149f296581cb8cacde57d1/-/blob/content/company-info-and-process/communication/index.md#sources-of-truth

42. David Segonds, "Which Team-Decided Punishments Are You Using for Tardiness to Daily Scrums?" *Stack Overflow,* February 6, 2009, https://stackoverflow.com/questions/518612/which-team-decided-punishments-are-you-using-for-tardiness-to-daily-scrums

43. Melissa Gratias, "What to Do When You're Perpetually Late," *MelissaGratias.com,* https://www.melissagratias.com/what-to-do-when-youre-perpetually-late/

44. Matt Rosoff, "Andreessen Horowitz Charges Employees $10 Per Minute If They're Late to Meetings," *Business Insider,* March 1, 2011, https://www.businessinsider.com/andreessen-horowitz-adds-fourth-partner-2011-3

45. Alexander Kjerulf, "How to Get People to Arrive on Time for Meetings," *Chief Happiness Officer Blog,* August 25, 2006, https://positivesharing.com/2006/08/how-to-get-people-to-arrive-on-time-for-meetings/

46. Emmie Martin, "Warren Buffett Writes His Annual Letter as if He's Talking to His Sisters—Here's Why," *CNBC,* February 25, 2019, https://www.cnbc.com/2019/02/25/why-warren-buffett-writes-his-annual-letter-like-it-is-for-his-sisters.html

47. Zachariah C. Brown, Eric M. Anicich, and Adam D. Galinsky, "Compensatory Conspicuous Communication: Low Status Increases Jargon Use," *Organizational Behavior and Human Decision Processes* 161 (2020): 274–90, https://doi.org/10.1016/j.obhdp.2020.07.001

48. Hillary Shulman et al., "The Effects of Jargon on Processing Fluency, Self-Perceptions, and Scientific Engagement," *Journal of Language and Social Psychology* 39, no. 5–6 (2020): 579–97, https://doi.org/10.1177/0261927X20902177

49. Kevin Lowe, "How American Express Is Redefining B2B with Content Marketing," NewsWhip, April 24, 2018, https://www.newswhip.com/2018/04/american-express-redefining-b2b/

50. Bruna Martinuzzi, "Unveiling the History and Meaning of Jargon," *American Express,* https://www.americanexpress.com/en-us/business/trends-and-insights/articles/the-history-of-jargon/

51. "What's the Best Way to Stay Awake in Meetings?," *BBC News,* July 23, 2019, https://www.bbc.com/news/world-us-canada-49050936

52. Katie Navarra, "Nearly Half of People Are Bored at Work. How Can You Avoid 'Bored-Out' in Your Staff?," *Society for Human Resource Management,* January 8, 2024, https://www.shrm.org/topics-tools/news/employee-relations/prevent-bored-out

53. Kirsten Weir, "Never a Dull Moment," *Monitor on Psychology* 44, no. 7 (July/August 2013): 28–31, https://www.apa.org/monitor/2013/07-08/dull-moment

54. John D. Eastwood et al., "The Unengaged Mind: Defining Boredom in Terms of Attention," *Perspectives on Psychological Science* 7, no. 5 (2012): 482–95, https://doi.org/10.1177/1745691612456044

55. Shishir Mehrotra, "Time for Another Rituals Post," LinkedIn, https://www.linkedin.com/posts/shishirmehrotra_time-for-another-rituals-postthis-time-an-activity-7160436403569401857-kBEH

56. Glenn E. Littlepage and J. R. Poole, "Time Allocation in Decision Making Groups," *Journal of Social Behavior & Personality* 8, no. 4 (1993): 663–72.

57. Eric Schmidt, Jonathan Rosenberg, and Alan Eagle, *Trillion Dollar Coach: The Leadership Playbook from Silicon Valley's Bill Campbell* (New York: HarperBusiness, 2019).

58. Schmidt, Rosenberg, and Eagle, *Trillion Dollar Coach.*

59. Jade Bonacolta, "Wow, Thanks for the Feature, Business Insider!," LinkedIn, https://www.linkedin.com/posts/jadebonacolta_wow-thanks-for-the-feature-business-insider-activity-7301223913332588544-UW4T

60. Matthew Laing, "Use POWER Start for More Purposeful and Effective Meetings," *Ekipa,* July 5, 2023, https://ekipa.co/insights/blogs/use-power-start-for-more-purposeful-and-effective-meetings/

61. Masahiro Toyoda et al., "Potential of a Small Indoor Plant on the Desk for Reducing Office Workers' Stress," *HortTechnology* 30, no. 1 (February 2020): 55–63.

62. Marlon Nieuwenhuis et al., "The Relative Benefits of Green Versus Lean Office Space: Three Field Experiments," *Journal of Experimental Psychology*: 20, no. 3 (2014): 199–214, https://doi.org/10.1037/xap0000024

63. Matt Day, "Take a Look Inside Amazon's Spheres as They Get Set for Next Week's Opening," *Seattle Times,* January 24, 2018, https://www.seattletimes.com/business/amazon/take-a-look-inside-amazons-spheres-as-they-get-set-for-next-weeks-opening/

64. Monica Nickelsburg, "Architect Behind Amazon's Massive 'Biospheres' Says They Aren't for Show," *GeekWire,* October 4, 2016, https://www.geek wire.com/2016/architect-behind-amazons-massive-biospheres-says-arent -show/

65. Glenn Fleishman, "A First Look at the Spheres, Amazon's Wild New Corporate Biodome," *Fast Company,* January 26, 2018, https://www.fastcompany .com/90158235/a-first-look-at-the-spheres-amazons-wild-new-corporate -biodome

66. "Inspiring Innovation with Biophilia," *Amazon News,* November 20, 2017, https://www.aboutamazon.com/news/amazon-offices/inspiring-innovation -with-biophilia

67. "Introducing Lab82, Adobe's Employee Experience Experimentation Engine," *Adobe Blog,* December 20, 2022, https://blog.adobe.com/en/publish /2022/12/20/introducing-lab82-adobes-employee-experience-experimen tation-engine

68. "Inside Adobe's Colorful, Redesigned Headquarters—WSJ Open Office," posted by *The Wall Street Journal,* YouTube, 6 min., 15 sec., January 13, 2020, https://www.youtube.com/watch?v=hgm1i-QXDgs

69. "Inside Adobe's Colorful, Redesigned Headquarters," YouTube.

70. Matthew Boyle, "Work Shift: Inside Adobe's Lab for the Future of Work," *Bloomberg,* December 20, 2022, https://www.bloomberg.com/news/news letters/2022-12-20/how-to-support-hybrid-employees-adobe-on-office -design-onboarding

71. "Inside Adobe's Colorful, Redesigned Headquarters." YouTube.

72. Alan Hedge and Duygu Nou, "Worker Reactions to Electrochromic and Low e Glass Office Windows," *Ergonomics International Journal* 2, no. 4 (2018): 166, https://doi.org/10.23880/eoij-16000166

73. Jeff Weiner, "Where I Work: I'll Take Walking 1:1s Over Office Meetings Any Day," *LinkedIn,* January 29, 2013, https://www.linkedin.com/pulse /20130129033750-22330283-where-i-work-i-ll-take-walking-1-1s-over -office-meetings-any-day/

74. Marily Oppezzo and Daniel L. Schwartz, "Give Your Ideas Some Legs: The Positive Effect of Walking on Creative Thinking," *Journal of Experimental Psychology: Learning, Memory, and Cognition* 40, no. 4 (2014): 1142–52, https://doi.org/10.1037/a0036577

75. Emily Peck, "Why Walking Meetings Can Be Better Than Sitting Meetings," *HuffPost,* April 9, 2015, https://www.huffpost.com/entry/walking -meetings-at-linke_n_7035258

76. "Shared Plates: How Eating Together Makes Us Human," *Gastropod,* June 2, 2020, https://gastropod.com/transcript-shared-plates-how-eating -together-makes-us-human/

77. Kevin M. Kniffin et al., "Eating Together at the Firehouse: How Work-place Commensality Relates to the Performance of Firefighters," *Human Performance* 28, no. 4 (2015): 281–306, https://doi.org/10.1080/08959285.2015.1021049

78. Mike Bloomberg, "Food Can Help Build Relationships and Encourage Communication," LinkedIn, August 17, 2023, https://www.linkedin.com/posts/mikebloomberg_food-can-help-build-relationships-and-encourage-activity-7203843358815834113-z3WZ

79. Ankit Bisht and Sangeeth Ram, "Fueling Growth Through Moments of Customer Delight," *McKinsey & Company,* August 13, 2024, https://www.mckinsey.com/capabilities/growth-marketing-and-sales/our-insights/fueling-growth-through-moments-of-customer-delight

80. Josh Bernoff, *Writing Without Bullshit: Boost Your Career by Saying What You Mean* (New York: HarperBusiness, 2016).

PRINCIPLE 6 TIMING: GET YOUR MEETINGS IN RHYTHM

1. Rebecca Hinds, Robert Sutton, and Hayagreeva Rao, "Adobe: Building Momentum by Abandoning Annual Performance Reviews for 'Check-Ins,'" *Stanford Graduate School of Business, Case No. HR38,* 2014, https://www.gsb.stanford.edu/faculty-research/case-studies/adobe-building-momentum-abandoning-annual-performance-reviews-check

2. Hinds, Sutton, and Rao, "Adobe: Building Momentum by Abandoning Annual Performance Reviews."

3. "HR Lessons from the Adobe Performance Management Overhaul," *PerformYard,* January 20, 2023, https://www.performyard.com/articles/adobe-performance-management

4. David Burkus, "How Adobe Scrapped Its Performance Review System and Why It Worked," *Forbes,* June 1, 2016, https://www.forbes.com/sites/davidburkus/2016/06/01/how-adobe-scrapped-its-performance-review-system-and-why-it-worked/

5. Shishir Mehrotra, "Rituals for Hypergrowth: An Inside Look at How YouTube Scaled," *Coda,* 2015, https://coda.io/@shishir/rituals-for-hypergrowth-an-inside-look-at-how-youtube-scaled

6. Robert Sutton, Hayagreeva Rao, and Rebecca Hinds, "BuildDirect: Constructing a Culture That Can Weather the Storms," *Stanford Graduate School of Business, Case No. E526,* 2014, https://www.gsb.stanford.edu/faculty-research/case-studies/builddirect-constructing-culture-can-weather-storms

7. Kevin Fishner, "Focus on Your First 10 Systems, Not Just Your First 10 Hires—This Chief of Staff Shares His Playbook," *First Round Review,*

April 2, 2020, https://review.firstround.com/focus-on-your-first-10 -systems-not-just-your-first-10-hires-this-chief-of-staff-shares-his-play book/

8. Fishner, "Focus on Your First 10 Systems."

9. Marc Benioff and Carlye Adler, *Behind the Cloud: The Untold Story of How Salesforce.com Went from Idea to Billion-Dollar Company—and Revolutionized an Industry* (San Francisco: Jossey-Bass, 2009).

10. Fishner, "Focus on Your First 10 Systems."

11. Yamini Rangan, "Whether You Think You Can," LinkedIn, https:// www.linkedin.com/posts/yaminirangan_mindset-matters-activity -7254282225653841920-6MO4

12. Marc Benioff, "Create Strategic Company Alignment with a V2MOM," *360 Blog*, Salesforce, December 11, 2024, https://www.salesforce.com/blog /how-to-create-alignment-within-your-company/

13. Rebecca Hinds et al., *2024 State of Work Innovation Report*, Asana, https:// assets.asana.biz/m/7247625de89a76e6/original/State-of-Work-Innovation -2024_Global.pdf

14. Hengchen Dai, Katherine L. Milkman, and Jason Riis, "Put Your Imperfections Behind You: Temporal Landmarks Spur Goal Initiation When They Signal New Beginnings," *Psychological Science* 26, no. 12 (2015): 1927–36, https://doi.org/10.1177/0956797615605818

15. Hengchen Dai, "Research Explores How 'Fresh Starts' Affect Our Motivation at Work," *Harvard Business Review*, February 4, 2019, https://hbr.org/2019/02 /research-explores-how-fresh-starts-affect-our-motivation-at-work

16. Laura W. Geller, "Katherine Milkman on Why Fresh Starts Matter," *Strategy+Business*, August 8, 2014, https://www.strategy-business.com/article /00266

17. Sutton, Rao, and Hinds, "BuildDirect: Constructing a Culture That Can Weather the Storms."

18. OnPoint Consulting, "Top 15 Uncommon Strategy Execution Quotes to Keep You Inspired and On Track," OnPoint Consulting, https://www .onpointconsultingllc.com/blog/15-inspirational-quotes-to-drive-strategy -execution

19. Ken Segall, *Insanely Simple: The Obsession That Drives Apple's Success* (New York: Portfolio, 2012).

20. Colin Bryar and Bill Carr, *Working Backwards: Insights, Stories, and Secrets from Inside Amazon* (New York: St. Martin's Press, 2021).

21. Rob Cross, "Looking to Actually Improve Workplace Productivity? Rethink Team Collaboration," *Institute for Corporate Productivity*, May 29, 2024, https://www.i4cp.com/productivity-blog/looking-to-actually-improve -workplace-productivity-rethink-how-your-teams-collaborate

22. Inga Carboni and Rob Cross, *Collaborative Practices of High-Performing Teams, Connected Commons,* July 2020, https://www.robcross.org/wp-content/uploads/2020/07/Collaborative-Practices-of-High-Performing-Teams-2020July20.pdf

23. Jared Spataro, "5 Key Trends Leaders Need to Understand to Get Hybrid Right," *Harvard Business Review,* March 16, 2022, https://hbr.org/2022/03/5-key-trends-leaders-need-to-understand-to-get-hybrid-right

24. Bryan Kitch, "How to Create a Team Working Agreement," *Mural,* September 7, 2023, https://www.mural.co/blog/team-agreement-guide

25. Shishir Mehrotra, "Supercharging Decision Making: 14 Ways to Dory/Pulse," *Coda,* 2024, https://coda.io/@shishir/dory-pulse

26. Daniel Kahneman and Amos Tversky, "Intuitive Prediction: Biases and Corrective Procedures," *TIMS Studies in Management Science* 12 (1979): 313–27.

27. Gary Klein, "Performing a Project Premortem," *Harvard Business Review,* September 2007, https://hbr.org/2007/09/performing-a-project-premortem

28. Shreyas Doshi, "Pre-mortems: How a Stripe Product Manager Prevents Problems Before Launch," *Coda,* https://coda.io/@shreyas/pre-mortems

29. Connie J. G. Gersick, "Time and Transition in Work Teams: Toward a New Model of Group Development," *Academy of Management Journal* 31, no. 1 (1988): 9–41, https://doi.org/10.2307/256496

30. Jacob Morgan, "Airbnb's Secret to an Amazing Corporate Culture," *HR Exchange Network,* February 11, 2019, https://www.hrexchangenetwork.com/hr-talent-management/articles/elephants-deadfish-and-vomit-the-secret-to-airbnbs-amazing-corporate-culture

31. Amy Edmondson, "Learning from Mistakes is Easier Said Than Done: Group and Organizational Influences on the Detection and Correction of Human Error," *Journal of Applied Behavioral Science* 32, no. 1 (1996): 5–28, https://doi.org/10.1177/0021886396321001.

32. Ed Catmull, "How Pixar Fosters Collective Creativity," *Harvard Business Review,* September 2008, https://hbr.org/2008/09/how-pixar-fosters-collective-creativity.

33. Jeff Bezos, "2016 Letter to Shareholders," *Amazon News,* April 17, 2017, https://www.aboutamazon.com/news/company-news/2016-letter-to-shareholders

34. Johanna Bolin Tingvall, "Why We Love Failure," *Spotify HR Blog,* October 30, 2017, https://hrblog.spotify.com/2017/10/30/why-we-love-failure

35. Amy C. Edmondson, "Strategies for Learning from Failure," *Harvard Business Review,* April 2011, https://hbr.org/2011/04/strategies-for-learning-from-failure

36. Flavor Graveyard, Ben & Jerry's, https://www.benjerry.com/flavors/flavor-graveyard

37. John Lunney and Sue Lueder, "Postmortem Culture: Learning from Failure," Google, https://sre.google/sre-book/postmortem-culture/

38. Molly Gamble, "The 15-Minute Meeting That Transformed Cleveland Clinic," *Becker's Hospital Review*, July 17, 2023, https://www.beckers hospitalreview.com/hospital-management-administration/the-15-minute -meeting-that-transformed-cleveland-clinic.html

39. Gamble, "The 15-Minute Meeting That Transformed Cleveland Clinic."

40. Gamble, "The 15-Minute Meeting That Transformed Cleveland Clinic."

41. Gamble, "The 15-Minute Meeting That Transformed Cleveland Clinic."

42. Krystina Martinez, "7 Strategies for Running Effective Remote Meetings," *Zapier*, March 27, 2020, https://zapier.com/blog/effective-remote-meetings/

43. Christoph Riedl and Anita Williams Woolley, "Teams vs. Crowds: A Field Test of the Relative Contribution of Incentives, Member Ability, and Emergent Collaboration to Crowd-Based Problem Solving Performance," *Academy of Management Discoveries* 3, no. 4 (2016): 382–403, https://doi.org /10.5465/amd.2015.0097

44. Christoph Riedl and Anita Williams Woolley, "Successful Remote Teams Communicate in Short Bursts," *Harvard Business Review*, October 28, 2020, https://hbr.org/2020/10/successful-remote-teams-communicate-in-bursts

45. Kevin Kruse, *15 Secrets Successful People Know About Time Management* (Philadelphia: Kruse Group, 2015).

46. Natasha Piñon, "No. 1 Lesson from 3 Years of No-Meeting Wednesdays, Says HR Expert: Meetings Aren't 'The Enemy,'" *CNBC*, February 1, 2023, https://www.cnbc.com/2023/02/01/top-lesson-from-no-meeting -wednesdays-canva-hr-head-jennie-rogerson.html

47. "State of Remote Work 2020," Owl Labs/Global Workplace Analytics, https://resources.owllabs.com/hubfs/website/sorw/2020/owl-labs_sorw -2020_report-download_FINAL_07oct2020.pdf

48. Gabriela N. Tonietto, Selin A. Malkoc, and Stephen M. Nowlis, "When an Hour Feels Shorter: Future Boundary Tasks Alter Consumption by Contracting Time," *Journal of Consumer Research* 45, no. 5 (2019): 1085–1102, https://doi.org/10.1093/jcr/ucy043

49. Benjamin Laker et al., "The Surprising Impact of Meeting-Free Days," *MIT Sloan Management Review*, January 18, 2022, https://sloanreview.mit.edu /article/the-surprising-impact-of-meeting-free-days/

50. Paul Holbrook, "Set Yourself a 'Meeting Budget,'" *LinkedIn*, https://www .linkedin.com/pulse/set-yourself-meeting-budget-paul-holbrook-dqvie/

51. "What We've Learned Our First Year as a Virtual First Company," *Dropbox Blog*, June 16, 2022, https://blog.dropbox.com/topics/company/what -weve-learned-our-first-year-as-a-virtual-first-company

52. "How to Stay Productive and Impactful in a Distributed Workplace," *Dropbox*, https://experience.dropbox.com/resources/how-to-be-productive

53. "Research Proves Your Brain Needs Breaks," *Microsoft WorkLab*, April 20, 2021, https://www.microsoft.com/en-us/worklab/work-trend-index/brain-research

54. Brent N. Reed et al., "The Hidden Toll of Meeting Hangovers," *Harvard Business Review*, February 12, 2025, https://hbr.org/2025/02/the-hidden-toll-of-meeting-hangovers

55. Deborah G. Ancona and Chee Leong Chong, "Entrainment: Cycles and Synergy in Organizational Behavior," *Research in Organizational Behavior* 18 (1996): 251–84.

PRINCIPLE 7 TECHNOLOGY: INNOVATE AND ITERATE

1. Eryn J. Newman and Norbert Schwarz, "Good Sound, Good Research: How Audio Quality Influences Perceptions of the Research and Researcher," *Science Communication* 40, no. 2 (2018): 246–57, https://doi.org/10.1177/1075547018759345

2. Rita R. Silva et al., "Make It Short and Easy: Username Complexity Determines Trustworthiness Above and Beyond Objective Reputation," *Frontiers in Psychology* 8 (2017): 2200, https://doi.org/10.3389/fpsyg.2017.02200

3. Hyunjin Song and Norbert Schwarz, "If It's Hard to Read, It's Hard to Do: Processing Fluency Affects Effort Prediction and Motivation," *Psychological Science* 19, no. 10 (2008): 986–88, https://doi.org/10.1111/j.1467-9280.2008.02189.x

4. Shaheen N. Awan et al., "The Effect of Microphone Frequency Response on Spectral and Cepstral Measures of Voice: An Examination of Low-Cost Electret Headset Microphones," *American Journal of Speech-Language Pathology* 31, no. 2 (2022): 959–73, https://doi.org/10.1044/2021_AJSLP-21-00156

5. "Global Travel and Expense Policy," *GitLab Handbook*, https://handbook.gitlab.com/handbook/finance/expenses/

6. Valentina Chilingaryan, "How to Remove Background Noise: A One-Click Solution," *Krisp Blog*, November 15, 2024, https://krisp.ai/blog/remove-background-noise/

7. GitLab Unfiltered, "Hear Nothing Say Something," uploaded by GitLab Unfiltered, YouTube, 1 min., 36 sec., January 22, 2020, https://www.youtube.com/watch?v=LZ5spXU5HbU

8. Priya Parker, "We're Using the Mute Button All Wrong: Part 2—Intimacy," *Art of Gathering Newsletter*, August 8, 2020, https://www.priyaparker.com

/art-of-gathering-newsletter/were-using-the-mute-button-all-wrong-part
-2-intimacy

9. Hailley Griffis, "How We Structure All Hands as a Fully Remote Team," *BufferBlog,* May 10, 2018, https://buffer.com/resources/remote-all-hands/

10. "Shush: Keep It to Yourself," Mizage, https://mizage.com/shush/

11. Linda K. Treviño, Robert H. Lengel, and Richard L. Daft, "Media Symbolism, Media Richness, and Media Choice in Organizations: A Symbolic Interactionist Perspective," *Communication Research* 14, no. 5 (1987): 553–74, https://doi.org/10.1177/009365087014005006

12. Kristen M. Shockley et al., "The Fatiguing Effects of Camera Use in Virtual Meetings: A Within-Person Field Experiment," *Journal of Applied Psychology* 106, no. 8 (2021): 1137–55, https://doi.org/10.1037/apl0000948

13. Abi Cook, Meg Thompson, and Paddy Ross, "Virtual First Impressions: Zoom Backgrounds Affect Judgements of Trust and Competence," *PLoS One* 18, no. 9 (2023): e0291444, https://doi.org/10.1371/journal.pone.0291444

14. Géraldine Fauville et al., "Nonverbal Mechanisms Predict Zoom Fatigue and Explain Why Women Experience Higher Levels than Men," *Social Science Research Network,* April 5, 2021, https://papers.ssrn.com/sol3/papers.cfm?abstract_id=3820035

15. Vyopta Incorporated and Wakefield Research, "The Challenges of Hybrid Work: Vyopta 2022 Survey," *Vyopta/Wakefield Research,* April 12, 2022, https://go.vyopta.com/vyopta_wakefield_survey_22

16. "Cameras On or Off? Professionals Weigh In on Video Usage During Virtual Meetings in Korn Ferry Survey," *Korn Ferry,* October 24, 2023, https://www.kornferry.com/about-us/press/cameras-on-or-off

17. "I'm Not a Cat: Lawyer Gets Stuck on Zoom Kitten Filter During Court Case," posted by Guardian News, *YouTube,* 48 sec., February 9, 2021, https://www.youtube.com/watch?v=lGOofzZOyl8

18. Mark Weiser and John Seely Brown, "Designing Calm Technology," December 21, 1995, https://people.csail.mit.edu/rudolph/Teaching/weiser.pdf

19. Amber Case, "Principles of Calm Technology," Calm Tech Institute, May 2024, https://calmtech.com/

20. "Love Them or Hate Them, Virtual Meetings Are Here to Stay," *Economist,* April 10, 2021, https://www.economist.com/international/2021/04/10/love-them-or-hate-them-virtual-meetings-are-here-to-stay

21. Lisa Masjutin et al., "Fatigued Individuals Show Increased Conformity in Virtual Meetings," *Scientific Reports* 14 (2024): 18807, https://www.nature.com/articles/s41598-024-69786-6

22. James E. Katz and Mark Aakhus, *Perpetual Contact: Mobile Communica-tion, Private Talk, Public Performance* (Cambridge: Cambridge University Press, 2002).

23. Gary P. Pisano, "The Hard Truth About Innovative Cultures," *Harvard Business Review,* January-February 2019, https://hbr.org/2019/01/the-hard-truth-about-innovative-cultures

24. James Thomas, "Death by PowerPoint: The Slide That Killed Seven People," *McDreeamie-Musings,* April 15, 2019, https://mcdreeamiemusings.com/blog/2019/4/13/gsux1h6bnt8lqjd7w2t2mtvfg81uhx

25. Vasudevan Mukunth, "The Risk of a Lab-Leak and the Columbia Disaster Have a Common Lesson for Us," *Wire,* June 3, 2022, https://science.thewire.in/external-affairs/world/lab-leak-risk-assessment-columbia-shuttle-disaster-information-design/

26. Elisabeth Bumiller, "We Have Met the Enemy and He Is PowerPoint," *New York Times,* April 26, 2010, https://www.nytimes.com/2010/04/27/world/27powerpoint.html

27. Guy Kawasaki, "The 10/20/30 Rule of PowerPoint," *Guy Kawasaki's Blog,* December 30, 2005, https://guykawasaki.com/the_102030_rule/

28. "GitLab Communication," *GitLab Handbook,* https://handbook.gitlab.com/handbook/communication/

29. William S. Pfeiffer and Kaye E. Adkins, "PowerPoint Presentations," chap. 16 in *Technical Writing: 21st Century Tools for Effective Communication* (Upper Saddle River, NJ: Pearson/Prentice Hall, 2006), https://ptgmedia.pearsoncmg.com/images/0131498630/samplechapter/rosenberg_ch16.pdf

30. Pfeiffer and Adkins, "PowerPoint Presentations."

31. "Read AI's David Shim on Making Meetings More Efficient with Intelligent Agents," *Madrona Venture Group,* May 29, 2024, https://www.madrona.com/read-ai-david-shim-efficient-meetings-intelligent-agents/

32. Umar Shakir, "Zoom 2.0 Relaunches as an AI-First Company Without Video in Its Name," *Verge,* November 25, 2024, https://www.theverge.com/2024/11/25/24305942/zoom-communications-rename-ai-first-company

33. "Meeting Scheduling Trends Report: 130+ Scheduling Links Stats," *Reclaim.ai Blog,* October 27, 2022, https://reclaim.ai/blog/meeting-scheduling-links-trends-report

34. Brendan Burke, "4 Myths and 1 Truth About Scheduling Meetings," *Boomerang,* June 12, 2023, https://blog.boomerangapp.com/2023/06/4-myths-and-1-truth-about-scheduling-meetings/

35. Robin Daniels, "One of My Favorite Guilty Pleasures Is Saying No to AI Bots Joining Meetings," *LinkedIn,* https://www.linkedin.com/posts/robingdaniels_ai-bots-activity-7243231244048633858-Ex6P

36. Sherin Shibu, "Is AI Accidentally Spilling Your Company's Secrets? A VC Firm's Private Conversations Were Included in Meeting Transcripts," *Entrepreneur*, October 2, 2024, https://www.entrepreneur.com/business-news/ai-transcription-services-are-spilling-company-secrets/480671

37. Ephraim Allon, "I'm Using AI to Prep for Meetings," *LinkedIn*, March 3, 2025, https://www.linkedin.com/posts/eallon_ai-2datasense-llm-activity-7270056757064806400-X9qi

38. Rebecca Hinds, "Turn Your AI Skeptics Into AI Innovators," *Inc.*, July 21, 2024, https://www.inc.com/rebecca-hinds/turn-your-ai-skeptics-into-ai-innovators.html

39. Katharina Lix et al., "Aligning Differences: Discursive Diversity and Team Performance," *Management Science* 68, no. 11 (November 2022): 8430–48, https://doi.org/10.1287/mnsc.2021.4274

40. Nilay Patel, "The CEO of Zoom Wants AI Clones in Meetings," *Verge*, June 3, 2024, https://www.theverge.com/2024/6/3/24168733/zoom-ceo-ai-clones-digital-twins-videoconferencing-decoder-interview

41. Matthew Boyle, "Meetings Won't Be the Same When the Boss Sends an AI Bot," Bloomberg, April 15, 2025, https://www.bloomberg.com/news/features/2025-04-15/meetings-won-t-be-the-same-when-the-ceo-sends-an-ai-bot

42. Boyle, "Meetings Won't Be the Same."

43. Ethan Mollick, "I Invited a Live HeyGen AI Avatar to a Zoom Meeting," *LinkedIn*, https://www.linkedin.com/posts/emollick_i-invited-a-live-heygen-ai-avatar-to-a-zoom-activity-7259367524222328832-g4sa

44. Lodewijk Gelauff et al., "Achieving Parity with Human Moderators: A Self-Moderating Platform for Online Deliberation," in *The Routledge Handbook of Collective Intelligence for Democracy and Governance*, ed. Stephen Boucher, Carina Antonia Hallin, and Lex Paulson (New York: Routledge, 2023), 202–21, https://doi.org/10.4324/9781003215929-15

45. Soohwan Lee et al., "Conversational Agents as Catalysts for Critical Thinking: Challenging Social Influence in Group Decision-making," *arXiv preprint* arXiv:2503.14263, March 18, 2025, https://arxiv.org/abs/2503.14263

46. Timothy R. Hannigan, Ian P. McCarthy, and Andrew J. Spicer, "Beware of Botshit: How to Manage the Epistemic Risks of Generative Chatbots," *Business Horizons* 67, no. 2 (2024): 123–33, https://doi.org/10.1016/j.bushor.2024.03.001

47. Ian P. McCarthy, Timothy R. Hannigan, and André Spicer, "The Risks of Botshit," *Harvard Business Review*, July 17, 2024, https://hbr.org/2024/07/the-risks-of-botshit

48. Paul Leonardi, *Digital Exhaustion: Simple Rules for Reclaiming Your Life* (New York: Riverhead Books, 2025).

49. Callum Borchers, "The Annoying Person in Your Work Meeting Might Just Be You," *Wall Street Journal,* August 15, 2023, https://www.wsj.com /lifestyle/careers/ai-meetings-work-feedback-bots-bc380d72

50. Prithwiraj Choudhury, Bart S. Vanneste, and Amirhossein Zohrehvand, "The Wade Test: Generative AI and CEO Communication," *CESifo Working Paper no. 11316* (2024), https://www.econstor.eu/bitstream/10419/30 5558/1/cesifo1_wp11316.pdf

51. "What Is Kaizen and How Does Toyota Use It?," *Toyota UK Magazine,* May 31, 2013, https://mag.toyota.co.uk/kaizen-toyota-production-system/

52. James Bessen, "The Automation Paradox," *Atlantic,* January 19, 2016, https:// www.theatlantic.com/business/archive/2016/01/automation-paradox /424437/

CONCLUSION DESIGN YOUR MEETINGS LIKE A PRODUCT OR PAY THE PRICE

1. "Paola Antonelli: Why I Brought Pac-Man to MoMA," uploaded by TED, YouTube, 18 min., 32 sec., May 28, 2013, https://www.youtube.com /watch?v=YzGjO5aHShQ

INDEX

ABOUT THE AUTHOR

REBECCA HINDS is a leading expert on collaboration in the digital age. She's helped dozens of organizations across industries and continents fix their dysfunctional meetings, improve team collaboration, and leverage technology to drive real business results. Her insights and research on meetings and collaboration have appeared in top outlets like *Harvard Business Review*, *Time*, *The New York Times*, *The Wall Street Journal*, Bloomberg, *Fast Company*, CNBC, *Forbes*, *Wired*, *TechCrunch*, and *Inc.*

Rebecca holds a BS, MS, and PhD from Stanford University, where her research focused on how new technology—especially collaboration tools and AI—is transforming the way we work. Her PhD research earned her the prestigious Stanford Interdisciplinary Graduate Fellowship, one of the university's highest honors for doctoral students pursuing cross-disciplinary research. While at Stanford, she was also inducted into Stanford's Cap and Gown Society, which recognizes the university's top women leaders.

In 2022 Rebecca founded the Work Innovation Lab at Asana, the work management platform. The lab produces cutting-edge research on the future of work, and its insights consistently appear in top business publications. In 2025, she founded the Work AI Institute at Glean to conduct cutting-edge research on how AI is transforming work and help leaders adapt. A sought-after keynote speaker, Rebecca has shared her research and work with global audiences at major events including SXSW, Dreamforce, and the Gartner Digital Workplace Summit.

Rebecca regularly advises organizations on how to fix meeting overload, improve collaboration, design smarter hybrid and remote workplaces, and use AI to fix broken ways of working—without sparking an employee revolt. In 2025, she co-instructed the CNBC *Make It* course "How to Use AI to Be More Successful at Work," teaching professionals how to wield AI effectively.

Rebecca's bias for innovation and challenging the status quo was shaped by her experiences as a multi-time founder. Her second company, Stratio, which she cofounded with Stanford classmates, was named one of the top fifty student-run businesses in the world by the Kairos Society.

Before she was fixing meetings, Rebecca was a competitive swimmer. She was a semifinalist at the Canadian Olympic Trials and a member of Stanford's women's swim team where she learned some of her most enduring lessons about teamwork and collaboration, in and out of the pool.

Rebecca is a columnist at *Inc.* and *Reworked*, where she writes about smarter ways of working.

Learn more at rebeccahinds.com.